A History of Glasnevin

Its village, lands and people

Tony O'Doherty

ORIGINAL WRITING

© 2011 Tony O'Doherty

All rights reserved. No part of this publication may be reproduced in any form or by any means—graphic, electronic or mechanical, including photocopying, recording, taping or information storage and retrieval systems—without the prior written permission of the author.
Reprinted with corrections and additions May 2011

ISBN: 978-1-908024-25-1

Maps approved and supplied by

A CIP catalogue for this book is available from the National Library.

Published by ORIGINAL WRITING LTD., Dublin, 2011.

Printed in Great Britain by MPG BOOKS GROUP,

Bodmin and Kings Lynn

Dedicated to the people of Glasnevin

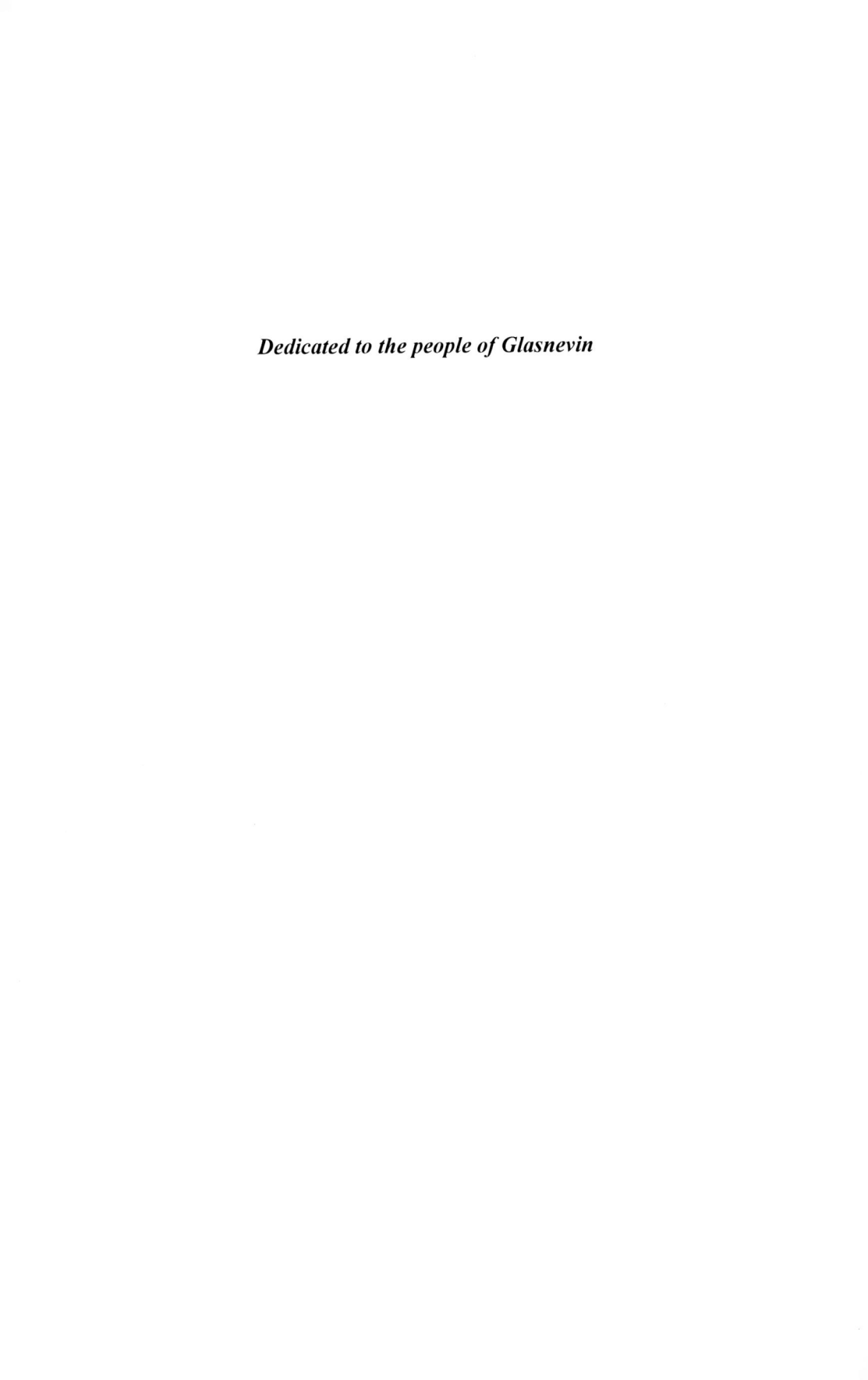

CONTENTS

Preface ix
Acknowledgments x
Introducing Glasnevin xiii

Chapter 1
PLACE-NAMES AND BOUNDARIES 1

Chapter 2
ANCIENT TIMES 6

Chapter 3
THE EARLY CHRISTIAN PERIOD: ST. MOBHI IN GLASNEVIN 8

Chapter 4
THE NORSE PERIOD 14

Chapter 5
CHRIST CHURCH CATHEDRAL AND GLASNEVIN 16

Chapter 6
MEDIEVAL GLASNEVIN: ITS CASTLE AND MOTTE 19

Chapter 7
THE MANOR FARM OF GLASNEVIN AND THE PRIOR 23

Chapter 8
GLASNEVIN IN THE 15TH CENTURY: TENANTS AND LEASES 26

Chapter 9
THE REFORMATION AND AFTERWARDS 29

Chapter 10
GLASNEVIN IN THE 17TH CENTURY: WARS, TURMOIL AND DECLINE 34

Chapter 11
A Survey of Glasnevin by Richard Francis in 1640 — 38

Chapter 12
The 18th century: From ruin to prosperity — 44

Chapter 13
The 18th century residents — 47

Chapter 14
Parish organization in the 18th century — 50

Chapter 15
The Alms House, the Poor Lott and the Washerwomen — 56

Chapter 16
The Parish School: The "Inkbottle" — 61

Chapter 17
Delville and Doctor Patrick Delany — 66

Chapter 18
The Second Mrs. Delany — 74

Chapter 19
Delville after the Delanys — 81

Chapter 20
The Barber Family and Carlingford House — 84

Chapter 21
Thomas Tickell, public servant and poet — 89

Chapter 22
James Belcher, patron of the arts, and Ardmore — 91

Chapter 23
THE LARGER LANDOWNERS AND THEIR HOUSES 1700 - 1840   93

Chapter 24
GENTLEMEN AND THEIR VILLAS FROM 1700 ONWARDS   98

Chapter 25
GLASNEVIN IN THE 19TH CENTURY   107

Chapter 26
FAMINE AND PESTILENCE: RELIEF MEASURES   110

Chapter 27
FROM PASTORAL AREA TO TOWNSHIP   115

Chapter 28
POPULATION AND HOUSING 1850- 1900   120

Chapter 29
PUBLIC HOUSES IN GLASNEVIN.   122

Chapter 30
THE MILL OF GLASNEVIN   129

Chapter 31
COLLEGES AND SCHOOLS OF THE COMMISSIONERS OF EDUCATION   133

Chapter 32
MARLBOROUGH HALL AND MARLBOROUGH HOUSE   137

Chapter 33
CLAREMONT INSTITUTE AND ST. CLARE'S   143

Chapter 34
THE EUSTACE FAMILY AND HAMPSTEAD HOSPITAL   147

Chapter 35
CONVENT OF THE HOLY FAITH GLASNEVIN   150

Chapter 36
ST. VINCENT DE PAUL MALE ORPHANAGE ST. JOSEPH'S MONASTERY,
AND ST. VINCENT'S SCHOOL.   158

Chapter 37
GLASNEVIN (PROSPECT) CEMETERY   161

Chapter 38
THE BOTANIC GARDENS: THE BRIGHTEST JEWEL   167

Chapter 39
THE 20TH CENTURY: A NEW ERA   177

Chapter 40
THE NEW SUBURB OF GLASNEVIN 1901-1935   181

Chapter 41
THE "GREAT WAR" AND THE TROUBLES   197

Chapter 42
BETWEEN THE WARS: A LITTLE LOCAL HISTORY   200

Chapter 43
THE "EMERGENCY" AND AFTERWARDS   203

Chapter 44
POST-WAR GLASNEVIN 1945-1960   205

Chapter 45
GLASNEVIN 1960-2000: RENEWAL   209

Chapter 46
PUBLIC TRANSPORT IN GLASNEVIN   211

Chapter 47
ST. MOBHI'S CHURCH OF IRELAND FROM 1706   221

Chapter 48
ST MOBHI'S CHURCHYARD   233

Chapter 49
THE ROMAN CATHOLIC CHURCH IN GLASNEVIN 1619-1900   239

Chapter 50
THE ROMAN CATHOLIC CHURCH IN GLASNEVIN IN THE 20TH CENTURY   244

Glossary of place names   *249*
Sources for the illustrations   *269*
List of historic maps of relevance to Glasnevin   *270*

Preface

The history of a locality must be considered in the wider context of events outside the area, and even outside the country that are part of our national history. For this reason, other relevant information and explanations are included to give the reader the broader national context.

In an age when old boundaries have been effaced and the suburban sprawl of Dublin City has engulfed the old country villages, it is important to preserve the histories of the ancient territories and manors such as Glasnevin, Finglas and Grangegorman This has been done for many other areas of the City and County of Dublin, and Glasnevin deserves no less. This history is the result of thirty years of active research, and local knowledge acquired over a period of several decades.

It is hoped that this publication will help to give the people of Glasnevin and others, in particular those interested in the history of County Dublin, a better knowledge and understanding of its long historic past.
Although written primarily for the people of Glasnevin, local historians and others may find some items of interest therein.

For ease of reading and research, a system of sub-headings is used in each chapter to facilitate the locating of particular items.

Acknowledgments

The author was fortunate in obtaining assistance from many people, private individuals and those working in various institutions, in fact too many to mention individually.

Many local Glasnevin people provided information that would otherwise be lost with time. Pride of place must be given to Brendan Scally and his late wife Doreen, former residents of Glasnevin who provided help and encouragement over those years. Brendan, well-known as a local historian of North County Dublin and an accomplished artist, and Doreen have been an invaluable and prolific source of information on Glasnevin past. Brendan's family have been in Glasnevin since 1852 when his great-grandfather Denis Scally established the Brian Boru public house, and Doreen's family the Cunninghams resided in Newton House from 1882 to 2005. Some of Brendan Scally's sketches of Glasnevin Village are included.

The author is grateful to the late Tom Healy, who ran a shoe-repair business in the village, and his late wife Maureen, who furnished many anecdotes and pieces of information about life in Glasnevin long ago.

Special thanks are due to the following:

Rev. Victor Stacey, former Rector of Glasnevin and Santry Parishes, and the late Leslie Mahon who allowed me access to the ancient parish records of St. Mobhi's Church,
Dr. Raymond Refausse. Representative Church Body Library, Churchtown for permission to reproduce the 1640 Survey Map of Glasnevin, and for the use of archival material of Christ church Cathedral,
Conor O'Toole who provided information on the early Irish Church.
Sister Theodore and the late Sister Assisi of the Holy Faith Convent Glasnevin for information on the Convent and its buildings,
Rachel Pollard for permission to use material from her book "The Avenue",
Diarmuid Fitzpatrick for information on Matthew Fitzpatrick. Headmaster of the Model School,
Fionan de Barra, who provided illustrations for the castle and the mill
Ruth McManus for permission to use material from her book "Dublin 1910 - 1940",
Sally Shiels for information on the Model School and the NDNSP.
Sheila McGilligan for information on Thomas Conolly, Master Builder,
Arthur McGuinness for information on the locality

Particular thanks are due to people in the following organizations:

The National Library
The RCB Library, Braemor Park, Churchtown,
The Architectural Archive, Merrion Square,
The Royal Society of Antiquarians, Merrion Square,
The National Archive,
The Registry of Deeds, King's Inns.
The National Gallery.

Principal sources

A considerable amount of material from Christ Church Cathedral sources was used for this publication. The sources are: Calendar of Deeds, Calendar of Records, Guard Books A and D, the Account Roll of the Priory of the Holy Trinity. The Vestry Books of Glasnevin Parish 1707-1901 (now held in the RCB Library) yielded considerable local historic information.

Other sources used were the Crede mihi, Calendar of Archbishop Alen's Register c.1172-1534, Berry's Wills in Trinity College Dublin, Registry of Deeds in King's Inns, Byrne's Dictionary of Irish Local History.

Some topics, e.g. the Botanic Gardens, Glasnevin Cemetery, Holy Faith Convent and the Claremont Institution, are dealt with comprehensively in various other publications, and whereas some information is provided on them, the reader is referred thereto for further information in each case.

Introducing Glasnevin

Dublin City and County have been well-served by historians since the early 19th century, for example D'Alton, W. St. J. Joyce, F. Elrington Ball, Dillon Cosgrave, Sir John Gilbert, and Samuel Fitzpatrick. Some deal with Glasnevin, but do not go into any great detail.

Glasnevin is one of the many areas of Dublin that once were country villages situated amid green fields, each with its own identity and history. From 1900 onwards, those villages and fields gradually became engulfed by the ever-expanding city, a process that continues to this day.

Glasnevin is a part of Dublin City, but its recorded history began four centuries before that city was founded. To those of us that live, or have lived, there, it is a gentle, almost old-world place in the hectic life of modern Dublin City, with its bridge over the River Tolka, its winding main street, and of course Dublin's "Brightest Jewel", the National Botanic Gardens. To ordinary Dubliners it is famous for its great cemetery where many of their forbears lie buried. For the locals, the cemetery is a place apart that belongs to all Dubliners, and indeed to the nation because of the many notable Irish people buried there.

The recorded history of Glasnevin begins in the sixth century when it became the site of the first Christian monastic settlement in North County Dublin. In the middle ages after the coming of the Anglo-Normans, the lands of Glasnevin became a manor belonging to the Priory of the Holy Trinity (Christ Church), and the village (or "towne" as it was termed) was a typical manorial village of the Pale.

Following the wars and tribulations of the seventeenth century, the village fell into ruin. It was rebuilt early in the 18th century, after which it became a very fashionable place wherein to reside. Its residents included some famous people from Dublin's administrative, literary and artistic circles, Dr. Patrick Delany, for example, whose friend Dean Swift was a frequent visitor.

In 1901, the Dublin City boundary was extended to take in the greater part of Glasnevin. The old village deteriorated over the years and by 1950, many of its eighteenth and nineteenth century houses had fallen into disrepair, and the village looked tired and shabby. The period from 1950 onwards saw the destruction of many old houses – Delville, the Turrets, Roseville, Ardmore and Carlingford House, to name a few.

The village was largely rebuilt during the latter half of the 20th century, with buildings in a variety of architectural styles, alas, not all in harmony. The village contains two pyramid-style structures – the new church and the controversial "Met Office", the "pointless pyramid" of its critics.

Chapter 1:

PLACE-NAMES AND BOUNDARIES

Place-names

A complete list of all place-names in Glasnevin is given in the "Glossary of place-names" at the end of this book. Many names are obsolete and some are so old as to be of antiquarian interest only. This chapter deals with some obsolete names, as well as some of the older names that have survived. Many of the older place-names survive only in the archive documents of Christ Church Cathedral and old title deeds.

Very few of the original Gaelic names, presuming such existed, are extant, and it is probable that most were ignored or otherwise forgotten after the arrival of the Anglo-Norman immigrants. The names documented during medieval times and later appear to have been allocated quite casually, without regard for any of the previous names and many are named after, say, the principal tenant at the time of the granting of the lease, for example "Draycott's Farm". The Survey of Glasnevin in 1640 by Richard Francis (q.v.) gives the names allocated to the various farms at that time, and most were in use up to 1800

The first Ordnance Survey of Ireland in the 1830s divided every parish into areas called "townlands" and gave them names, usually based on the original Gaelic. However, most of the townlands in Glasnevin are designated by obviously English names which were derived at the time from the names of estates and holdings. Apart from Clonmel, Daneswell and Drishoge, those names bear little or no relation to the older names. Moreover, the townlands bear little resemblance to the old farms in the 1640 Survey.

The name *Glasnevin* meaning the "Stream of Nevin" is mentioned in the Annals of the Four Masters as the place where St. Mobhi established his monastic school in the 6th century. It occurs in Archbishop Alen's Register of Deeds in a variety of spellings.

The name "*Clonmel*", (Meadow of Honey) spelt variously as Cloonemell or Clynemel survives in the modern townland of Clonmel, and dates from before Norman times. It is mentioned in the Calendar of Archbishop Alen's Register and is listed as a "farm" in the Survey of 1640, (also called Wicomb's or Wickham's Farm).

Draycott's (or Wadd's) Farm was the name given in the 1640 Survey to the area occupied approximately by the present townland of Wad which is directly south of Clonmel.

The townland *"Drishoge"* in Glasnevin, which is the area around Botanic Avenue, was known in medieval times as *"The Lord's Mede"*, a direct benefice of the Lord Prior of the Priory of the Holy Trinity (Christ Church), and after the Reformation, *"The Deane's Farm*. The Bath family from Drishoge in Drumcondra acquired this land in 1570 and the name *Drishoge* (meaning "brambly") was apparently then extended to the area.

Daneswell Road. Takes its name from the *Deane's Well* (see below). The name "Daneswell" was given to two townlands in the 19th century, to a terrace on Whitworth Road (*Daneswell Villas)*, and to this road in 1927.

Figure 1: The Deane's Well, Glasnevin

The Deane's Well A well situated in a field (the "Bull's Field"), now occupied by Fairfield Road and Cliftonville Road, was called the "Deane's Well" (pronounced "Dane's Well"). This field formed part of the old Fairfield estate and is shown on 19th century maps as having a "Curious Well"). The name "Deane's Well" undoubtedly is derived from its location in or near the area called "The Deane's Farm".

The Deane's Well is mentioned in the Dublin Historical Record 1957 Vol. 17.1 pp 23-24 "Curative wells in old Dublin" by Mrs. M.J.F. Daly, who writes of "...another well some distance from the Tolka known as Danes Well which gave its name to two separate portions of the townland and Daneswell Road. It is known that fallen statues were found lying in a ditch near the well, which were part of the well's adornment, thus indicating that it had the reputation of being a holy well, and probably a curative one".
The inference in this article is that the statues were of religious significance, but this is highly unlikely from a historical viewpoint. The statues were very likely secular ornamentation for this "Curious Well", probably dating from the eighteenth or early nineteenth century.

The *Great Farm* occupied most of the area east of the Naul (now Ballymun) Road, including Bank Farm, Hampstead and Wadelai.

The Great Meadow or "Moche Mede" as it was called in medieval times (also called the *"Long Meadow"*.) lay on the south bank of the Tolka

River. It is triangular in shape and forms part of the Botanic Gardens, and it was originally reserved for growing hay, (It is designated D3 on the 1640 Survey map).

The *Fee Farm* was mainly the present townland of Prospect (north side of the Finglas Road, including the cemetery and the Iona area) along with a large area from north of the village as far as the Nevin Stream.
It included the Delville estate, now the grounds of the Bon Secours Hospital.

Cross Guns (The). This was the name given to Glasnevin's second village at the junction of the Finglas Road and the Glasnevin Road. It comes from the tavern of that name in the area, which existed there before 1700.

Cross Guns Bridge is the local name for *Westmoreland Bridge* (its official name since 1789) on the Royal Canal.

Goose Acre, a small townland comprising Addison Lodge grounds and the land to the north as far as Botanic Avenue, is probably of much earlier origin.

The Cinder Path was the name given up to about 1970 to the lane connecting Church Avenue with St. Mobhi Road.

Roaches Hole was an inlet on the north bank of the River Tolka, located eastward of the Bridge on St. Mobhi Road.

The *Old FInglas Road* was called *"Finglas Road North"* before 1900. It formed part of the original road to Finglas until the building of the Finglas Road sometime around 1600.

Corey Lane was the old name for *Botanic Avenue* which dates from 1901, called locally *"Slut's Alley"* from the 1700s when the area was impoverished. The origin is not known.

The *Naul Road* was the old name for Ballymun Road (R108) up to 1900.

Washerwoman's Hill has been a local name for Glasnevin Hill since about 1750, but was never an "official" name. In the 1700s, it was called *"Glasnevin Streete"*. The eponymous washerwomen lived in the Parish Alms House which was located beside the Hill in the present River Gardens area.

Wadelai is a recent name, dating from about 1900. This area is designated *"Cullenagh"* in the 1640 Survey.

Ballygall is designated *Ballinagall* "(the way of the foreigners") in the 1640 Survey.

After the area of Glasnevin was incorporated in Dublin City in 1901, many of the older street names were replaced with their modern versions and a house-numbering system. Various little terraces with their quaint names were rendered obsolete, mainly on the present Botanic Road and on Ballymun Road . Some of the original terrace names are still visible on the old wall plaques that survived, Details will be found in the Glossary and in Thom's Directories from 1847 to 1900.

Parliamentary parish boundaries

Glasnevin is a civil parish in the Barony of Coolock in the County of Dublin, bounded by the Parishes of Finglas, Santry, Drumcondra and Clonliffe. Like many former rural areas of County Dublin, it became a part of the City of Dublin, and it has been one of the "leafy suburbs" of our capital for over a century.

From the year 1185 in the time of Archbishop Laurence O'Toole until the setting up of the township in 1878, the parish was the basic unit of administration. One of the results of building development in the general area in the 1950s and 1960s was the physical defacing of the old parliamentary boundaries between Glasnevin and Finglas Parishes, and Glasnevin and Santry Parishes as the defining streams,fields walls and hedges gave way to concrete. The new suburb known as Ballygall is situated partly in Glasnevin, Finglas, and Santry Parishes, and has no definable boundaries.

The old parliamentary boundaries are shown on OS maps up to 1936

One of the very few boundary markers is part of an old masonry wall on the Old Finglas Road between two houses facing Tolka Estate Road, which marked the boundary between Finglas and Glasnevin Parishes. The northern and eastern boundaries with Santry and Drumcondra take in the Clonmel estate, and were marked by the old course of the Wad River (or Stream), which crossed Ballymun Road under the long-gone "Wad Bridge", and entered the River Tolka through the present Griffith Park past the back gardens of Walsh Road in Drumcondra. South of the River, the parish boundary bisects the Iona district, St. Alphonsus Road being in Drumcondra, and Iona Road and the church in Glasnevin.
The Royal Canal marks the southern boundary, although the original line lay a short distance to the south, as may be seen on the older maps. The western boundary commences a little to the west of Finglas Road, and

turns right just before Finglas Bridge to turn north toward Tolka Estate Road.

The Violet Hill Estate, while technically just outside the parliamentary boundary, is generally accepted nowadays as being part of Glasnevin

These old parish boundaries are perpetuated in the Church of Ireland system, unlike those of the Roman Catholic Church which have been changed many times as their congregations expanded during the twentieth century.

The townlands of Glasnevin

The Townlands of Glasnevin according to the 1837 Ordnance Survey are as follows:

North of the River Tolka:

Ballygall (part of)
Bank Farm
Claremont
Clonmel
Glasnevin Demesne
Hampstead North

Hampstead South
Violet Hill Little

Wad
Walnut Grove

South of the River Tolka:

Goose Acre
Greenmount
Daneswell
Fair Field
Botanic Garden
Cross Guns North
(or Daneswell)
Prospect
Slut's End
(also called West Farm)
Drishoge
Tolka Park

These townlands are shown on the OS maps issued before 1940.

Chapter 2:
ANCIENT TIMES

The road to Glasnevin

The ancient road ran northwards from the River Liffey crossing known as the Ford of the Hurdles (Ath Cliath), branching westwards towards Tara and proceeding northwards through the wooded countryside, following the route of the present-day Church Street, Constitution Hill, Phibsborough, and Botanic Road. Approaching the River Tolka, it veered slightly westwards past the present Botanic Gardens towards the ford where the river is wide and shallow. The first bridge was built here in medieval times, and this has remained the location of Glasnevin bridge to this day.

From this point, the road continued uphill towards Finglas by way of the present-day Ballygall Road (Bealach na Gall - the "Way of the Foreigners" as it became known at a later date).

The River at Glasnevin

The River Tolka (from "Tulach" meaning a flood, in Latin "Tulga"; also Tulghe) rises near the railway station in Batterstown in Co. Meath and flows through Dunboyne, Clonee, Mulhuddart, Blanchardstown, Ashtown, Cardiff's Bridge, Finglaswood, Finglas Bridge, Glasnevin, and Drumcondra, before entering the sea beyond Ballybough, a total distance of 30 km.
True to its name, the Tolka has a long history of flooding its hinterland. Recent floods happened in 1946, December 1954, 1967 and November 2002, causing severe hardship and distress to many of the residents in Glasnevin, Drumcondra and Fairview.

The Tolka has several small tributaries, including the Wad and the Nevin stream in Glasnevin, and the Finglas River that joins it at Finglas Bridge. The Wad, a small stream, formed part of the northern boundary of Glasnevin, and it and Wad's Farm, were apparently named after a tenant of that name.

The Nevin Stream

A tributary of the Tolka, the Glas Naoidhean or "Nevin Stream" gave the area its name. The origin or meaning of the word "Naoidhean" is not known. Various guesses as to its meaning have been made, including "Infant Stream" but its true meaning or derivation is lost. Its original course is shown on John Taylor's map of the environs of Dublin (1816)

The stream rises in Charlestown, to the north of Finglas Village, and today flows underground for most of its course. It flows under the Jamestown Road through the old Ballygall Estate, under Ballygall Road near the shopping area and flows above ground through the grounds of St Clare's Home, passing under an old bridge. It goes underground once more before crossing Ballymun Road at its junction with Griffith Avenue. It then turns southwards and flows, still below ground, through the grounds of the Bon Secours Hospital (where its one-time glen is still identifiable), and underneath River Gardens to enter the River Tolka at a point just downstream of Glasnevin Bridge. Unfortunately, it has been designated "The Claremont Drain" by Dublin Corporation, which is a debasing of its historical significance.

Until the late 18th century, the Nevin stream flowed through the glen in Delville and out in front of the Alms House to the roadway on Glasnevin Hill and it is shown on some old maps flowing down the side of the street, joining the River Tolka at the bridge. The stream today is much smaller as a result of agricultural and later building development over the centuries.

North County Dublin: Fingal

Glasnevin lay at the most southerly part of the area traditionally called Fingal. The Fingal area stretched from the River Tolka in the south to the Delvin River in the north of the County of Dublin. Its western boundary seems to have varied over time, but it was roughly on a line going northwards from the Cappagh area of Finglas. The present county of Fingal covers a somewhat different area. The area took its name from the Norse settlers - the Fine Gall ("fair-haired strangers"). In ancient times, the area was called Maigh Breagh, after a legendary chieftain who, supposedly, lived around 2000 B.C. In the early years of the Christian era, the area was the homeland of the Ciannachta clan, who took the surname O Cathasaigh in the 11th century.

References: Fair Fingal, by Patrick Archer. (Raven Press)
           Annals of the Four Masters

Chapter 3:
THE EARLY CHRISTIAN PERIOD: ST. MOBHI AND GLASNEVIN

The early Irish Church

The Monastery and Monastic School of Glasnevin was an important institution during the early Christian period. This history would not be complete without a description of the Irish Church at that time.

The early Irish Church was imbued with a fervour for sanctity and learning, and it subsequently became the light of the "Dark Ages" in Europe. It differed in many ways from the rest of the Christian Church in Western Europe. Ireland had no cities or towns, and therefore the church was rural in character. Instead of having the diocesan system ruled by bishops, it consisted of monastic settlements in various locations, each ruled by an abbot who was both spiritual and territorial governor. An early Irish monastery consisted of a church, the Abbot's house and separate huts for the monks.
The monks and students spent their time in prayer, instruction, study and copying the Scriptures. Each had a writing table or desk. They usually had to fend for themselves.

An Irish bishop then was merely a functionary with no territorial powers or responsibilities and the offices of abbot and bishop were often borne by one individual.

Irish monks of that period wore a simple habit with a hood. The so-called "Celtic" tonsure they adopted gave them a strange appearance by our standards (and even by contemporary standards elsewhere!) in that the head was shaven across the front half of the scalp and the hair was allowed to grow long at the back. This style may have been of druidic origin.

Ireland and the Eastern Churches

There is strong evidence that the early Irish Church owed its origins mainly (although not exclusively) to missionaries from the East, in particular Egypt, who probably came by Syrian and other merchant ships plying their way from Alexandria westwards. Its organization, liturgy and practices were in the eastern tradition rather than that of the west.

Hermits and anchorites who chose a solitary existence were common in both Ireland and the East, and they have given us Irish place names such as "Desert", "Dysert" and "Kildysert" which are not Irish in origin (the word "desert" comes from the Egyptian "deshret" meaning "red land").

Some of the early Christian monuments bear ornamentation similar to that found in the Middle East: an Egyptian "tau" crozier is depicted on the High Cross in Kilfenora in County Clare, while the Cross of Dysert O'Dea, also in County Clare, is in the form of the Greek "Tau".

St.Mobhi

St Mobhi is the patron saint of Glasnevin and one of the twelve "Apostles of Ireland" (the designation "Saint" was not used in the early Irish Church). His genealogy is given in the Book of Ballymote. His real name was Berchan, and he came of a noble family – the Fotharta - in County Mayo. He was born, probably, around 500 A.D. He became a monk and took the name Mo Bhi (sometimes spelt Mo-Bii), meaning the servant of Bi, another monk, as was the custom then (the names Molaga and Mochua are similarly derived).He became known as Mobhi Clarainach, "clarainach"meaning "flat- or board-faced" because of a facial deformity not uncommon at the time. A somewhat credible account of his time is found in the "Life of Colmcille" by Adamnan, Abbot of Iona, written in the following century and transcribed by Manus O'Donnell in the 16th century.

The Monastic School

Mobhi studied at the Monastery of Clonard with his kinsman St. Finian. He departed and travelled to Glasnevin where he founded a monastery and a monastic school - the ancient equivalent of a seminary, and certainly the first "third level" establishment in the Dublin area. The monastery grounds comprised the present site of the Bon Secours Hospital with the area bounded by Church Avenue, Ballymun Road and upper Glasnevin Hill, including the site of the Met Eireann Office, which was the burial ground.

The Nevin Stream provided a convenient fresh water supply for the monks and the students.

The monastic establishment consisted of the church, the Abbot's house and the huts of the students, surrounded by a circular enclosure. The entrance to the monastery was probably where Church Avenue is today.

A deed map of Delville estate dated 1799 (now the Bon Secours Hospital site) shows the curved outline of what is almost certainly part of the original boundary of the monastic site. The surviving 18th century east wall of the present site may well follow part of this outline.

The lives of the students

The number of students is reckoned by scholars of the period to have varied from about twenty-five to fifty at most. Each student and monk lived in his own hut, which was made of mud and wattles (willow branches) with a roof made of reeds and strips of turf. Each hut contained a desk or table of some sort, and a crude bed. Each student had to provide his own food and fuel. The River Tolka provided a plentiful supply of fish, and wild life would have abounded in the surrounding woodland.

Amongst those that studied under Mobhi were Saints Colmcille (or "Columba" in Latin). Comgall, Canice and Ciaran (of Clonmacnoise) who came from Clonard Monastery about 542 A.D. to complete their studies.

The "Life of Colmcille" contains some stories about his time in Glasnevin under Mobhi.
At one time, the Church and the Abbot's house lay on the east side of the Nevin Stream, and the students' huts lay on the other side. One evening, when the bell rang for Vespers, the Nevin Stream was in flood. The students were afraid to cross, with the exception of Colmcille who was a tall energetic and impulsive Northerner. He jumped into the water and swam across. Mobhi, on beholding this escapade, met Colmcille with a rebuke "Is calma tecar annsin anocht, a huai Neill" ("You are a daring man to come here to-night, descendant of Niall"). Colmcille replied: "God is able to remove this hardship from us!" When Mobhi and his pupil emerged later from the Church after Vespers, they beheld the huts of the students now sitting on the east bank of the stream. Although some writers give this a miraculous interpretation, the real explanation, if there is any truth in the story, is probably very mundane, as the light structures would not have been too difficult to shift after the flood had abated.

A new church

Following the incident involving Colmcille and the subsequent crowding of the east bank (which was much less extensive than the rest of the grounds, as can be seen to-day), Mobhi decided to build a new Church on the west side, very likely where the present church of St. Mobhi stands.

In the course of a discussion with his students, Mobhi asked them how they would furnish this church.
Ciaran replied: "Many holy men to please God"
Canice replied: "Godly books for the better serving of God"
Comgall replied: For the chastening of my body, illness and disease" (which turned out to be prophetic)
Colmcille replied:" Gold and silver, not for the love of wealth, but for establishing monasteries and reliquaries, and to give for God's sake, to those in need"

Mobhi pronounced: Thus it shall be: The monastery of Colmcille shall be richer than any in Eire or Alba.

When Colmcille departed to begin his mission in 543 A.D., Mobhi instructed him that he should not take or accept land until he, Mobhi, gave him permission.

The Plague

Not all that came from abroad was good. In the year 543.A.D. word came to Glasnevin of a great plague that had reached Ireland, the "Buidheach Conall" – "jaundice the colour of stubble". This was called the "Antonine Plague", a severe form of hepatitis, which had originated somewhere in the Middle East, and over the following years it spread throughout Europe by land and by sea, eventually reaching Ireland.

The death of Mobhi

On hearing of the plague, Mobhi told his students to leave and disperse to save themselves. He himself stayed behind in Glasnevin to minister to the people there until he succumbed to the plague. Mobhi died in Glasnevin "on the banks of the Tolka to the north" in the year 544.A.D. (The Annals of the Four Masters). The conventional date of his death is 12th October 544, but such dates were usually allocated by the annalists and cannot be authenticated.

St Colmcille, St. Ciaran, St. Canice and St. Comgall

Four famous students of Mobhi went on to found monasteries. Canice founded monasteries at Finglas and Kilkenny (which derives its name from him). Ciaran founded the famous monastery at Clonmacnoise, and Comgall founded monasteries at Clontarf and Bangor.

Colmcille, having left Glasnevin journeyed northwards, staying in various places including Swords (Sord Colmcille). He was then aged twenty-five years. Eventually, he arrived at Derry where he was welcomed by the local chief, Aodh Mac Ainmire. The chief gave him hospitality and offered him land for a monastery. Colmcille, mindful of Mobhi's command, felt bound to refuse the offer. However, as he was leaving the fort of the chief, he met two men whom he recognized as being from Glasnevin. They told him that, before he died, Mobhi had sent them to say that Colmcille now had permission to accept land. The men gave him Mobhi's girdle or cris as a sign of this. Colmcille replied thus:

> "Mobhi's girdle
> Never was closed around fullness
> it was not opened before satiety
> it was not shut around lies"   (from Leabhar Breac).

The girdle or "cris" (crios in modern Irish) in the Irish monastic tradition had a special significance: it was worn to prevent overeating and could be tightened as a form of penance. Some were preserved in "Belt Shrines", as was that of Mobhi. The accuracy of this story, and of other stories of the period, has been questioned by modern historians.

The Annals of Ulster record three successors to Mobhi: Cialltrog, who died in 741 A.D., Elpin who died in 753 A.D., and Maolbuille ("Princeps Glasnoide") who died in 882 A.D.

The memory of Mobhi

The memory of Mobhi was revered for centuries after his death. The name Mobhi was adopted by some other religious persons and there was a Saint Mobhi in North County Dublin in the Skerries area who has been confused by some writers with the original saint. Kilmovee in County Mayo commemorates another saint of that name.

An account of the life of Saint Colman, who lived in the seventh century, which was discovered in the town library in Rennes (Brittany) by Kuno Meyer (the renowned Celtic scholar) tells that Colman on his return to Ireland visited Glasnevin "to sleep and pray on the grave of Mobhi Clarainach".

The latter days of the monastic settlement

There is a dearth of information on the monastery in Glasnevin towards the end of the first millennium.

Around 1000 A.D. there was a re-organization of the monasteries whereby Finglas Abbey (now restored) became the "mother house" for the monasteries in the area, including Glasnevin. We can assume that the church in Glasnevin and a monastic residence of some sort were rebuilt, and they lasted until the twelfth century. There is no trace of the original church or huts which, being constructed of timber or wattles, could not have lasted more than a few years at a time.

The burial ground of the monastery

As described above, the monastic site stretched as far as the present Ballymun Road. In the summer of 1914 during the building of an extension to Marlborough House (on the site of the present Meteorological Office), a number of early Christian graves were unearthed. These consisted of about ten "slab graves" or tombs made of limestone slabs, lying east-to- west, containing human remains and some artifacts including a bone implement resembling an apple- scoop (National Museum Registration No. 1915: 42, a letter from a Professor. Dixon). The graves were thought to date from the 10th century.

No other artifacts were found, which seems to have discouraged further interest, presumably not helped by the outbreak of the Great War.

References: The Life of Colmcille by Adamnan, translated by Prof. O Cheallachuir
Dublin Historical Record 1957 Vol. 17

Medieval Dublin: Pre-Norman Dublin, by John Ryan S.J. (Irish Academic Press)
"The Early Irish Church" by Kathleen Hughes (Cambridge University Press) .

Chapter 4:
THE NORSE PERIOD

The Norsemen

The Norsemen devastated much of the country until they eventually settled down to build Ireland's first towns. Glasnevin could not have escaped their ravages, but there is no specific reference to Glasnevin in the monastic accounts of the period.

The Lindsay Hoard

In 1838, a small hoard of Hiberno-Norse coins was found in the Claremont area of Glasnevin, and it was subsequently given the name "the Lindsay Hoard". It consisted of seven coins minted in York, England, in the tenth century, and two Arabic coins ("Kufic Dirhams"). These coins may have some association with the expulsion of the Hiberno-Norse dynasty from York in 927 A.D.

References: The Hiberno-Norse Coins in the British Museum by H.M. Dolley M.R.I.A, F.S.A. (British Museum)
Ms catalogue of Dawson cabinet in Royal Irish Academy.

The Battle of Clontarf and the weapon-finds

The only major event here in this period was the Battle of Clontarf, possibly the most famous battle in Irish history, which was fought on Good Friday 1014 between Brian Boru's forces and a huge Norse army that included reinforcements from overseas. Notwithstanding the historical name, the battle was fought mainly in the areas of present Glasnevin, Clonliffe and Phibsborough and as far south as Mountjoy Square. The last stage of the fighting took place in the present Clontarf and Fairview areas when the Norse were retreating to their ships. The combatants numbered about thirty thousand in all, and the burial of the dead and clearing the battle area afterwards must have taken a long time. The dead and their weapons were scattered over the entire battle area, from Glasnevin to Fairview, judging by discoveries made in the 20th century.

When Marlborough Hall (later "Colaiste Caoimhin", the Dept. of Defence) was being built in the early 1900s, excavations revealed several pits containing human remains and rusty weapons which must have dated from this event. The National Museum appears not to have been informed, and the find was used and dispersed by the local children at the time. Similar but smaller finds were made during the building of houses on Home Farm Road in the 1930s.

There is a field on the banks of the River Tolka, lying just north of the Cemetery, designated "The Bloody Acre", which name some accounts ascribe to the "Battle of Tolka Wood". This battle supposedly took place some time before the Norman Invasion. There is so far no evidence for the origin of the name.

Source: Brendan Scally

Chapter 5:
Christ Church Cathedral and Glasnevin

The reform of Christ Church

After a succession of Danish prelates, Laurence O'Toole, Abbot of Glendalough, became Archbishop of Dublin in 1163. He was the first Irishman to occupy the See, and the last one for many centuries.
 He introduced major reforms in the diocese, including the establishment of parishes. Fingal was divided into forty parishes of which Glasnevin was one. These parishes were taken over by the new Church of Ireland after the Reformation, where, despite amalgamation, they remain almost unchanged to the present day.

The Church of the Holy Trinity, better known as "Christ Church Cathedral", or to be precise, its associated Priory, was to play a major part in the history of Glasnevin. The Cathedral was founded in 1038 A.D. and the associated Priory of the Holy Trinity was established as a monastic chapter to the Cathedral. The Priory was placed in the charge of the "Canons Secular", who were monks of an English Benedictine Order introduced by the Danish Bishop.

 Laurence O'Toole, as the new Archbishop of Dublin introduced major reforms in his diocese during the period before and after the Normans arrived. He reformed the Priory of the Holy Trinity by changing its constitution from Canons Secular to Canons Regular who observed the Rule of Saint Augustine. There were twelve "Canons" or priests in the Priory who, with the Prior, were responsible for the administrative affairs of the Priory lands. The work on the lands was performed by lay brothers, by employees such as ploughmen, and by the tenants as part of their leases.

The lands of Glasnevin under the new order

In the new order in England, and now in Ireland, the development of towns and cities, as distinct from villages and hamlets, meant that the supply of food had to be organized to produce surpluses on a large scale to feed urban dwellers

In 1178, the Archbishop granted certain church lands to the Priory of the Holy Trinity attached to Christ Church Cathedral. These included the present Dean's Grange, Grangegorman (which occupied approximately the same area as Phibsborough and Broadstone today), and the Lands of Glasnevin which were transferred from the Abbey of Finglas. The Lands of Glasnevin are bounded by Santry to the North and East, by Finglas to the North and West, by Grangegorman to the South, and by Drishoge (now part of Drumcondra) to the East. (CC Deed 364).

The Archbishop requested the Pope, Alexander III to take the diocese into his care and to confirm the possessions of the See of Dublin. The Pope granted this in his decree issued 20th April 1179 A.D. The decree mentions "Glasnevin with its Mill" (" Glasnedin cum Molindino") as granted to the Priory of the Holy Trinity. ("Crede mihi"). A Bull issued in 1186 by Pope Urban III again confirms the arrangement and mentions "Glasnoyden with its Church" amongst the possessions of the Priory. (CC Deed 6).

When King John granted Dublin its Charter in 1192, he confirmed, as temporal ruler, the Church possessions in the Papal Decree, including "Glasnedan" to the Priory of the Holy Trinity (he was later to fall out with the Pope over payments, bringing England under interdict for a long period).

In 1228, the "Grange of Glasnevin" with its "Church and Appurtenances" was confirmed once again as belonging to the Priory of the Holy Trinity, this time by Archbishop Luke.(CC Deed 44).
The Prior, as Lord of the Manor, had absolute jurisdiction over all tenants and inhabitants, and he held his own "Courts Baron" to administer justice. "Courts Leet" were another form of assizes which were held annually by the steward or bailiff of the Manor, and dealt with petty crime.

Tenancies and rents

In the twelfth and thirteenth centuries, money did not form part of the rent, and payment was in the form of produce such as poultry, grain, and one or two days work for the landlord at times of ploughing, sowing, weeding, haying and harvest.

Taxation matters

The "Crede mihi" has an entry for 1230 A.D. stating that "the Church in Glasnevyn in the Deanery of Tachny (Taney)" was worth 30s. after all deductions.

According to the Account Roll of the Priory (or the" Black Book" as it was also called), in 1306 A.D. the Priory's possessions in Glasnevin were *"a Manor with three carucates of land valued at 48 shillings in tithes.*

In 1339 A.D. Archbishop Alexander established the right of Visitation by the Archdeacon of Dublin in the church of Glasnevin and the right to receive by proxy 20d from that church (CC Deed 208)

References: Archbishop Alen's Register of Ancient Deeds,
Crede mihi
Christ Church Deeds.

Chapter 6:
MEDIEVAL GLASNEVIN:
ITS CASTLE AND MOTTE

The arrival of the Normans in Glasnevin

The earliest recorded mention of a newcomer to Glasnevin concerns one William of Glasnevin and his wife Juliana, who granted lands at Kinsealy to the Priory. No further details of the transaction or of the individuals are extant.

The church in Glasnevin, up to then a wooden structure like many, was rebuilt by immigrant stonemasons and other artisans, and consecrated to "Saint Movus" in 1240 A.D. It was refurbished and enlarged in 1345 A.D.

The Motte on the hill

Before building a castle, the Normans used to erect a temporary defensive earthwork called a "motte" consisting of a high conical mound of earth, formed by the soil from excavating a surrounding trench or ditch. The motte had a small fortification or palisade of stone or wood on top, and it was surrounded by a circular enclosure called a "bailey".

Figure 2: Norman Motte, River Gardens, Glasnevin Hill

Evidence of a Norman presence in Glasnevin lies in the *motte,* a large circular mound situated in the present River Gardens apartment development. Its strategic position would have afforded views up and down the River and way to the south. The circular stone wall at the summit is shown on some 19th century maps and it was gradually dismantled during the 20th century.

The Castle of Glasnevin

Figure 3: Glasnevin Castle ruins c.1944

A small castle – the Grange or Manor Hall – was erected just south of the Church, probably at the same time as the rebuilding of the church in 1240 A.D. The castle was of a type now designated a "hall house", or "hall castle" which was common in England and Scotland in the thirteenth and fourteenth centuries. It should not be confused with the "hall keep" and the later "tower house" type. Unlike the hall keep which was part of a larger complex, a hall house stood alone. A typical hall house, for example, would consist of a two-storey rectangular building, with a small turret at one corner. It would have been surrounded by an external stockade, usually of timber.

The Castle was the centre of administration for the Manor of Glasnevin, wherein was held a Court Baron. The "Chamberlain" or "Bailiff" who managed the manor would have resided here along with some of his staff and servants. The building contained chambers for the Prior for use during his regular visits as Lord of the Manor when, for example, he would preside at the Court Baron.

Figure 4: Glasnevin Castle ruins: Doorway

The castle was probably refurbished in 1345 A.D. and continued in use until the dissolution of the monasteries in 1545. It fell into ruin sometime afterwards, and its ruins lasted until they were levelled in 1950 in the course of the building of the new Bons Secours Hospital.

Figure 3 is a photograph taken of the ruins of the Castle in 1944, (the Gothic arch is possibly an 18th century embellishment by Dr. Delany). Figure 5 gives an architect's impression of how it may have looked originally.

Figure 5: Impression of the original Glasnevin Castle c.1340

Glasnevin Village

A village (or "towne" as it was termed) was established wherein resided the newcomers - tradesmen and labourers - that worked the farm. Their houses would have been of mud or stone with thatched roofs, and having a rectangular shape unlike the circular dwellings of the native Irish. Each small dwelling would have included a strip of land (designated a "messuage") which was intended to provide food for the family. Historical documents show that the smallholders' dwellings or "messuages" consisted of strips of land between the main road and the river Tolka, starting at Glasnevin Hill, and continuing down the present Old Finglas Road. Each messuage had access to the river bank.

The new residents

By the year 1300 A.D. the centre of Glasnevin had become a typical Anglo-Norman village. The following tenants are listed for the year 1325 A.D. by Thoma Beuly in the Account Roll of the Priory:

John de Barry
John Fox (farmer)
Geoffry Finch (farmer)
Thomas Caman
Matilda Kyngham
Cecilia Knyt
Iyvar Vertator (turner)
Maurice the Dryver
Annota Attehill
John Baret
Alice Othyre
Alice Salmon
Nicholas the Clerk
Thomas Callagh
Nicholas le Grete
Robert Richard
Thomas the Chamberlain
John Crobok
Thomas Lang
Richard Braceator (Brewer)
Adam Mayn
Hugh the Smith.
Margery Kakhen
Alice Lambe
Eva the Widow
John Lambe
Sir David the Chaplain
Simon Kynche
Robert Olay
William Bodenham
Mariota Salmon (Salmon by the water)

We can see here the hierarchy of people that worked the Manor: In charge of the Manor, a Chamberlain (variously termed "steward" or "bailiff") who was assisted by a clerk, farmers, a brewer, a driver, and a smith. Sir David, as priests were addressed at that time, looked after their spiritual welfare. He paid an annual rent of 6d for his cottage.

Apart from, possibly, Thomas Callagh, none of the names given above are Gaelic, from which we may infer that no Irish remained.

Source: Christ Church Deeds (RCB Library).

Chapter 7:
THE MANOR FARM OF GLASNEVIN AND THE PRIOR

The source of the information below is the Account Roll of the Priory of the Holy Trinity, which was kept by Thomas de Beuly.

The Manor Farm

A part of the Manor was farmed directly by the Priory, which seems to correspond to the area designated later as the "Fee Farm". The produce of the Manor farm comprised cereals, vegetables, hay and sheep.

In 1345 A.D., the Manor work-force consisted of a *"serjeant"* (a privileged tenant - originally a retainer that had rendered signal service to his lord in battle), one carter, six ploughmen, one shepherd and one doorkeeper. These men were assisted, at the busy times of sowing, mowing, haying, weeding and harvesting, by tenants who were obliged to do so under the terms of their leases.

Ploughmen were paid wages of five shillings a year, and the workmen were paid in grain as the following entries for 1343 show:

Allowances of one serjeant, one carter, 6 ploughmen, of Glasnevin, from the Sunday 18 May) next before the feast of S. Dunstan to the feast of S. Margaret the virgin (20 July) for 10 weeks, 7 crannocs 1 peck, at 7 pecks, heaped to the crannoc, and each takes 8 pecks, level measure, for 10 weeks, which is, by heaped measure, 6 ¼ peck.

(A peck was the dry measure equivalent of a gallon, and was in use until the early part of the 20th century).

The rebuilding of the Church and the Castle

From the Account Roll of the Priory entries for the year 1345 A.D. it may be adduced that the Church and the Castle underwent some form of refurbishment or, more likely, rebuilding. The following are the entries:

a censer bought for Glasnevin, 7d.

repair of one small hammer for breaking stones at Glasnevin, 2d

hire of a certain man making straw chairs, seats and straw stools for the Prior's chamber at Dublin as well as at Glasnevin, 16d.

to Brother John Dolphin for making 2 glass windows for the chancel at Glasnevin, with bars, nails and hooks of iron, for the same, 2s 2 1/2d.

iron bought to make bars for the windows of Glasnevin, 2s 7d.

The Prior of the Holy Trinity

The Prior of the Convent of the Holy Trinity was Lord of the Manor of Glasnevin. The office was a prestigious and powerful one, which controlled vast wealth. For this reason, the Prior had a status similar to that of an abbot, despite the nominal seniority of the latter. The establishment at Christ Church was a centre of Anglo-Norman power in that it contained the original Four Courts, and also maintained a school for the education of children in the English tradition.

The Prior visited Glasnevin regularly, and his arrival with his entourage would have been a cause for some stir in the village. The usual purpose of his visit was to preside over the Court Baron which tried minor miscreants. Serious offences were dealt with at the Priory in Dublin.

The Prior's table

The Prior would normally be served three full meals each day. The fare was lavish and varied. For instance, breakfast on one particular day consisted of roast goose, pigeon, and wine. Other meals would include lark pie, oysters from Clontarf, chicken, rabbit (the domestic variety), onions (the only vegetable mentioned), followed by pears and imported figs and dates. On Fridays and other days of abstinence, fish provided the main course. Such elaborate meals often concluded with sweet dishes called "subtletys" – cakes of marchpane (or "marzipan" as it is called today) fashioned into shapes, the medieval equivalent of "petit fours".

The Account Roll for 1343 and 1344 contains quite a number of items pertaining to food and drink that were bought in Glasnevin for the use of the Prior and his guests, including wine and ale.

In Glasnevin at this time the local ale-house was run by a Mariota Dawenoy, with whom the Prior had an account. (An entry reads *"Also to Mariota Dawenoy for a debt of ale from the time of Robert the Bailiff at Glasnevin, 2s"*. The location of the premises is not known, but for a number of reasons, its most likely site would have been beside the bridge where the 18th century Bull's Head Tavern stood, and the present Tolka House stands today.

The Black Death.

The Black Death – the Bubonic Plague – was probably the most virulent disease ever to afflict Europe.
In Ireland, the plague entered by the seaports of Howth and Dalkey. It affected mainly the Anglo-Norman settlers in the towns and cities, including Kilkenny, where a Franciscan, John Clyn, recorded the events for posterity. Its severity was such that three quarters of the victims died within a week. Crops perished in the fields and livestock were untended and abandoned. It appears that at least half – perhaps two thirds - of the total population perished. In Dublin, all the Canons of the Priory of the Holy Trinity died, including Thomas de Beuly, and the Account Roll ceased then. There is no account of what happened in Glasnevin, but it could not have escaped the plague.
Outbreaks occurred again in 1362, in 1368-69, and in 1374-75, further reducing the population. On the other hand the native Gaelic population escaped largely due to its rural structure and its low density.

"It's an ill wind that blows no one any good" is an old saying that proved true in this event. The decrease in the numbers of labourers eventually led to higher wages, despite the efforts of the Crown in England to peg wages by issuing the Statute of Labourers. On the other hand, farmers and others whose rents comprised so many days labour found that they could no longer afford the cost, and many in Glasnevin and elsewhere abandoned their holdings. This gave rise to changes in the system of land-leasing and the type of tenant involved, and this is described in the next chapters.
Further plagues were to occur at intervals over the following centuries causing more devastation of Dublin's population.

References: "The Great Dying" by Maria Kelly, published by Tempus
The Account Roll of the Priory of the Holy Trinity

Chapter 8:
Glasnevin in the 15th Century: Tenants and leases

The Tower House

In 1429, a statute was passed with the effect that a subsidy of £10 would be paid by the Commons of every county to every "liege man of our Lord the King" (Henry V) who would build "a tower sufficiently embattled or fortified", at least twenty feet by sixteen feet by forty feet high. These small castles or "tower houses" were merely fortified houses which were occupied by the gentry of the Pale. A large number of tower houses were built, but few have survived.

A tower house was built in Glasnevin about this time in the Hampstead area. It was called Hampstead Castle in the eighteenth century by the new owner, and it is shown thus on early 18th century maps. Strangely, it is not shown in the Survey of 1640, although the approach avenue thereto is shown. The ruins existed until 1875, when its stones were used in the building of the Elmhurst, the convalescent home of Hampstead Hospital.

Leases to the Canons

In the 1400s, some of the monks or canons of the Priory were given leases of small lots in Glasnevin for a nominal rent – " a red rose", for example, and the Sacrist or Treasurer of the Priory had the lease of the Mill and a part of the Mill Field. The larger part of the Mill Field was the benefice of the Canons (later "Vicars Choral") of Christ Church. These two plots were a source of substantial income, and tenants were obliged to have their corn ground at this mill. The Mill Field, seeing that it was beside the bridge and the ale-house, was probably the area where trading was carried and traders would have had to pay for the use of the ground.

The Great Farm and the Fox Family

The earliest lease on record of a large property was that of the Great Farm which was occupied by the Fox family in the 14th and 15th centuries.

Documents surviving from the period and published in "Berry's Wills" include an inventory of all the goods, "moveable and immoveable", for the year 1473 of Geoffrey Fox and his wife Jonet, following her demise. Also included are the wills of Jonet Fox (1473), and of Geoffrey's second wife, Margaret (nee Lawless) (1476), the domestic details of which make interesting historical reading.

The Farm of Clonmel: Housing for the farm labourers

In 1475, Robert Fitz Symond, of Dublin, obtained a lease of lands in Clonmell for 41 years at 20s for 14 years p.a. and 2 capons and 2 geese annually. He was bound to perform the *"customary service"* on meadow, ploughing, reaping and weeding days (CC Deed 931). In addition, he was to erect, over a period of six years, a house *"seven couples long"* with mud walls and a roof of straw, a gate with wood and planks of oak, and to make suitable ditches to protect the premises. This building was to house some of the farm labourers of the Manor.

The word *"couple"* denotes a simple type of house of a modular construction with an A - shaped roof provided by a couple of naturally-curved timber trusses, termed *"crucks"*, secured by a horizontal tie- beam at wall level, and a "collar beam" near the apex. This arrangement - called a "cruck truss" - was supported independently, or almost independently, of the walls.
The word "ditch" here meant a low wall of mud and stones, as used up to recently in Munster.

The small tenants: rent and responsibilities

For smaller tenants, rents at this time usually consisted of payment partly in money, along with the provision of labour during harvest, a "ridge" of corn, "watch hens" at Christmas, and "heriots", "hocks" or "hartells" (A heriot was a tribute paid to a lord on the death of a tenant, consisting of a live animal, a chattel, or, originally, the return of borrowed equipment. A hock was special payment usually made at festival times. The exact meaning of "hartell" is not known). Some tenants were obliged to provide the keep of a horse at Christmas, when the Prior, and later the Dean, visited Glasnevin.

The care and preservation of trees was of particular importance, perhaps even more than in modern times. Trees could not be cut down without a licence, and where a full-grown tree was felled, ten young trees had to be planted instead. Ash wood was much in demand, since it was used to make carts and cart wheels.

Details of various small tenancies will be found in the Deeds of the Priory of the Holy Trinity

For example, in 1473 there was a lease to *Thomas Fyche*, Canon of the Cathedral of the Holy Trinity (Christ Church) and *Thomas Petyt*e, Clerk, and *William Fyche* of a vacant place in the croft of William Dullant, of Glasnevin, for the life of Thomas Fyche. The annual rent was "one red rose". (CC Deed 1003).

The lessees were bound to erect a dove- cot nearby. Dove-cots to house pigeons and doves were common at this time: a typical one consisted of a large bee-hive shaped masonry- structure up to 20 feet high, with an opening at the top for entry, and recesses for nesting inside. A door at ground-level provided access.

In one case, where a tenant took over a house in which Margaret Yoye, a widow, lived, there was a condition that she was not to be ejected for as long as she lived.

Reference: Byrne's Dictionary of Irish Local History.

Chapter 9:
THE REFORMATION AND AFTERWARDS

The clergy and religious of Glasnevin before the Reformation

As the 15th century moved to a close, the momentous event of the Reformation began in Germany. In Ireland, life continued at its usual pace, inside and outside the Pale, unaware of coming events that were to culminate in the greatest religious and political upheaval since the fall of the Roman Empire.

The available information gives the names of some of the clergy that served in Glasnevin in this period:

John Neil (c. 1470)
John Wolfe (d.1481)
Patrick Lowe, who obtained a lease of two messuages in Glasnevin in1508. He died in 1514.

John Wolfe and Patrick Lowe (or Law) are mentioned in the "Obits and Martyrology of Christ Church Cathedral" as being worthy of remembrance annually.

Also mentioned in the "Obits" are Richard of Glasnevin, Canon ("Canonus Noster"), and William Stratyn of Glasnevin, Brother, ("Frater nostri congregationis").

Reference: Obits and Martyrology of Christ Church Cathedral

The Priory of the Holy Trinity after the Reformation

King Henry VIII declared himself Head of the Church of England in 1535. However, he was a schismatic rather than a reformer, and Protestantism did not obtain a hold in England until later.
His first act was the suppression of all the religious houses and the acquisition of their wealth.
Following the King's decree in 1538, the Commission for the Suppression of all Abbeys recommended that six houses, including three in Dublin, should be allowed to continue "changing their habit and rule after such sort as shall please the King's majesty should stand". The three houses in Dublin were St. Mary's Abbey, Grace Dieu in North County Dublin, and the Priory of the Holy Trinity. However, despite the Commission's

recommendations, a royal decree closed down all the monasteries except the Priory.

The reason for this exemption was that the Priory was, along with Dublin Castle, an important centre for the English establishment in Ireland. The Deputy and Officers used to lodge there, and it ran a school for "young men and children in virtue, learning and the English tongue and behaviour". The original Four Courts used to sit there, and Parliaments, Councils and the Commons could resort thereto in term time for definition by Judge. Closing down this establishment was clearly out of the question.

From Prior and Priory to Dean and Chapter

In 1537, Robert Payneswyke was installed as the Prior of the Holy Trinity, with Richard Ball as sub-Prior, and John Mosse as Precentor and Sacrist. In 1539 a royal decree changed the title and office of Prior to that of Dean of Christ Church, with, among other benefices, the Church of Glasnevin for his prebend.
The sub-Prior became Precentor, having one half of the tithes of Glasnevin, and the Seneschal and Precentor. William Whyte became the Chancellor, having the other half of those tithes.

The sub-Precentor and Sacrist became the Treasurer, and he enjoyed the benefices of Balscadden, Punchestown, and the Water Mill of Glasnevin, with the small piece of land adjoining (the Mill Field).
Six "Vicars Choral" replaced the monks, and they were allocated the piece of land beside the Mill Field, which is today the island in the Botanic Gardens formed by the River Tolka and the mill stream.

(Surprisingly, perhaps, a decree dated 1542 states that the Vicars Choral were obliged, under penalty, to celebrate Mass regularly including "*Roode Masse in Lent and one ladie mass daily*").

Merchants and aldermen: the new land owners

After the dissolution of the religious houses, their lands were forfeited to the Crown. This gave an opportunity to the Dublin merchants to acquire the properties that were now on the market, and they lost no time in doing so. The Corporation was given the task of granting leases of the lands, and the Aldermen, by virtue of their position, were able to take full advantage of the opportunities presented.

The Reformed Church in Dublin, despite its official status and the zeal and sincerity of its adherents, was not faring well. Not least among its problems was shortage of money, now that the former church lands were in the hands of laymen. If the new landlords were Protestant, they supported the new clergy, but the records show that, for a considerable period, the majority of Aldermen, gentry and merchants remained Catholic.

A change in the leasing system of the Lands of Glasnevin

The lands of Glasnevin remained under the direct ownership of the Dean and Chapter of the Cathedral of the Holy Trinity (Christ Church) for some time. The Dean and Chapter decided that they would no longer be involved directly in running their farms or in small leases, and accordingly, they farmed out their lands to "large" tenants. Dean's Grange, Grangegorman and Glasnevin were among the manors of Christ Church that were divided and leased to the new tenants.

With this change came a new type of lease known as the "Fee Farm". This was a tenure by which an estate was held in "fee simple", that is, free from conditions or limitations on inheritance, and without any other services beyond a perpetual fixed rent. This did away with all the complex medieval services, hocks and heriots and made the rent a straightforward monetary payment. However, many leases continued under the old system until the 17th century.

The lease of the Manor of Glasnevin

Until 1540, there had been only one large tenancy, namely, the Great Farm of Glasnevin. In 1542, the Dean and Chapter began the division of the lands of Glasnevin with a lease to *Alderman Thomas Stephyns*, *Alison* his wife, and his son *Oliver Stephyns*, merchant, of the Manor of Glasnevin, with lands in Glasnevin and Drumcondra, the Mill of Glasnevin with "tacht and watercourse thereof" (the mill meadow, watch hens and customary hocks of the Manor exempted) for 31 years. The rent was £19-12s-8d with the moiety of the heriots or hartells during the term. The usual covenant applied for re-entry in the event of non-payment of rent.

The lessors would give two ash trees annually to build wheels and carts, and the lessees were to set 20 young ash trees in lieu thereof. The lessees were bound by covenant not to cut down any of the great trees of the Manor without licence. (This was at a time when timber had become scarce in Ireland generally and special measures were necessary for its conservation).

The Seven farms

In 1579, Alderman Richard Fagan obtained a lease for £10 for the Seven Farms. There was a covenant for cultivating the land. The Dean also demised to him the "church house" in Glasnevin for a rent of 14s, payable to the Curate of Glasnevin, with two hens at Christmas.

The return of the native Irish

As a result of the hardships of the 1400s, many of the older tenants had died, or had abandoned their holdings which quickly became derelict. The Prior (later the Dean) had no choice but to give the leases to newcomers. The terms of some of the newer leases appear to be rather harsh – a form of "rack-rent"- and included a provision for rebuilding the derelict dwellings.

A glance at the names of the smallholders of Glasnevin village after the year 1500 shows that many of the newcomers were the "mere Irish". This was due to an immigration of ordinary people from Gaelic Ireland, probably in the expectation of a better life, or at least one that provided more stability and security than the Gaelic system. Their names include *John Cane, Gylle christe O Cayn, Dermod O Many, John Mannyng (1532), Laurence Ennis (1581), Carroll (or Kerral) Doyne (Dunne)*. Some of them even attained the higher social position of yeoman.

The locations of some of those leases can readily be identified, e.g. Gylle christe O'Cayn, a tailor, was leased "a ruinous messuage with a garden" beside the bridge, and in 1592, Dermod O Many was leased a messuage on the west side of Glasnevin Hill. In 1542, John Cane was the tenant of a messuage and house opposite the *Bull Ring*. The Bull Ring was situated on the Common, the site of the present national school on Botanic Avenue.

Taxation immunity for Glasnevin

The inhabitants of Glasnevin enjoyed immunity from cesses and carriage by an Act of Parliament, but by 1577 some cessors (tax officials) had gone about "to vex and bother" the inhabitants of Glasnevin. To counter this state of affairs, the Lord Deputy and the Council declared in 1578 the town and lands of Glasnevin exempt from "leases of subsidy and carriage". (CC Deed 453). This was renewed in 1592 by an Order of the Council. On 4th November 1645, an Act of Council again declared that the Town and Lands of Glasnevin in Co. Dublin ought to be free from all costs of subsidy, carriage and all other charges whatever.(Acta Capituli Trinitatis MS 97). This privilege ceased in 1696 when a poll tax was levied instead.

Further reading: The Lords of Dublin in the time of the Reformation by Dr. Colm Lennon
Dublin City and County from Prehistory to Present, Chapter 6. (F.H. Aalen and Kevin Whelan edit.)
Source: Christ Church Deeds

Chapter 10:

GLASNEVIN IN THE 17TH CENTURY: WARS, TURMOIL AND DECLINE

A century of turmoil

The seventeenth century in Ireland was a period of tremendous political and social upheaval. The old Gaelic way of life crumbled away after the flight of its aristocracy, and the Irish people faced a new period of insurrections, wars, massacres and persecutions on a scale unheard of even in Tudor times. Life was hard, and the bitter winters that had begun in the previous century continued to inflict famine and other hardships on a hapless people.

The insurrection of 1641

A period of comparative peace followed the collapse of Gaelic Ireland at the Battle of Kinsale.
In 1641, the situation changed with the outbreak of rebellion in Ulster, which quickly spread throughout Ireland. The Irish forces comprised a confederation of the native Irish and the Old English, which later took the Royalist side in the English Civil War against Cromwell and the Parliamentary Army. The alliance was an uneasy one, despite their common Catholic religion, because many of the Old English had a residual loyalty to the Crown. In the event, all were to suffer after the war.

The area of Glasnevin does not seem to have featured in the war, except for one incident early in 1642 which was recorded by Robert Bysse Junior in his account of events in the Dublin area.

" *News was sent by the state; that the enemy from Drogheda was come to Dublin, at least 4,000 of them and so it was the night before Candlemas Day, Colonel Hugh Byrne and Colonel Lysaght Moore were in the town of Glasnevin, being about 1,000 horse and foot, and were sent for by Colonel Luke Netterville, who also met them with more men. He had given them notice that the English Army was all gone to the County of Kildare, and the town being empty, at least Oxmantown might be fired and pillaged. Netterville and his men kept at Drumcondra, the others were at Glasnevin and these marched nearer the (Abbey) Green to Glasmochonoge (the present Broadstone area),* but the day breaking, they returned, nothing being done, and they hardly discerned (sic) by the *town; only Captain Scout and his company, that night watching about the Bridge of Drumcondra, took a sentry of the enemy early in the morning, who told them he would bring them upon thirty of the enemy close by.*

Apparently, this was a trap, and they found themselves surrounded by at least 500 men, but they managed to escape.

Hearth Rolls

The Hearth Roll of 1657 gives the following information for the Parish of Glasnevin:

William Corbe: 2 hearths
John Griffin: 2 hearths
John Allen: 2 hearths
Alderman Hutchinson: 2 hearths and 1 oven.
18 others with one hearth each.

According to the Hearth Roll of 1664, there were only ten houses, none of which had more than one hearth. The names of the occupiers were: William Hill, a soldier, Widow Allerton, Thomas Jackson, Edmond Gillshaw, Flone Cushlan, Donnell Grymlay, Richard Harris, John Lummond, William Cooper and John Neales.

There is no ready explanation for the discrepancy between the two hearth rolls, or between them and the Survey of 1640

Daniel Hutchinson: Cromwellian supporter and financier

According to the Civil Survey of 1654, the lands of Glasnevin were in the possession of Daniel Hutchinson. Hutchinson was a merchant, an Alderman, and an Elder of the Independent Church and he lived in Winetavern Street in Dublin. He was an ambitious and powerful man who took advantage of the situation to advance his commercial and political interests.

After the Cromwellian campaign, all ecclesiastical lands and revenues were seized by the Commonwealth Government and administered as public property. The supporters of Oliver Cromwell fared well on both sides of the Irish Sea, and one of most prominent of those was Daniel Hutchinson. He became a prominent member of Cromwell's Parliamentary Party and government in Dublin, and he acted as Treasurer to the Commonwealth. He advanced £1000 to supply the Cromwellian forces in Ireland, and was rewarded with a grant of land in County Kildare. He sat in the Westminster Parliament as one of the representatives of Dublin from 1654 to 1656.

After the Restoration of the English monarchy in 1660, Hutchinson found himself in a precarious situation. It says much for his astuteness and political acumen (and perhaps his wealth) that he managed to survive the political and social upheaval, and to hold on to his property. In 1663, a joint petition by the Dean, Dr. Mosson and Daniel Hutchinson to the Duke of Ormond made the case that, since the farm in Glasnevin consisted of eighty small parcels and some larger parcels, it would be impossible to distinguish them, and much trouble might result in law. A surveyor Richard Francis was ordered to give expert evidence.

New leases and the Glebe

Hutchinson stated that he was willing to surrender all his leases and take a new lease, under such covenant for the benefit of the Dean and the Curate or incumbent, and for the repair of the church. This was granted on 27th July 1664. This time, however, he was to be a tenant of the Dean and Chapter to whom the lands had been restored. The lands leased were the Great Farm, Draycott's Farm, and the Seven Farms, now at a rent of £40 per annum, instead of £12-8-6 that he had to pay previously.

Under the terms of his lease Hutchinson was obliged to provide six acres as a glebe for the Curate, convenient to the church, or if the curate should not reside there, he had the use of it at a rent of 40s. This was probably the site of the modern housing development called "The Haven" (off Church Avenue). There was no permanent curate until after 1700, and it appears that the glebe was ignored over this period. The matter was not raised again until the 19th century, when the Curate sought legal advice on the matter. Daniel Hutchinson died in 1676, and was succeeded by his grandson John Weaver.

In 1675, Maurice Berkeley obtained a lease of 200 acres of land lying north of the village. His widow Dorothy would later sell her house and remaining land to Dr. Patrick Delany.

The 1662 Act of Settlement and afterwards

After the restoration of the English monarchy, the authorities set about undoing the acts of the Parliamentarians, in particular, the allocation of property. In 1666 under the Act of Settlement, James, Duke of York, later King James II, was granted lands in England and Ireland. These included the Fee Farm of Glasnevin. After the deposing and flight of King James in

1688, all his lands were forfeited, and in 1693, King William III granted the Glasnevin lands to Henry Guy and others.

The decline of Glasnevin Village

Whereas the Black Death had caused a drastic loss of population in the 1300s, the Cromwellian wars and clearances were at least as devastating in that they caused the death of more than six hundred thousand people. To make things worse, the remaining "Irish" were forced to quit the area around Dublin, Those that were left fled to the cities and towns for their safety, with the result that Glasnevin and the other villages of County Dublin became derelict.

References: The Lords of Dublin in the time of the Reformation
              Radcliffe's paper on Glasnevin (RCB Library) .

Chapter 11:
A Survey of Glasnevin by Richard Francis in 1640

Richard Francis, Surveyor to the Council

In 1640, Richard Francis was appointed Surveyor to the Council by the Lord Deputy. In the same year, he produced the results of his survey of the Town and Lands of Glasnevin belonging to the Dean of the Holy Trinity in Dublin. This document lists in detail every parcel of land in Glasnevin, with the acreage and names of the tenants and under- tenants. Forming part of the survey report is a remarkable map, which shows the all the various holdings, rivers, roads and substantial dwellings. It is on a scale of twenty perches to one inch, and appears to be reasonably accurate for its time. It uses an alpha-numeric system for identifying the holdings in the survey and on the map: The main farms are identified by letters of the alphabet, and the parcels, into which they are subdivided, by number.
The sheer complexity of the parcels of land and their extremely irregular boundaries must have posed great difficulties for the Surveyor.

The Farms of Glasnevin shown on Richard Francis' Map 1640

Many of the farms consist of separate parcels of land lying in different parts of the Parish, and some parcels are very small indeed, particularly in the area around the village. The main farms and their identifying letters are as follows:

A. Draycott's farm (later Wadd's Farm), which was an area south of Clonmel stretching from the Naul Road westwards as far as Ballygall, It also included a small parcel (A27) on the corner of Church Lane and the Naul Road. It comprised a total of 38 Irish Acres.

B. The Seven Farms, which comprised about twenty separate areas scattered throughout Glasnevin comprising a total area of 88 Irish Acres. It included the present Cross Guns area, most of the southernmost area of Glasnevin and various parcels scattered over the parish.

C. Common - a triangle of land designated "D common" at the northeast corner of the parish.

D. The Dean's, which comprised the former Lord's Mede (later called

Drishoge), the Great Meadow (part of the present Botanic Gardens) and various other parcels. This should not to be confused with the nineteenth-century townland of Daneswell.

E. The Vicars of Glasnevin, the area adjoining the churchyard (today called "The Haven") and forming part of the benefice.

F. The Treasurer of Christ Church, the water mill and its immediate surroundings.

G. Gough's farm, which included two parcels in the village (the later townland of Goose Acre stretching from Addison Lodge to Botanic Avenue, and the Carlingford property). This took its name from John Gough, Alderman from 1569 to 1594. It comprised a total of 16 Irish Acres.

H. Clonmel or "Cloonemell" or "Clynmell" which approximated to the present townland of the same name. Its name dates from before Norman times. It is also referred to as Wickam's or Wicomb's farm and Charles' farm. It comprised a total of 53 Irish Acres.

I. The Great Farm, unchanged since 1300 and at one time with 125 Irish acres, the largest holding. It encompassed the greater part of the area north of the River Tolka and to the east of the village, It also included a small parcel on the west side of the highway, referred to as Cullenagh which is approximately the present Wadelai area.

K. Forster's farm, which comprised part of the present Dublin Industrial Estate and a few other areas including a messuage in the village in the area of the present Botanic Villas. It took its name from John Forster, Alderman in 1580. It was previously known as "Broughall's Farm". It comprised a total of 31 Irish Acres.

L. The Fee farm was one of the larger holdings, and included the area of the present cemetery (Prospect), part of Iona area and a large area north of the present Old Finglas Road.
It also included the site of the present Bon Secours Hospital (formerly Delville) and of the now - demolished Roseville. It comprised a total of 156 Irish Acres.

V. The Vicars of Christ Church: The Mill Field adjoining the Treasurer's mill property.

The Seven Farms

By 1640, the under-leasing of the Seven Farms by John Fagan had become quite complicated. Patrick Stronge held 88 acres of the Seven Farms directly from Michael Fagan and another 102 acres under Sir William Anderson. George Carruthers was another under-tenant here to Sir William Anderson. (Actis Capituli 65, CC Deed 1399).

The Dean's Farm

The Survey gives James Bathe of Drumcondra as the main tenant of the Dean's Farm (previously "The Lord's Mede" and afterwards Drishoge),

Draycott's Farm (Wadd's Farm) and the Chamberlain Family

Draycott's Farm, later called Wadd's Farm and North Farm, took its name from lessee Henry Draycott, Master of the Rolls, described as "a weak old man". The Draycotts came from Mornington in County Louth.

In 1594, in consideration of a contribution towards the steeple of Christ Church Cathedral, the farm was leased to Aarland Ussher, of Dublin, for 99 years at a yearly rent of £66-8s and on the expiration of the old lease, for a rent of £3-6s-8d "payable at the Mary Chapel of Christ Church". The lessee was obliged to build and repair the house on the premises, and to keep the same quantity of land under tillage as previously required. (CC Deed 1417).

In 1602, George Ussher of Dublin, Administrator of the affairs of Aarland Ussher assigned a lease of Draycott's Farm to Alderman Michael Chamberlain, a Catholic who came from Athboy, County Meath. His son, also named Michael was the main tenant in 1640. At this time, Chamberlain was also a tenant of part of the Great Farm. Unfortunately for him, he was attainted as an Irish Papist under the Commonwealth of Oliver Cromwell and his lands were forfeited.

After the Restoration he was fortunate, when, as a result of his mother's efforts, his lands were restored to him. Unfortunately, his luck did not hold. After the "Glorious Revolution" that resulted in the defeat and flight of King James II, Michael Chamberlain was once again attainted, this time permanently.

Forster's Farm (Broughall's farm)

The later name comes from Alderman John Forster, who in 1594, obtained a continuation of the lease of the farm which he had held "as amply as John Quatermass or Broughall held same" for 99 years (he was married to a Rose Quatermass). The Survey of 1640 gives William Ball, of Ballygall, as the main tenant.

The Fee Farm.

The Survey gives Mr. James Bath (of Drumcondra) as the main tenant of the 156 Irish Acres of the Fee Farm, with Edward Wickham as under-tenant.

The Vicars' Meadow and the Great Meadow

Some parcels were directly held by the Chapter of Christ Church. These included the island formed by the River Tolka and the mill stream, known today as the "Mill Field".
The mill, with the small strip of land adjoining was a benefice of the Treasurer of Christ Church.

Houses and their occupants in Glasnevin in 1640

The 1640 Survey map shows a number of buildings inside and outside the village, including the church and the mill house with its mill wheel. Three were substantial dwellings: One large house on the site of the present Met Eireann Offices, was the residence of Patrick Stronge (B26). On a later map of the 1688 forfeitures, this house is marked "Baron Echlin's house". (Sir Henry Echlin was Baron of the Exchequer from 1690 to 1714).

Another large house stood on the corner property bounded by Church Avenue and the Naul Road occupied by Jenico Preston (A27). Further up the road, on the site of the present Church Hill House, was a house occupied by John Richards (I22).

On the site of the present Bon Secours Hospital stood a large house occupied in 1640 by Edward Wickam, probably the principal dwelling here, which would later become the "Delville" of Dr Patrick Delany (reference L26). Edward Wickham appears to have been the most prosperous of the residents, and in addition to his own fine residence, he owned four other houses in the village. One was on the site of the present Melville on The Naul (Ballymun)Road, another on the site of the present Holy Faith Convent, a third on the Old Finglas Road on the site of the former

Roseville and a fourth on the west side of the Hill. He also held 156 acres of the Fee Farm under James Bath.

In the Cross-Guns area we find two houses, one occupied by George Carruthers which is on the site of the present Dalcassian Downs and the former orphanage (B7), and another on the opposite side of the road occupied by Robert Bath (E2), beside a lane going southwards (the present Whitworth Road).

Inferior dwellings such as mud cabins and hovels of the poor are not shown.

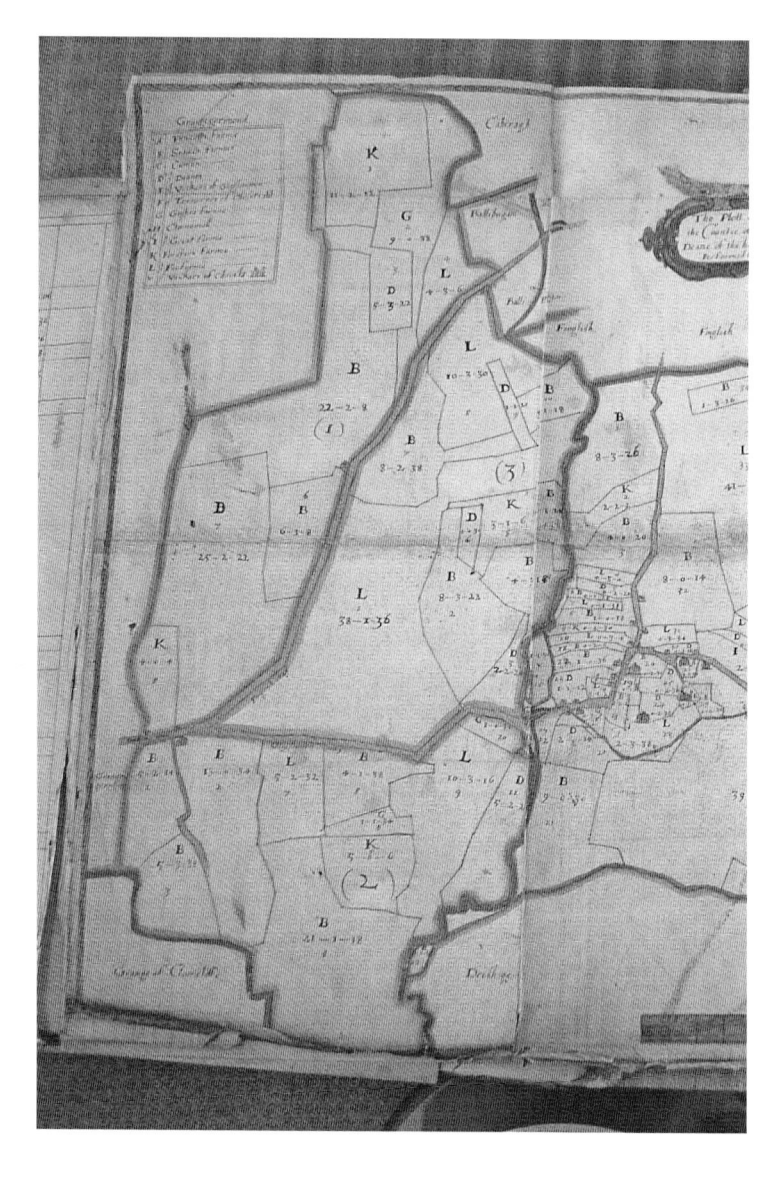

*Figure 6: Survey of Glasnevin by Richard Francis 1640.
Copyright© Representative Church Body*

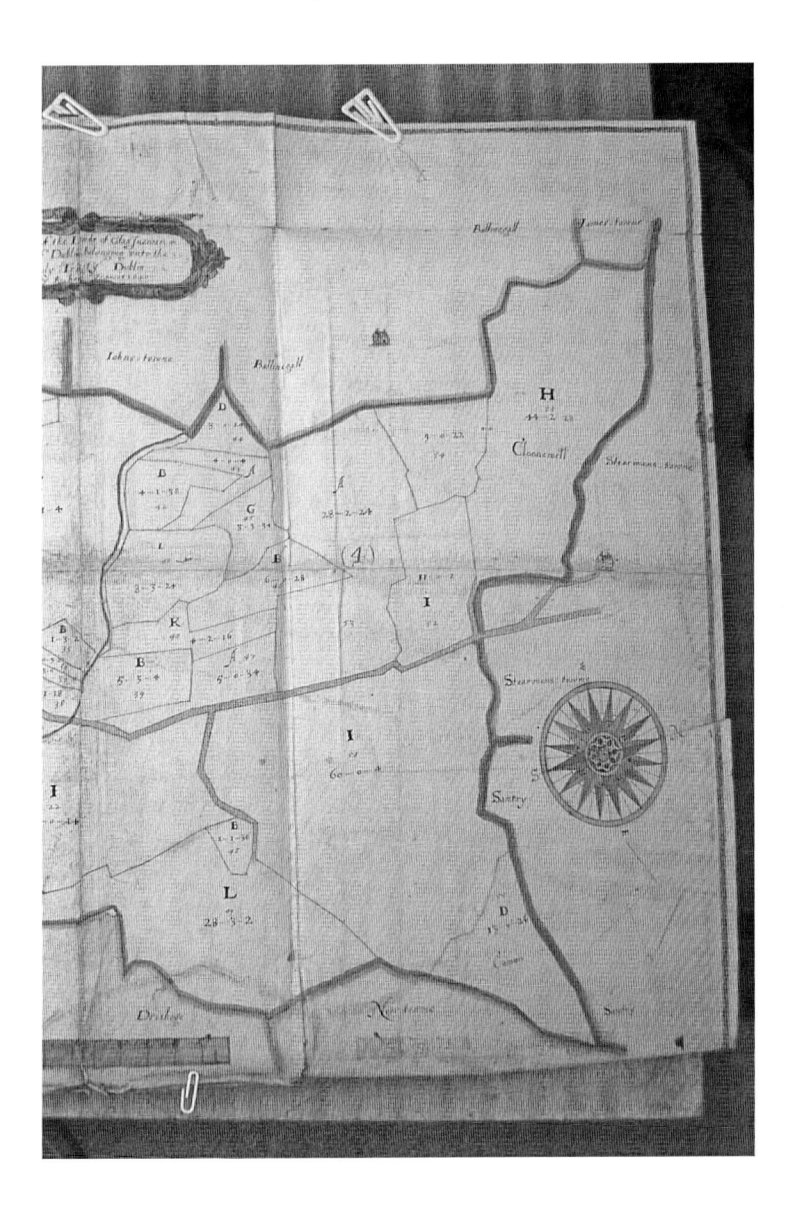

Chapter 12:

The 18th Century:
from ruin to prosperity

A derelict village

County Dublin had fared badly during the 1600s: Fifty years of intermittent warfare and civil disturbance had taken its toll. Its villages and churches were largely in ruins, and Glasnevin was no exception. Archbishop King, in a letter to the proprietors of Grange Gorman dated 8th October 1725, describes the state of Glasnevin village at the turn of the century as follows:

"It was the receptacle of thieves and rogues, the first search when anything was stolen was there; and when any couple had a mind to retire to be wicked, there was their harbour".

Glasnevin Village was a scene of dereliction. There were, it appears, only a few substantial dwellings, and rows of mud cabins and hovels in varying degrees of squalor. The church was roofless and in ruins. What was more, uncertainty regarding the tenancy of the land discouraged investors.

Disposal of the Lands of Glasnevin

The Westminster Parliament decided that it needed money to defray the expenses of the continental wars and the reduction of Ireland. As part of this plan, the lands of King James which had been granted to Henry Guy and others were "resumed" by the English Parliament and vested in trustees for the purposes of sale. The lands of most of Glasnevin were sold on 1st June 1703 to Sir John Rogerson for £2687. Part of the price was paid in money, and the remainder in soldiers' debentures which he had bought from their owners, very likely in public houses and various other locations.

Sir John Rogerson, Knight and property developer

Within fifteen years, a great improvement had taken place, and Glasnevin had become a prosperous and prestigious place in which to dwell. The individual mainly responsible for this was Sir John Rogerson, a man with wide commercial and political interests and one of the most enterprising gentlemen of his day. As well as being a successful business man, he was a merchant, a ship owner, a Member of the Irish Parliament, and Lord Mayor of Dublin. The quay named after him has preserved his memory.

Rogerson also purchased 195 acres from Maurice Berkeley's widow Dorothy, containing arable meadow, a garden and orchard on the north side of the street, also a stone house with conveniences all in good repair, with a garden and orchard (probably Exchequer Baron Echlin's residence), and another house and garden with a large court surrounded by a stone wall on the Naul Road (possibly the site of the future Clermont, which eventually became St. Clare's).

The rebuilding of Glasnevin Village

Rogerson rebuilt most of Glasnevin village and its church. He built for himself a house at the end of the village street facing the Naul road which later became known as "Glasnevin House" and ultimately the present Holy Faith Convent. Rogerson built several other houses in the area, and these would have been in the Jacobean or Queen Anne style. Some of those, including Glasnevin House, were rebuilt in a Georgian style later in the century.

Three of the original houses survived well into the twentieth century. These were: The Turrets, Ardmore, and Beechmount House, the last of which is the only one to survive to this day. One of his achievements in Glasnevin was the rebuilding of the church, with the financial help of friends and neighbours.

Archbishop King wrote, in the continuation of his letter to the proprietors of Grange Gorman, *"but since the church was built, and service settled, all these evils are banished. Good houses are built in it and the place civilized "* In another letter, the Archbishop writes, somewhat cynically, that *"Sir John Rogerson got a church built at Glasnevin, and contributed effectually to it, and it has doubled and trebled his rent".*

Sir John Rogerson died in 1724, and his estate included a dwelling house, stables, a coach house and some land behind the house which were left to his widow for her lifetime and then passed to his sons William and John. The coach house still stands, and is of interest for its unique fenestration.

The Berkeleys

One of the largest landowners in Glasnevin at the turn of the century was Maurice Berkeley, whose wife Dorothy was a daughter of Major Joseph Deane of Crumlin.

The Berkeleys had leased property of more than two hundred acres in 1667 from the Fee Farm that had been settled on James Duke of York (the future King James II) after the Restoration. The lease was renewed in 1675 and again in 1688 after the deposing of King James. Their land was mostly situated to the north of the village, and included the future Claremont Estate and Delville.

In 1703, Mrs. Berkeley, now widowed, sold most of her land to Sir John Rogerson, but retained her dwelling house and the land surrounding. This land comprised about fifteen acres, including four acres described as "The Glynn" (the glen of the Nevin Stream), a plot with a front on the street. In 1717, Mrs Berkeley demised this plot to Hugo Batho, the Huguenot merchant whose house and garden adjoined it.

In 1719, she demised her property, including "The Glen", to Dr. Richard Helsham and Dr. Patrick Delany. Mrs. Berkeley purchased a new and smaller villa close by, called the "Garden House", on Gough's Farm, the site of the later Carlingford House, from Sir John Rogerson.

She died in 1728, leaving her house to her eldest daughter (also called Dorothy) whose husband was John Charlton, Justice. They leased the house to George Bannister of Dublin (Deed 71/39) with the use of a pew in the church.

In 1737, the younger Dorothy Charleton, now widowed, made a new lease of the house- the "hobbledehoy" as Swift called it - to Doctor Delany.

Source: Registry of Deeds, King's Inns

Chapter 13:

18ᵀᴴ Century residents

New names

As the village developed, gentlemen from Dublin City acquired or built villas in the area, and Glasnevin became a fashionable place of residence for the literary, artistic and professional classes of Dublin. Many of the names in the early parish records of Glasnevin are clearly English, with a few French Huguenot names. These people were mainly prosperous middle class and tradesmen. There were also, of course, the poor, who were of native stock.

The villagers.

Many of the names of the villagers for the first half of the century appear to be mainly from the North of England: The names include Cooke, Blundell, Williams, Wolfinden, Gass, Hudson, Tickell, Beele, Eltaph, Jenkinson, Teeling, Fairweather, Pilkington, Cliburn, Atkinson, and Knightly.

Andrew Macilraith, a man from Belfast, set up a paper mill on the site of the Mill of Glasnevin, and the family lived there until the beginning of the next century.

Irish names begin to appear after 1710, for example Leinagh, Reilly, Kelly, Kane, Ogan, Barry, Tracy, Carroll, and Doyle. The very poor that lived on the south side of the river were almost certainly native Irish and nominally Catholic. The majority of the other residents were Protestant, regardless of surname, and this was to continue until the mid-nineteenth century.

The Huguenots.

The first Huguenot to settle in Glasnevin was Hugo Batho, a merchant. His house still stands - the impressive Jacobean Beechmount House that crowns Glasnevin Hill. He was a Church Warden in 1714 and in 1721 he was made an overseer of the roads. He died in 1724, survived by his wife and daughter.

Other Huguenot names recorded in the Parish Records are:

Dean Drillincourt, (of Armagh),
Lewis Chaigneau, a merchant,
Will Chaigneau (his son?),
Jjaack (sic) Rabateau, who was a Church Warden in 1717,
J. Regnant, who was a Church Warden in 1725,
M. Junadine,
Capt. Theo. Desbrisney,
Will. Eliot.

Distinguished residents of Glasnevin in the 18th century

Sir John Rogerson's venture in Glasnevin was successful in attracting the prosperous professional and upper middle classes, and Glasnevin became a fashionable place in which to reside. Possibly its most famous resident then was Doctor Patrick Delany, whose fame, such as it is, would appear to be derive from his association with Dean Swift, and from his second wife, Mary Delany.
Distinguished residents included the Barber family Mary, poetess, and her sons Constantine, physician and Rupert, painter, James Belcher, Supervisor of the King's printing press, Pursuivant of Arms and patron of the arts, Thomas Tickell, another very senior civil servant and poet of some note, and a friend of Joseph Addison, Hugh Mitchell M.P. for Bannow, a prominent business man and politician.

Other prominent residents were Henry Singleton, Master of the Rolls and Chief Justice of the Common Pleas, Isaac Ambrose who was Clerk of the Irish House of Commons, Samuel Fairbrother, a noted publisher, and John Cotton, poet, philosopher and mathematician.

Joseph Addison and Richard Steele, founders of the "London Spectator" and friends of Swift, did not reside in Glasnevin at any time, as incorrectly asserted in many historical references. Addison died in London in 1719, the same year in which Delany took up residence in Glasnevin. Richard Steele lived most of his life in London, and he appears to have been confused with another gentleman, Sir Richard Steele, who acquired Hampstead in 1769.

References: Vestry Book Glasnevin Parish, RCB Library
　　　　　　The Oxford Literary Companion

The population of Glasnevin Village in the 18th century

In 1766, a census of the population of Glasnevin Parish made to the Parliamentary Gazette recorded a total of 825 residents and 142 houses. These consisted of 344 Protestants and 481 "Papists", a total of 825 which would not vary to any appreciable extent over the next eighty years.

The applottment list for 1772 contains the names of the residents and valuations of their properties in Glasnevin. Not all "Papists" were poor, for example Gregory Byrne, a property owner, who occupied the late Thomas Tickell's house. The following extract contains the names of some of the property-owning residents of the Village:

South of the River: John Coffee ("Coffee Cabins" on site of Addison Terrace), Gregory Byrne (the Tickell Estate, now the Botanic Gardens), Mrs Mackleworth (The Mill).

Glasnevin Street east side: Mr. Rupert Barber: (Carlingford House), Alex Mackleworth (mill owner).

Glasnevin Street west side (later Vincent Terrace): Mrs Leathly, .Mrs Leonard.

Glasnevin Street north side: Mr.D. Meredith (Delville), Rev. Mr. Chambre, (Minister). Mr. Ford, Mrs .Davis.

Glasnevin Street south side: Mr. Watson, Mr. Doyle, Edmund Netterville. Hugh Henry Mitchell (Mitchell Estate, now the Holy Faith Convent).,

References: Vestry Book Glasnevin Parish - RCB Library.

The Cross Guns

Glasnevin's second village - The Cross Guns- took its name from a former public house in the area. The village that grew up in the area became known as Cross Guns, and it is also the name of a townland there. The bridge over the Royal Canal, formally named Westmoreland Bridge (1789), is better known as Cross Guns Bridge. On the east side where a row of shops now stands, stood Daneswell, a large Georgian house, which was demolished in the early 1920s.

Chapter 14:
Parish organization in the 18th century.

The Grand Jury

In the 1700s and up to 1840, the administration of County Dublin was the responsibility of the Grand Jury, the forerunner of the modern county council, under the County Governor, the chief official (styled Lord Lieutenant after 1831). Grand Juries were appointed by the County Sheriff, and were originally set up to assess whether a case existed for a prosecution to proceed (as in the United States today). Later, they assumed responsibility for the public services such as roads, bridges and health matters. Like the modern county councils, they were authorized to raise money under a system called "The County Cess", the equivalent of our present rates system.

The Parish Vestry

The responsibility for running the temporal affairs of each parish was relegated to the Vestry, which was a committee of parishioners under the Minister of the local Church of Ireland. The Vestry of Glasnevin was legally answerable to the Grand Jury and, ultimately, to the Lord Lieutenant of County Dublin. The Vestry met every month or so in the church which became the centre of administration for the parish. The Vestry comprised the Minister, two wardens, about four sidesmen (to assist the wardens), and a few ordinary members, drawn from all social classes.

The first meeting of the Vestry was held on 21st May 1706 for the purpose of rebuilding the church. This project had been approved by the Archbishop of Dublin (Dr. King) following his visit to Glasnevin on 13th May previously. He had appointed Sir John Rogerson and Charles Ryves Esq. to be Church wardens, with two sidesmen, who were given the responsibility for repairing the church.

The responsibilities of the Vestry were wide-ranging and onerous, which included raising money for the parish fund by "applottment", that is, assigning a valuation to all properties and striking a rate, similar to the modern municipal rates system.

Roads

Maintenance of the roads was to be a continuing problem in Glasnevin until the twentieth century. After the church was built, the first task undertaken by the Vestry was the repair of the roads. On 6th April 1708, it was agreed *"in the first place to gravelle well and make good the Road from the Avenue of His Grace the Lord Primate and Lord Justice of Ireland to the Parish Church of Glasnevin, for that His Grace hath been a benefactor to the said Church"*. Since the time of Laurence O'Toole, the Archbishop of Dublin had held the lands of Finglas which included Johnstown, and the road in question consisted mainly of the modern Ballygall Road, part of the Old Finglas Road and Church Lane (now Avenue).In 1709, two highway overseers were appointed: John Hudson and Henery Clyburn.

Legislation for maintaining roads under an Act of 1710 (replacing an earlier Act of 1613) required all landowners, tenants and residents generally to provide six days of free labour annually. This system proved unpopular and the Act was repealed in 1760. The responsibility was transferred to the Grand Jury, which raised the required money through the county cess.

On 12th April 1721, the Vestry decided that *"the Roads leading from the Cross Guns on the Dublin Road to Glasnevin, and from thence to Johnstown and Ballygall, and most of the High Roads of the Parish were out of repair, and that they should be repaired by the six days of labour of the several inhabitants of the Parish "pursuant to several Acts of Parliament"*. Hugo Batho and Arthur Thurston were appointed overseers. (This is the earliest mention of the Cross Guns, Glasnevin's "second village"). On 23rd April 1728, the Vestry appointed supervisors and overseers "to examine all abuses committed in the Roads and to prosecute persons impairing them".

Toll gates (turnpikes)

Toll gates (or turnpikes) were created in 1729 on major roads north of the City in order to divert the cost of road maintenance from the local denizens. Two toll gates were erected at the Cross Guns, one at the beginning of the Finglas Road, and the other on what is now Botanic Road. The income from those gates went towards the repair of the roads of the Parish.

The income from toll gates was never really sufficient for the purpose, and the condition of the roads continued to be poor. The tolls caused widespread resentment at what was seen as double taxation, and they were officially abolished in 1855. In any event, the advent of the railways would have put paid to the toll system.

Tree planting

The cultivation of trees continued to be an important item in the parish. On 10th February 1712 – 1713 (this way of writing the date shows that the Gregorian Calendar was in the process of adoption by the English Parliament) the Vestry decided, "pursuant to an order from the Clerk of the Peace of the County" that sixty trees should be planted at a rate of about one to every ten acres. The residents were applotted accordingly, and the three biggest plantings were Sir John Rogerson – 7 trees, William Emes - 13 trees, and W. Fairbrother - 5 trees.

Deserted children and abandoned infants

Later in the century, a sub-committee was set up to deal with the problem of destitute and deserted children. Local fosterage appears to have the usual way of dealing with those children, who were thus spared the horrors of the notorious Foundling Hospital attached to the Dublin Workhouse.

A century later, on 24th April 1832, a sum of £12 was allocated to the support of two deserted children, and in 1833, £18 was allocated to the support of three deserted children. Usually, two members of the Vestry were appointed as overseers.
In 1840, a foundling, Mary Ann Cottage, was entrusted to a Mr. Fenlon at his request.

Parish officials

The running of the parish was the responsibility of a group of laymen, who, with two exceptions, were unpaid. They were:

Wardens (or "church wardens") who were the leading members of the Vestry and were responsible for the administration of the Parish and acted as the legal representatives.

Sidesmen who were responsible for taking up the collections and for assisting the wardens.

Overseers who were responsible for applottments and collecting the cess, for distributing relief to the poor, and for the care of the roads.

The Sexton, who was responsible for the care of the Church.

The Parish Clerk who was a paid official responsible for the parish records and correspondence.

The Parish Constable, later designated "the Beadle", a type of local policeman who was responsible maintaining public order, particularly where children were concerned.

The Parish Clerk

The first recorded Parish Clerk was Thos. Jervis in 1708. In 1724, Matt Walls, it seems, combined the duties of Parish Clerk with those of school teacher and various other parish functions including that of constable. He did not have a salary, but payments were made to him from time- to-time, for example in 1727, he was paid £2. The cottage on Church Avenue nearest the church gate was, very likely, his residence. (The terraced cottages date from the mid 1800s).

Law and order

Grand Juries were responsible for erecting "Watch Houses" for the accommodation of watchmen and their arms. The early Ordnance Survey maps for Glasnevin show a building called a "watch house" in Glasnevin Demesne on the lower end of the Old Finglas Road (or "Finglas Road North" as it was called then). This building survived as a farm-worker's cottage until about 1952.

The first mention of a Parish Constable in Glasnevin is in 1706, when this official was asked to help with the rebuilding of the church. The Constable was appointed annually by the Court Leet in Grangegorman. The Parish Constable was occasionally given other duties, as in the case of Matt Walls, who was appointed school teacher in 1730.

The Parish Beadle

In 1829, we find the constable now designated "Beadle", the figure immortalised by Charles Dickens as Mr. Bumble in "Oliver Twist". Unlike his city counterpart, the rural Parish Beadle's duties were fairly light, such as dealing with minor offences by children and others. The Parish Beadle in Glasnevin was paid five guineas annually and he was provided with a uniform at a cost of £3-10s every two years. The conditions laid down were that the uniform was to be worn only while attending to his duties, and that it should last three years.

In 1832, the Beadle's salary was raised to ten pounds in consideration of additional duties that were imposed on him, in addition to his normal duties.
These were as follows:

- to keep the lanes and walks to the church in a clean state
- to attend to the gallery (of the church) on all occasions
- to ring the bell.

With the establishment of the Royal Irish Constabulary (the RIC) in 1822, the positions of Parish Constable and Beadle became obsolete afterwards.

The Parish pound

On 29th June 1741, the Vestry directed that a pound be built for stray animals in the Parish. The specification was as follows:

"The Pound to be built six foot high, coping included, to be built of lime and stone in a workmanlike manner. The gate four foot wide, to turn upon a pin of iron at the bottom, and swing on a iron hook coaded (sic) to the stone at the top. The stuff to be of good red deal, the jambs four inches of the lathe of red deal, with strong hasps and padlock". The pound was situated near the bridge and on the east side of the street.

A house was allocated to the Keeper. On completion, James Plunkett was appointed Keeper of the pound. He was succeeded by Edward Fitzimons in 1766. The Parish Pound was closed down in 1869 when Disestablishment took place.

Public houses

One of the parish committees was charged with overseeing the public houses in the area. At one time, its membership consisted of twelve men, making it the largest of the committees.

Soldiers of the King

During the Napoleonic wars, very many Irishmen served in the British Army and Navy, either voluntarily or by coercion from the Press Gangs. In August 1803, the Governor of the County notified the Parish that it must procure three men for the Army of Reserve, under pain of a heavy penalty. A "handsome bounty" would be given by application to the Minister. It was decided to raise £23-12s-9d for the purpose. This obligation was to last for the duration of the war.

References: Vestry Book Glasnevin Parish, RCB Library
            Byrne's Dictionary of Local History

Chapter 15:
The Alms House, the Poor Lott and the Washerwomen

The poor

Despite the growing economic prosperity in the eighteenth century, the majority of the population in Ireland continued to live in poverty, and despite disease and famine, the numbers increased. As early as 1703, the Dublin Workhouse was founded to cater for the destitute poor, and its harsh regimen was for many the only means of survival.

The destitute poor in general had not been cared for since the religious houses were dissolved in 1545. In 1707, the Church of Ireland - the Established Church - was given the responsibility for the temporal welfare of the parishioners. In Glasnevin, the parish charitable funds were allocated mainly to the elderly and widows who were unable to look after themselves, those on the Poor List and those in the Alms House.

The Poor Lott: A gift to the Parish

In 1723, a plot of land *"and the cabbins thereon"* was demised to the Parish. This was a gift from the Hon. George Forbes, eldest son of the Earl of Granard. Known as "The Poor Lott" it comprised about three roods (i.e. three quarters of an acre) on the east side of Glasnevin Hill, a site now occupied by part of River Gardens apartments and houses.

It was held in trust for sixteen years from 1724 for the use of four people: James Stott and his wife, and Thomas Cormick and his wife, who occupied the Alms House. Afterwards, the premises were demised to the benefit of the poor generally.
There was a prohibition on quarrying or "waste committed" under pain of making the grant void.

Part of the Poor Lott was leased for one pound yearly to the Barber family, owners of Carlingford House (or Florence Court as it is named in the 1738 Directory). This part continued to be occupied by the successive owners of Carlingford House.

A group of apartments called River Gardens was built on the Poor Lott and adjoining land in the 1980s. The ground was finally sold by the Parish in 1985.

Figure 7: Old Glasnevin Village from the Mound above Carlingford House (Courtesy of The National Library of Ireland) (showing the old Alms House to the right).

Glasnevin Parish Alms House

The original Alms House (or Poor House, as it was called sometimes) was set up in 1723 in a new building, or possibly a converted old one, on part of the Poor Lott.
The part of the plot on which the Alms House stood was maintained directly by the Parish, and the remainder was set to tenants, the rent from which went towards the support of those on the Poor List and those in the Alms House.

The first recorded occupants were "old Byrne and his wife" who were allocated a room on 16th April 1723 "under such regulation as Mr. John Travers (the Minister) shall think fit". This and subsequent entries show that, until 1816, both men and women had the right to a place. They were granted an allowance of eight pence a week each at this time. In 1724, two more couples were admitted: James Stott and his wife, and Thomas McCormick and his wife.

The new Alms House

After 1724, the next two recorded inmates admitted to the Alms House were Esther Rainy and Mary Hannagan, on 1st October 1740. There is a lack of entries after that date until 1757, possibly because the house had fallen into disrepair during this period. In any event, a new Alms House was built in 1757 by the artist Rupert Barber, apparently as part of the conditions of his lease. The new Alms House was a two-storey building containing eight rooms, evidently built to a good standard, possibly with a slated roof and with its gable-end facing the street.

On 5th May 1757, Elinor Cavanagh and Michael McLane were admitted to the two vacant rooms in the new Poor House, and to "a distributive share in the annual fund", followed in 1758 by Martha Mills, in 1760 by John Plunket ("a fit and proper person") and in 1761 by Mary Howard, Widow. Others admitted during this period were James Darling, Mary Johnson, Widow, and Sarah Brazille in 1771, Alice Darling in the place of deceased James Darling, Bridget Hamilton in place of Ann Duan in 1772, and Eliz. Mecan in 1773.

The washerwomen

Building the Alms House on the more prestigious side of the river caused one problem.

Since the foundation of the Alms House, the inmates had received an allowance of eight pence a week for their needs. However, over the years, this amount had become inadequate, and some of the women took in washing to earn more money. They were fortunate in that the Nevin stream flowing alongside the Alms House provided a convenient water supply. The washing would have been laid to dry on shrubs and trees, open to public view on the side of Glasnevin Hill, and, apparently, to the annoyance of the neighbours who, apparently, saw it as "letting down the area", and very likely, lodged a complaint with the Vestry.

On 23rd April 1771, the Vestry decided that the allowance of eight pence given to most of the Poor on the Church List was inadequate and that it should be increased to 1s – 1d. This evidently did not achieve the desired result, and it was followed on 16th March 1772 by an order *"that no publick washing be carried on in the Alms House"*.

The name "Washerwoman's Hill", by which Glasnevin Hill has been popularly known, was never an official or formal designation, but it has continued to be used in local parlance up to the present day. It is very likely that the name owes its origin to the activity of the women in the Alms House, and it may well have been a term of derision used by the poorer dwellers on the other side of the River Tolka.

According to local lore, the name "Washerwoman's Hill" was at a later period applied also to the part of Ballymun Road opposite the present "Rise". It appears that workmen coming into Dublin in the morning used to leave their washing with a woman that lived there, and collect it on their way home in the evening.

Other inmates

In 1795, Mary Fitzimons was removed from the Poor List on account of "misconduct" (no details given) and Alice Fagan was put in instead. In 1797, John Arnet was evicted from the Alms House.
An entry for 31st May 1803 is as follows: "Charlotte Leighlin being a Protestant and there being no other claim for admission, be admitted to the Poor House same benefit as Widow Dennison entitled. Remainder of rent paid by Ed. Farrell divided among the other inmates".
There existed an Alms House Poor Book for the years 1760 to 1813, but, unfortunately, it has been missing for a very long time.

New rules for the inmates 1815

The Vestry on 25th October 1815 drew up new rules for the inmates as follows :
1.	The right of appointing persons to reside in the Alms House rests jointly with the Minister, Church Wardens and Parishioners in Vestry.

2.	Funds permitting, it would be more beneficial to the Poor to increase their weekly allowance when necessary, to keeping up the numbers of poor on the list.

3.	No more females should be admitted on the Poor List than the Alms House can contain, being eight in number.

4.	Males would be in future eligible for the Poor List, but all males would be externs, and the Alms House kept for females.

5.	The beds and bed clothes should be examined once a month by the Vestry Clerk and any person not having theirs to produce would be turned out of the Alms House.

6.	In the case of the death of any of the inmates, the Vestry Clerk should see the parish bedding and bed clothes given in charge to one of the females of the House, who should be answerable for same as of her own, and produce them when a vacancy is filled up by the Vestry.

In 1818, the widows of the Alms House were granted an addition of seven pence per week, bringing the weekly allowance to 1s – 8d. On the other hand, the 5s given to them on festivals would be discontinued (this is the first mention of such a bounty).

Rules and penalties

In 1838, the Vestry decided that the deserving poor had become rather lax in both religious observance and in temporal matters, and that new measures were needed. On 17th May 1838, the Vestry decreed that the poor receiving relief out of the church fund had to attend after service on every Sunday to receive their money and in June, it decreed *"that any of the pensioners upon the poor list who were seen intoxicated, or may be convicted of drinking their weekly pension, be struck off the list"*.

The last years of the Alms House

The demand for places in the Alms House began to lessen during the nineteenth century, as may be deduced from the records. In 1839, the Vestry decided to appoint "a person, an object of charity and a Protestant to occupy a vacant room according to the provision of Lord Forbe's lease". A woman named Esther Patterson was the person chosen.
Widow Joseph Murphy was admitted to the Alms House on 23rd December 1847, she being the only needy Protestant widow in Glasnevin at the time, and probably the last person to be admitted. There are no records of any more admissions from that time until 1869, when the Alms House was closed down following the disestablishment of the Church of Ireland. The building was used as an outhouse by the occupiers of Carlingford Lodge until it was knocked down in the 1960s to make way for River Gardens apartments and houses.

The Poor List

Besides the Alms House, there was the "Poor List" for those parishioners that were given aid in cases of particular hardship. In 1771, there were thirty people on the Poor List.

In 1778, the Christmas Poor List raised £19.13.10, but usually, the returns from the collections held during Sunday Service were quite low, averaging about ten shillings. This seems to indicate either low attendances, or a somewhat ungenerous congregation.

The house on the Poor Lott (Carlingford Lodge).

Part of the Poor Lott, including some mud cabins, was first leased to a Michael Sullivan for 20s yearly with an obligation to build a house on the property. The house, a two-storey building with a slate roof, faced the street, and adjoined the Alms House. It lasted until the mid 1950s

Reference: Vestry Book, Glasnevin Parish, RCB Library.

Chapter 16:
THE PARISH SCHOOL – THE "INKBOTTLE"

Figure 8: The Parish School – the "Inkbottle" 1730-1900

Origins

One of the best-known Glasnevin land-marks for almost two centuries was a quaint-looking circular building with a conical roof, situated on the south bank of the river eastwards of Glasnevin Bridge. This was the Parish School from 1730 to 1900, affectionately known as "The Inkbottle", its chimney, resembling a bottle - stopper, perched on the top of the roof. In fact, this nick-name continued to be applied locally to the building that replaced it in 1901. It was originally known as "The Round House" and this name is used in the Parish records

One of the oldest primary schools in County Dublin, it was founded and paid for in 1727 by Dr. Delany of Delville, with the help of his friends including Dean Swift. There is no information as to why the particular design was chosen, and it has been ascribed by some to Dean Swift. The particular site chosen was the Common where the Village Bull-Ring had been located some centuries before. The building had two storeys, the upper one for occupation by the schoolteacher, and occasionally used as a Board Room by the school governors.

An Act of Vestry in 1727 enacted the constitution which placed the Parish School under the control of Governors and Governesses. At a vestry meeting on 26th March 1760, Dr. Delany handed over the school to the Minister, Church Wardens and Protestant parishioners of the Parish *"forever thereafter"*. The Vestry decided that the schoolhouse should forever be a Parish School.

The schoolmasters

The school -building was intended for "the reception of a schoolmaster to reside and dwell therein and to teach and instruct the children of the poor Persons residing or dwelling in the Parish". The first reference to a schoolmaster is on 7th May 1730, when Matt Walls, Clerk of the Parish, was appointed at a wage of 13 pence weekly to teach six poor children to read and write. Later entries refer to the existence of a schoolmistress "from the beginning", but there is no reference to any such before 1800.

The school was frequently in difficulty both with the standard of teaching and with the lack of funds. As might be expected, the main cause of the problem was a shortage of money, so that the Parish could not afford a proper schoolmaster. (The schoolmaster in Oliver Goldsmith's " Deserted Village" was "passing rich on forty pounds a year", a sum seemingly way beyond the Parish resources which could only afford £25 a year).

In1763, the job was combined with another parish post when a John Reily was appointed schoolmaster in the Parish, to reside in the school-house, and in addition, to be Keeper of the Parish Pound. Three years later, he was sacked because of the condition of the school and because he was "an improper master". A new master, Daniel Keenan, "a proper and fit person on the recommendation of several gentlemen" was appointed on 21st April 1767.

In 1768, a payment of 2s was made to Coogan for "reading" (sic) children, and in 1770, a payment of 2/2 to David Evans, Schoolmaster. Unfortunately, three record books for the next thirty years of the school are missing: The School Book of resolutions 1760 – 1813, the school account book 1771 – 1796, and the second school account book 1796 –1815.

Crisis

The school finances depended on special collections held at random. In the eighteenth and nineteenth centuries, a popular and successful means for raising funds for charity was the Charity Sermon given by a well-known preacher. On 22nd June 1794, the Reverend William Magee raised £60 for the school in this way.

Despite these efforts, there never seemed to be enough money. Unfortunately, matters were allowed to drift, and by 1815, the school was 60 guineas in debt. On 29th May 1815, the Vestry considered closing the school, but it postponed its decision until 26th June following. Remedial measures were hurriedly put into effect within days, and a charity sermon preached in St George's Church by a Mr. Barber raised £41-10s for the school. Mr. Barber was persuaded to preach another sermon, and a yearly grant of £15 was obtained from the "Society for promoting religion and discountenancing vice".

The crisis over, it was decided to appoint a committee to examine the state of the school and the manner in which children had been educated.

The Schoolmaster

Henry Beele was a local man who happened to be a member of the Vestry. In 1807, he was made Parish Clerk at a salary of twenty pounds yearly, and schoolmaster at a salary of twenty guineas, with the use of the school as a family residence. His unsuitability for the post was well known in the Parish, and there was a condition that he employ a "respectable competent assistant" who would reside in the school with the Beele family.

George Payne was appointed assistant schoolmaster, but he had to suffer some discomfort in the small closet that constituted his sleeping quarters. Following an investigation by the Minister, George Payne was finally appointed to his rightful position as schoolmaster, and it was decided that he should be instructed in the Bellian method of teaching.

A conscientious teacher, he was not a good disciplinarian, and he obviously found things difficult. In 1819, a want of discipline in the school was investigated and by 1820, things had deteriorated to such an extent that a meeting was called of the Governors of the School to consider the state of the school, to which the parents were summoned to attend. The irregularity in the attendance by some children was found to be "altogether attributable to the misconduct of their parents in this respect".

The girls' school

The investigation found that the schoolmistress Mrs. Maxwell was exemplary in her moral character and conduct, unremitting in her attention to the school, and perfectly qualified for her situation.

Another crisis

By December 1823, the Governors of the School had resigned on account of "the embarrassed state" of its funds, and the Master and Mistress were ordered to close the school on the 15th of December. However, it appears that things were left to drift, and George Payne soldiered on until his resignation in 1826. He was admitted to the Alms House, where he died in 1834, a conscientious teacher that deserved better. He was succeeded by a William Cusack in June 1827, and this man resigned in September 1827, after a bare three months.

New school regulations

On 8th October 1827, the Vestry re-established the fund for the maintenance of the Parish School, and a subscription list was opened, headed by Mrs. Lindsay, the wife of the Bishop of Kildare. The management of the school was delegated to the Minister Dr. Grier and a list of regulations was drawn up.

Trouble again

Despite the reforms in 1827, all did not go too well over the ensuing decade. A meeting of parishioners was held on 13th June 1837 with the Vestry members and the Bishop of Kildare. The meeting decided that there was "an improbability"(sic) appearing in the school expenses, with an amount of £13s-19s outstanding.
This meeting made three decisions:

1.   The Schoolmistress Mrs. McKelvey would be sacked because her yearly salary of £20 was more than the Parish was prepared to afford for the future.

2.   A subscription list would be opened to pay off the debt.

3.   Provision would be made in the parish applottment for the support of the Parish School and the Sunday School. This would not apply to the Infant school which had been established and supported by the Bishop of Kildare.

Raising funds for the school

It was obvious to all concerned that secure funding was necessary for the continuance of the school, which had been dragging from "post to pillar" almost from its beginning. The Vestry of 25th June 1837 resolved the matter with a set of reforms that included the patronage of Bishop Lindsay, annual donations of one guinea from willing parishioners, and a subscription list: In addition the school would revert to the original constitution of 1727 placing it under the control of Governors and Governesses

The last years of the Inkbottle

Following the re-organisation, the school prospered and by the middle of the century it was described as *""undoubtedly a most useful school. At a time when there were not many of its kind, it was doing good and faithful work, and not a few of its scholars of those days have succeeded well in life"*.

The school continued to be supported by the Parish, and in latter years to some extent by the Church Education Society. In 1896, it was placed under the National Board and it became a national school. At this time, the numbers on the Roll had increased to one hundred, and the building, besides being far too small, was not suitable any more for many reasons. It was decided that the best thing to do would be to build a new school, which would also serve as a parish hall. The building was knocked down in 1900, and this famous landmark was no more. It was replaced by the familiar building on Botanic Avenue today.

Reference: Vestry Book, Glasnevin Parish, RCB Library

Chapter 17:
DELVILLE AND DOCTOR PATRICK DELANY

Doctor Patrick Delany D.D.

Patrick Delany was of native Irish stock, born in 1685, one of two brothers from a Kilkenny family of humble standing. His father was the servant of Sir John Russell, a judge. A clever student, he attended Trinity College as a "Sizar" or scholarship student, and eventually gained a Fellowship and a Doctorate of Divinity. He was subsequently appointed to the Chair of History in the College.

An ambitious man, he aspired to the life of a wealthy churchman and gentleman and ultimately to a bishopric. In an age when bishoprics were the preserve of wealthy families, this was a futile ambition for a mere clergyman in his position. Nevertheless, this did not deter him from attempts to curry favour with the establishment. He was introduced by Swift to Lord Carteret, Lord Lieutenant in 1727 to whom he subsequently wrote the following "begging" verse:

Figure 9: Dr. Patrick Delany D.D (By permission of the National Gallery of Ireland)

> " My Lord, I wish to pay the debts I owe.
> I'd wish beside to build and to bestow"

His efforts were moderately successful soon afterwards when he was presented to the Parish of St. John. He was awarded the Chancellorship of Christ Church Cathedral in 1728.

Dr. Delany and his friends

Patrick Delany was a member of an elite Dublin circle of writers that gathered around Dean Swift. It included Thomas Parnell the Rector of Finglas, George Berkeley the famous philosopher, Thomas Sheridan D.D. father of Thomas Sheridan the actor, and Thomas Southern, the dramatist. Delany was introduced to Swift by Dr. Sheridan and he became his loyal lifelong friend and defender. His initial attraction for Swift was, according to one source, his physical resemblance to the great Joseph Addison of Spectator fame (*"a severely - reduced facsimile of Addison"*).

Dr. Richard Helsham

A close friend of Delany's was a Dr. Richard Helsham. A wealthy and influential man, he was born in Kilkenny in 1682. Helsham was a Fellow of Trinity College, a distinguished physician and a lecturer in mathematics and experimental philosophy (as science was termed in those days). He became Professor of Physic in 1729, and subsequently President of the College of Physicians. He was Swift's physician, who referred to him as "Doctor Arrogance".

Heldelville

The story of Dr. Delany's association with Glasnevin begins in 1719, when he and Dr. Helsham were demised the house and grounds belonging to Dorothy Berkeley, widow of Maurice Berkeley
The two Doctors took possession with a lease dated April 1719 but only Delany actually took up residence. Helsham was familiar with Glasnevin since he owned land there (the Dean's Farm or Drishoge) in the present Botanic Avenue area.

The two doctors built a new house in the Georgian style, and they gave it the somewhat inelegant name "Heldelville" derived from their own names, which name drew scorn and derision from Dean Swift in the form of a satirical verse. A few years later, Helsham relinquished his interest, leaving Delany in sole possession. Delany renamed the house "Delville" by which it was known until its demolition in January 1951. The original house appears to have been left standing to the rear of the new house, as happened with some other houses in the locality.
Richard Helsham died in 1738 ("A portrait of Irish Medicine", Chapter 3 gives details of his rather eccentric funeral arrangements).

Delville: The house

Delville was modest by comparison with many of the gentlemen's residences of the period, having a façade devoid of any external ornament or distinguishing feature. The interior plasterwork, however, was noteworthy, and it is described and illustrated in C.P. Curran's book "Dublin decorative plasterwork of the 17th and 18th centuries". The rooms downstairs were spacious – in particular the impressive entrance hall – but the bedrooms upstairs were pokey.

The second Mrs Delany in her correspondence some years later describes the house in detail.

Figure 10: Delville: 1944

Travels abroad: Pope at Twickenham

Delany decided that his garden would be an outstanding one, and he spent the next few years planning and making preparations. He accompanied Swift on a visit to London in 1727 where he was introduced to many influential people. He even succeeded in obtaining an invitation to the Royal Court of King George II. One of his introductions was to the home of the famous English poet Alexander Pope. Pope lived in Twickenham, and his main interests included gardening and landscaping.

Delany devoted much of this time to designing and laying out his garden in accordance with Pope's ideas, and, like many a good gardener, he never ceased making improvements. His garden, the first one in Ireland in the new landscaped style, became quite famous in the Dublin area and beyond.

A perimeter walk enabled views of the garden from its various sections: Informal paths, secluded arbours and seats including a "Beggar's Hut" set in a rock placed *"at the end of a cunning path set with trees, and overlooking the brook which entertains you with purling rill"* (Mary Delany), a popular feature of the period. Many other attractive prospects were laid out throughout the grounds.

"*The purling rill*", in other words the Nevin Stream, flowing through his grounds was a central feature of his design. The stream was spanned by rustic bridges, and formed cascades and the islets "Swift's Island" and "Swan's Island". The garden is shown in a number of sketches by the Mary Delany in 1745.

A mock satirical poem found in Mary Delany's papers, attributed to Thomas Parnell, describes the garden in the following words:

> *Would you that Delville I describe?*
> *Believe me sir I will not jibe*
> *For who could be satirical upon a thing so small?*
>
> *Yet in this narrow compass, we*
> *Observe a vast variety*
> *Both walks, walls, meadows and parterres,*
> *Windows, and doors, and rooms and stairs,*
>
> *And round this garden is a walk*
> *No longer than a tailor's chalk;*
> *Thus I compare what space is in it,*
> *A snail creeps round it in a minute.*
> *One lettuce make a shift to squeeze*
> *Up through a tuft you call your trees;*
>
> *And once a year, a single rose*
> *Peeps from the bud, but never blows;*
> *In short, in all your boasted seat,*
> *There's nothing but yourself that's great!*"

The Temple

North-west of the house was a large fruit and vegetable garden, and close by, a famous artefact called "The Temple", a summer house in the shape of a small Greek temple near the church wall, which was built about 1730. On the frieze overhead was an inscription in Latin *"FASTIGIA DESPICIT URBIS"*, meaning "it looks own on city spires", which is attributed to Dean Swift. The decoration included a medallion commemorating Stella, and a fresco painting depicting St. Paul. Although robust in appearance, the Temple was in fact mainly made of timber and plaster which was easily demolished when Delville was torn down in 1951. To the west of the Temple stood the remnant ruins of the medieval Glasnevin Castle which Delany retained for his garden, and, apparently, embellished with an archway.

A nine-pin bowling green was added in the 1740s. On a small parterre around the house there grew orange trees and peach trees. The recorded evidence is that the 18th Century winters were severe and the summers often dismal, but some summers were extremely hot and dry with drought conditions, which could explain the growing of oranges and peaches.

Figure 11: The Temple, Delville 1944

Dean Swift, Stella and Delville.

Dean Swift was a frequent visitor to Delville during the 1720s and 1730s. and he was often accompanied by Stella (or Esther) Johnston. They would spend time in the garden of Delville, she sitting with her chaperon Mrs. Dingly, he vigorously walking around. This may seem a romantic scene, but it must be recalled that at this time Swift was in his late fifties and Stella was in her forties and putting on weight. Stella died in 1728, to his great grief.

Delany did not escape the barbed wit of Dean Swift who wrote in his poem "Christmas Box for Dr. Delany":

> *"But you, forsooth your all must squander.*
> *On that poor spot called Delville yonder*
> *And when you've been at vast expense*
> *In whims, parterres, canals and fences.*
>
> *Your assets fail and cash is wanting*
> *Not further building, further planting,*
> *No wonder when you raise and level*
> *Think this wall low, and this wall bevel".*

He indulged in a lengthy correspondence in verse with Swift – a sort of duel by verse – in which the affable Doctor was no match for the acerbic Dean. Delany's financial difficulties were a by-word at the time, and Swift described them as

> *"quite ruin'd and bankrupt, reduc'd to a farthing,*
> *By making too much of a very small garden.*

In 1734, Swift persuaded the Lord Lieutenant, Duke of Dorset to visit Delville for dinner, which was undoubtedly the first major social event in Delany's life. Although their friendship had cooled by the end of the 1730s, (possibly due to Swift's illness) Delany remained a loyal friend and defender even after Swift's death in 1745.

The benevolent doctor: flood relief measures and charities

After a particularly severe of flooding caused by the River Tolka, Delany organized and paid for relief works for which he received praise in the following terms from a local poet (possibly John Winstanley):

> "The labourers all rejoice at his call
> and readily work wet or dry-a
> so well he does pay
> and treat them each day
> with bread and meat, ale and brandy-a.
>
> so public a spirit
> but few do inherit
> for generous actions renowned
> a friend to the nation
> deserves commendation
> let him with a mitre be crowned".

Dr. Delany was a founding member of the Dublin Society (afterwards the RDS) in 1731, which would later establish the Botanic Garden within sight of Delville.

The Doctor takes a wife

A clergyman and scholar in Dr. Delany's position was expected to marry, but his choice was necessarily limited, not least by the dearth of suitable ladies. He courted Margaret Tenison, (nee Burton) the wealthy widow of Richard Tenison, from Thomastown in County Louth, and after a courtship of four years, they were married in 1732. Shortly afterwards, secure in his new-found wealth consisting of an income of £2000 a year, he procured a house in Stafford Street (now Wolfe Tone Street) in the city.

Dr. Delany, widower

Margaret died in 1741, leaving a daughter by her first marriage. She was buried in the churchyard nearby, and her settlement devolved to Delany. Some years later, it was to be his misfortune to become involved in prolonged litigation with the Tenison family on the disposal of his late wife's estate.

Poet, writer and preacher

During the period of his wife's illness and after her death, Dr. Delany wrote and published a great deal of material, secular and religious, none of it particularly outstanding or memorable. His theological opinions and statements were bizarre to say the least. In 1754, he published a pamphlet denouncing the docking of donkeys' tails. He was castigated by

Swift for his tract condemning the use of blood in food products (*"sermons on black puddings!"*). He was happier on secular ground with his "Selected poems from Ireland" (1730) and "The fable of the pheasant and the lark"(1730).

References:
A Portrait of Irish Medicine, by Eoin O'Brien
Swift, the man, his works and the age, by Irven Ehrenpreis (Methuen).

Chapter 18:
THE SECOND MRS. DELANY

The Doctor seeking a second wife

Finding a suitable wife for the second time was no easy task for a man of Dr. Delany's mature age and social standing. In spite of his circumstances, a singularly fortunate sequence of events was to bring him to a second and even happier marriage. The lady of his choice was an attractive English widow whom he had met ten years beforehand in Dublin, by name Mrs. Mary Pendarves, nee Granville.

Mary Granville (1700 – 1788)

The story of the life of Mary Granville could be a typical work of popular romantic fiction. She was born in Coulston, Wiltshire in the year 1700 into a noble but temporarily impoverished Jacobite family. At the age of eighteen, she was forced by her uncle into a marriage with Alexander Pendarves, a wealthy Cornish squire, who was forty years her senior, who lived in a dilapidated old castle near Falmouth. Her uncle had hoped by this alliance to expand his political influence and connections. She thought her new husband "ugly and disagreeable".

Squire Pendarves died in 1724, on the eve of the day on which he had arranged to change his will in her favour. Mary was left a young widow, and, to the dismay of her family, penniless once again.

Figure 12: Mary Delany, 1731
(By permission of the National Gallery of Ireland)

Mrs. Pendarves, widow

Mary, now the Widow Pendarves, was taken back into the bosom of the Stanley Family in London, who may have regretted what they had done. There she became popular in high society.
She travelled to Dublin in September 1731 with her friend Miss Ann Donnellan who belonged to an old Galway aristocratic family, and spent more than a year there. She mixed in Dublin's high society and her letters to her sister describe life therein in great detail. In January 1733 she was entertained by Dr. Delany at one of his Thursday Dinners.

A second marriage

Having decided that he would marry Mary Pendarves, Dr. Delany lost no time in pursuit of his chosen lady, and to this end he travelled to England in spring 1743. It was fortunate that he did this, since Mary was about to embark on a Grand Tour of the continent. After some reflection, and perhaps tired of her widowed status and London society, she accepted and they were married in London on 9th June 1743. Delany was now a mature 59 years of age and Mary was 44.

Her family did not approve of her marrying a parson who was of humble origin *and* an Irishman. Nevertheless, now that the deed was done, Mary persuaded her family to obtain preferment for her new husband.

The Dean of Downe

The first step in Delany's preferment was an invitation to preach before King George II, when he acquitted himself in great style. Within a year, he was elevated to the position of Dean of Downe, which gave him another source of income.

The new mistress in Delville

The new Mrs. Delany was enraptured by Delville and its garden. She wrote: "*There never was a sweeter dwelling…I never saw a more delightful place.*

On the left of the hall is another large room designed for a chapel (this was eventually completed in 1753). Behind the staircase, below, is a little hall and to the right, a small parlour where we breakfast and sup; out of it is our present bed-chamber, and as we sit by the fireside, we can see the ships ride in the harbour".

She describes the drawing room with its tapestry curtains and chairs of crimson mohair, and tables and looking-glasses, and the bed-chamber within hung with crimson damask.

She was delighted with her new garden. In one of her letters home, she describes its features as follows:

" About half-way up the walk there is a path that goes up that bank to the remains of an old castle (as it were) from which there is an unbounded prospect all over the country. Under it is a cave that opens with an arch to the terrace walk that will make a very pretty grotto. At the end of this terrace is a very pretty portico (the Temple?) prettily painted within and neatly finished without".

Garden improvements

Mary was a prolific artist, and she made a number of drawings of the garden.

Landscape gardening seems to have been one of Mary Delany's many skills and she and her husband set about improving and re-arranging their garden. New features included a nine-pin bowling green behind the house, a green-house and an ice-house.

They acquired a herd of sixteen deer, which was somewhat pretentious for an eleven- acre estate. Mary, in a playful moment, named these animals after her friends. As might have been expected, the deer attracted poachers and there were some violent incidents in one of which a poacher was seriously wounded.

Figure 13: Delville garden: The Beggar's Seat, by Mary Delany (1745)
(By permission of the National Gallery of Ireland)

Figure 14: Delville garden: Stream and Swift island, by Mary Delany (1745)
(By permission of the National Gallery of Ireland)

Hospitality unbounded

Whereas previously Delville had been a meeting place for Dublin's literary elite, Mary strove to make it a salon for fashionable and upper-class society. To this end, the Delanys embarked on a programme of entertainment that was lavish by any standards.

Mary's letters describe the feasts in great detail, including the seating arrangements. The high point of their social life came about on one morning in 1745 when the Lord Lieutenant Lord Chesterfield (of Phoenix Park fame, one of the most liberal and philanthropic men to hold this position) arrived for breakfast at very short notice. The Delanys rose to the occasion admirably, and the visit was repeated in the year following. Patrick Delany, son of a servant, was now an accepted member of upper class Dublin society.

That year was also a sad one for the Delanys when their great friend Dean Swift died after his long tragic physical and mental illness.

House improvements

In 1747, the library was extended, and in 1759, the chapel in the house was completed. The chapel was decorated by Mrs. Delany with shells in a rose foliage design, and a star in the glass window, and also on the floor, to commemorate Stella. Shell decoration was fashionable at the time, and Mrs. Delany was quite accomplished in this art. The Temple was also decorated by her in like fashion, but the weather took its toll and the shells gradually became loose and fell off.

Friends and neighbours

Patrick and Mary Delany had a wide circle of friends including her next-door neighbours the Barbers, the Hamilton Family, Letitia Bushe an artist and an old friend, William Clayton, Bishop of Clogher with his wife Katherine, the blind Mary O'Hara, and the ill-starred Pilkingtons Matthew and Letitia.

The Parish Pastor.

Dr. Delany acted as curate to the local Church of St.Mobhi during the 1740s. Mary Delany describes the procession to morning and evening services on one Sunday with the Doctor, eight of their friends attended by their numerous servants in train as they walked up through the garden to the postern gate in the wall separating the garden from the churchyard (this entrance is still to be seen, although now bricked up).

Trouble in Paradise

In 1750, the Tenison family took Dean Delany to court to render an account of his first wife's estate. She had died in 1741, and there were conditions in her will that gave her family cause to contest her legacy to her husband. Unfortunately, he had destroyed documents crucial to his defence, and in 1752, a Dublin court ruled against him. This, involving a possible loss of income, caused him great distress. In 1758, however, the Tenison lawsuit was eventually resolved in Delany's favour, which meant that he now had money to spend on completing the chapel and improving their home.

Mary Delany the artist

Apart from her literary efforts, Mary Delany had many artistic talents. Her sketches – including those of Delville - have survived and have been published in various books. What she is most famous for are her cut-paper flower pictures or collages in colour, of which no less than 970 have survived and have been published in more than one book.

In 1754, the Delanys bought a house in London, and began to spend a considerable amount of time in London and Bath, as well as their normal visits to the Deanery in Down. They spent two and a half years there from 1759 until mid 1761, after which they returned home to resume their old life-style.

The death of Dr. Patrick Delany

Dr. Delany's health began to deteriorate and in 1767 he and Mary went to live in Bath. He made his will in London in order to make sure that Delville and his London house (which constituted virtually his sole assets) would pass to his wife. In his will he protests his innocence in the Tenison affair which still trundled on in complexity and rancour. He died in Bath in May 1768 aged eighty-three years. His body was brought home and he was buried in a grave beside that of his first wife in St. Mobhi's churchyard in Glasnevin. His headstone, at the east end of the churchyard, bears the following inscription:

> Here lyeth the Body of Patrick Delany
> Formerly Senior Fellow of
> Trinity College Dublin
> Late Dean of Downe
> An orthodox Christian Believer
> An early and earnest Defender of Revelation
> A constant and zealous preacher of the Divine laws
> For more than fifty years
> And an humble penitent
> Hoping for mercy in Christ Jesus
> He died the sixth day of May
> MDCCLXVIII
> In the Eighty-fourth year of his age.

His widow Mary did not return to Ireland. Instead, she went to live in London, in St. James's Place, where she rejoined the high society, mixing with aristocracy and even royalty. She enjoyed the patronage of King George III and his queen, and in 1785 they granted her a Grace and Favour residence in Windsor along with a pension.
Mary Delany died peacefully in 1788, and she was buried in St. James's Church in Piccadilly in London.

Delville: vanished glory

Mary Delany left the disposal of Delville and its effects with the Sandfords who had been residing there in the meantime. Faulkner's Dublin Journal of 10th April 1770 carried the following advertisement:

"To be sold by Auction by Gabriel Whistler, Upholder and Auctioneer, on Thursday 19th inst. April 1770 and the succeeding days, the entire Household Furniture of the late Rev. Dean Delany, at his house in Delvin (sic) in Glassnevin, the furniture consists of crimson Silk Damask Four post Beds with Mahogany carved and ornamented pillars, Window Curtains and the hangings of Rooms to match ditto; green Damask Four-post Beds, Paragon, Callimanco and cheque ditto with Window curtains and Chairs to match, stuffed Back and Seat Chairs covered with crimson English Mohair and Window Curtains of the same, best seasoned Feather Beds, Blankets and Quilts, large Pier and Chimney Glasses allowed to be as good Plates as any in this Kingdom, Indian and Mohogany Cloaths, Chests with every Requisite in the Furniture way, and in the present Taste, which will be more fully expressed in Hand Bills".

Thus ended the Delany period in Delville. The Delanys had lived the comfortable if somewhat frivolous life of the privileged of their time, albeit on a relatively modest income. Patrick Delany's literary writings were not particularly distinguished, and but for his friendship with Dean Swift, and his wife's memoirs, he would have been forgotten before long.

References: Letters from Georgian Ireland, edited by Angeline Day (Friars Bush Press)

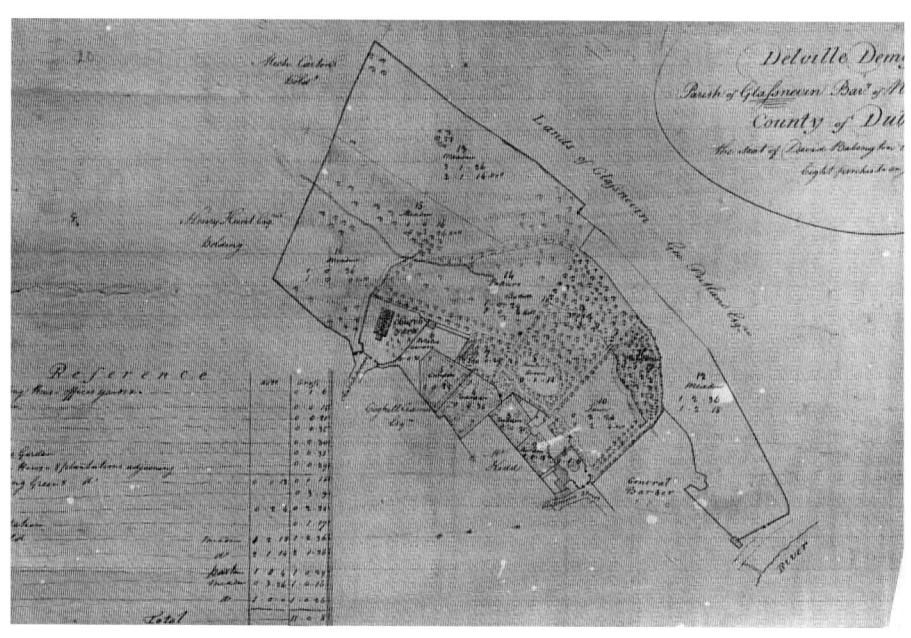

Figure 15: Map of Delville Demesne 1799
(Courtesy of The National Library of Ireland Ref. 21 F53 (51))

Chapter 19:
DELVILLE AFTER THE DELANYS

The subsequent owners

After the Delanys, the house came into the possession of John Westlake, a landowner who died in 1799, although the applottment list for 1772 shows a Mr. Meredith in residence. A deed map dated 1799 shows Delville to be the seat of David Babingdon, Esq. The next occupant was Dr. Thomas Percy, Bishop of Dromore and editor of "Reliques of Ancient English Poetry", who resided there for a short while, followed by Sir Marcus Somerville whose name appears on a deed map of 1807.

Robert Emmett: a tradition

A tradition handed down through successive owners of Delville tells the tale of how the headless body of the unfortunate Robert Emmett was brought to Delville after his execution in 1803, and carried through the house, out by way of the bay window at the side, and up the garden to the postern gate leading to the churchyard of St. Mobhi. (q.v.).

Robert Mallet FRS: Scientist, engineer and seismologist (1810-1881)

In a society where the humanities, rather than the sciences, have long been revered, we find that Delville's most celebrated residents were the Delanys, despite the fact that their contributions to literature and the arts were peripheral.

The name of Robert Mallett is not very well known, yet it is one of the greatest in the history of Irish science and engineering. Born in Dublin in 1810 into a family engaged in the iron and steel industry, he graduated from Trinity College in mathematics and classics in 1830 and subsequently joined the family business.

Figure 16: Robert Mallet

Robert Mallett lived in the nineteenth century, the Victorian era, when engineering was in the process of changing society. Their family Victoria Foundry supplied the steel for the new Railways, and for the railings around Trinity College. About 1822, his father Richard had established an iron foundry at Cross Guns beside the Royal Canal, nick-named "Mallett's Folly" at the time because he had assumed, wrongly, that he had the right to use the water of the canal, The factory building subsequently became a flour mill (the North City Milling Co.), and is now an apartment block.

Robert Mallet's fame rests on his engineering and scientific discoveries. He was responsible for many inventions, and he was involved in some water pipe schemes and in the Dalkey atmospheric railway. His enduring fame derives from his contribution to the science of seismology.

Robert Mallet was above all responsible for creating the science of seismology, and he coined its name. Applying his engineering knowledge, he carried out historical research and experiments in Ireland (on Killiney Strand), and, more effectively, abroad in Italy. He produced a catalogue of major earthquakes world-wide from the earliest records and in 1846, he presented a paper to the Royal Irish Academy: "The Dynamics of Earthquakes".
Following an earthquake in Naples, he produced a Report: "The Great Neapolitan Earthquake of 1857: The First Principles of Observational Seismology".

He was a founding member of the Institution of Civil Engineers of Ireland in 1835.
He was elected a Fellow of the Royal Society in 1854. He was responsible for advances in metallurgy which he put into practice in the design of cannons for the Crimean War.

Robert Mallett lived in Delville from 1830 to 1858, where his father remained as caretaker during the later years. He moved to Clapham, London in 1860, where he died in 1881.
He has been largely forgotten, but in 2006, the Dublin Institute for Advanced Studies announced the setting up of a Mallet Professorship of Seismology in the School of Cosmic Physics: at last, a fitting tribute to the man that invented the science. He is commemorated by a plaque at Ryder's Row, off Capel Street in Dublin.

Sir Patrick Keenan: A society wedding

A Mr. Patrick Joseph Keenan, Commissioner for Education, and his family, occupied Delville from about 1870 until 1900. He received the Order of Companion of the Bath and was subsequently knighted as Sir Patrick Joseph Keenan C.B. KCMG.

For one brief and happy day on 15th May 1883, Delville relived the glory of its past. On that day, Keenan's niece Elizabeth (Daisy) Burke from Galway married the 11th Earl of Fingall in the union of the two Catholic families at a ceremony in the Archbishop's private chapel in Rutland (now Parnell) Square. The wedding celebrations were held in Delville afterwards. The guests included the Viceroy and Lady Spencer with all the vice-regal court and many from the judiciary and public service, and a Catholic priest, a Fr. Healy from Bray. The new Countess was very much taken with Delville and the event is described in full in her memoirs: "Seventy years young: The memoirs of Elizabeth Countess of Fingall," first published in 1937.

After Patrick Keenan's demise in or about 1890, his two sons Norbert Keenan B.L. and Captain Keenan lived in Delville until 1900. According to local accounts, the Keenans kept cattle on the estate and were reputed to have sheltered them in the famous Temple.

Lanigan-O'Keefes

In 1900 Stephen Lanigan-O'Keefe, a member of the prestigious Dublin family of lawyers took over Delville, and it remained in possession of this family until 1932. The house was leased to a succession of tenants during this period.

The end of Delville

In 1932, a merchant from Limerick, a Mr. John O'Brien, acquired Delville, but neither he nor his widow were able to preserve the house as it deserved. The house gradually became more shabby and the once-famous gardens suffered from neglect. Various tenants leased rooms there in the late thirties. At one time, the widowed Mrs. O'Brien offered to sell land for the building of a new church, but this came to naught.

In 1943, Mrs. O'Brien sold the house and land to the Bon Secours Sisters for the building of a hospital. The house was used as a nursing home while the new hospital was being built, but the end came during the second week of January 1951 when Delville was razed to the ground. The event was reported in the newspapers of the time. The Temple and castle ruins suffered the same fate, and soon the classic Delville was no more.
Some of the stonework was incorporated in the new hospital building, as well as one of the magnificent marble fireplaces.

During the excavations for the foundations of the new hospital in 1951 some human remains were discovered which may have been buried there illicitly in the early 1800s instead of in the nearby churchyard.

Chapter 20:
THE BARBER FAMILY AND CARLINGFORD HOUSE

Carlingford House

When Mrs. Dorothy Berkeley demised Delville to Doctors Helsham and Delany in 1719, she went to live in a more modest dwelling nearby, one of the many built by Sir John Rogerson, called "The Garden House". She died at her home in 1728 (notified in Exshaws Magazine). She left the house to her daughter Mrs Dorothy Charlton who demised it first to a John Bannister, and afterwards to Dr. Delany in 1737 who used it as an annex for his many guests and relations. It is named "Florence Court" in the Dublin Directory for 1738, but it is better known as "Carlingford House".

The coming of the Barbers to Glasnevin

Dr. Delany was a very generous and kind landlord to two friends of his, a couple, by name of Rupert and Mary Barber. Rupert seems to have been a resident tenant in Delville in Mrs. Berkeley's time. The records of St. Werburgh's Church indicate that the Barber family lived in Werburgh Street in the early 1700s. The first mention of the Barbers in Glasnevin is that of Rupert who in 1719 was witness to the lease between Mrs. Berkeley and the Doctors Helsham and Delany.
Rupert Barber was originally a wool draper, or "clothier" who lived in Capel Street. He was an unsuccessful businessman, lazy, fond of his claret, and an indifferent husband and father. His wife Mary was one of the many women that belonged to Dean Swift's circle of friends and she achieved some reputation as a poet at the time.

The Barbers were evidently very good friends of Dr. Delany's. Following the acquisition by Delany of Garden House (later Florence Court, later Carlingford House), he apparently carried out some rebuilding and let it to the Barbers for a nominal or peppercorn rent.
This is commemorated in a satiric verse by Dean Swift as follows:

> " Here a convenient box you found
> Which you demolished to the ground
> Then built, then took up with your arbour
> And set the house to Rupert Barber".

In 1719, Doctors Helsham and Delany took a lease of the following:

"one walled garden walled with lime and stone, bounded on the south by Mrs. Berkeley's garden, on the west side by Hugo Batho's garden, for the use of Rupert Barber, his wife Mary and his son Constantine", situated just the south of Delville ground. (Deed 23/273).
This garden produced fruit and vegetables and would have provided a modest income for the Barbers. It remained in use as an orchard until about 1950.

Mary Barber, Poet

One of Dean Swift's most loyal friends, Mary Barber was a very forceful woman who had long nurtured an ambition to be a famous poet. Having reared four children, she describes herself thus in verse:

"A mother who vast pleasure finds/ in modelling her children's minds".

She was single-minded in her pursuit of fame and she sought patronage at every level.
She had written a poem in praise of Delany's eulogy of Lord Carteret in 1725 and Delany, her friend and neighbour, introduced her to Dean Swift in 1728.

She finally succeeded in achieving publication of her work, and dedicated it to Lord Orrery.
It was about this time that she went to live in Bath, where she stayed for some six or seven years before returning home.

The Barbers had four surviving children, Constantine, Rupert Junior, Mira and Lucius. Mira, as far as is known, did not marry.

In 1755, Mary Delany wrote that "Old Mr. Barber is alive, drinks his claret, smokes his pipe and cares not a pin for any of his family who, if they had not met with better friends than himself, might have starved". Mary Barber died in 1755, and is buried in the local churchyard (St. Mobhi's), along with her errant husband who died in 1760.

Rupert Barber Junior

Rupert, the second son, was born in 1719. It would appear that he accompanied his mother when she went to England in 1734, and he studied art at Bath. He became a well-known painter, particularly of miniatures and cameos, and he was particularly noted as an enamel miniaturist. His subjects included Dean Swift and Dr. Delany. One of his portraits of Dean Swift depicts him without a wig, the only such portrait known, which hung in Shankill Castle in Kilkenny until the 1990s. In 1745, he painted a portrait of Mary Delany.

Figure 17: Carlingford Lodge, Glasnevin Village (1965)
(Courtesy of The National Library of Ireland)

Rupert, now established as a successful artist, took possession of the family home in Glasnevin, at some time after 1740.
The house adjoined the Poor Lott and the Alms House. In 1757 Rupert took a lease of the "Poor Lott" and rebuilt the Alms House as part of the arrangement. He knocked down the original "Garden House" and built a new and imposing residence called *Florence Court*, later known as *Carlingford House*. This house lasted until the 1970s, when the River Gardens scheme was built on the site.

Of particular architectural interest was the imposing gateway with its stone pillars and wrought-iron gates which remained a prominent feature of the village street until 1970.
Rupert Barber continued his work until he died in 1772.

Author's note: Many writers and historians have assumed from Mrs. Delany's letters that the Barbers lived in a small house at the bottom of Delville garden. The applottment list for 1772 shows Rupert Barber as the occupier of a house (Carlingford House) with a rating of £16 along with twenty acres. Its original name "Garden House", it seems, is very likely the cause of this misunderstanding. Furthermore the deed map of Delville in 1799 shows no such house.

Doctor Constantine Barber

The eldest son, Constantine, was born in 1714. He entered Trinity College in 1730, where he is listed as the son of Jonathan Barber (*Alumni Dublinensis*). He rose to become one of Dublin's most eminent physicians and he became one of the three King's professors. He was Professor of Materia Medica in TCD, and President of the College of Physicians.

His listing in Trinity College as the son of "Jonathan Barber" rather than Rupert Barber remains somewhat of a mystery. It is suggested that this was probably an error made by the Registrar, seeing that there was a Jonathan Barber, of Capel Street, also a clothier, whose wife was also named Mary.

Constantine Barber is best remembered as the physician to Dean Swift in his later years. Mary Delany refers to him as "a very good sort of man and a very good physician", and mentions "his agreeable gentle wife". He was also family physician to the Delanys.
The applottment list for 1773 shows that Doctor Barber lived in Glasnevin in "Ardmore" on the opposite side of the street, succeeding James Belcher therein.

General Lucius Barber

Lucius, the youngest son, was born in 1720. He joined the British Army and rose to the rank of Lieutenant-General. He is mentioned in the "Recollections" of John O'Keefe, the actor and stage director, as a classmate. A Mrs. Barber, presumably his wife, died on 28th October 1801. Lucius, it appears, was also a miniaturist, one of whose subjects was the noted Irish actress Peg Woffington. He lived in the family home until his death on 12th December 1808, followed by the death of his daughter Miss Jane Barber twelve months later. They were both buried in the family grave in the churchyard nearby.

Carlingford House after the Barbers

The next occupier of Carlingford House was Sir William Somerville, probably a son of Sir Marcus Somerville who had lived at Delville for a short time. In 1840, the property was leased as a "Private Lunatic Asylum" run by Doctor Joseph Duffy M.D. which is advertised in Battersby's Complete Catholic Registry 1840.

The house continued to be occupied in tenement fashion by a number of families until the 1950s. It was damaged by floods in December 1954 and

subsequently fell into disrepair.
The house was demolished in 1970 to make way for the building of River Gardens, a development of apartments and town houses. The development retains the medieval Norman motte in its midst. The ground with its rent was finally sold off by the Parish in 1988.

References:
A Georgian Celebration, by Patrick Fagan
A Portrait of Irish Medicine, by Eoin O'Brien,
Letters from Georgian Ireland, edited by Angeline Day (Friars Bush Press).

Chapter 21:

THOMAS TICKELL,
PUBLIC SERVANT AND POET

Thomas Tickell

An Englishman, Thomas Tickell came to live in Glasnevin in 1736. Thomas Tickell was a member of the London literary circle of Joseph Addison and Richard Steele of "Spectator and Tatler" fame, and he was well acquainted with Dean Swift and Dean Delany. Born in Cumberland in 1685, he studied at Oxford and became a Fellow of Queen's College. He was a close friend and protégé of Joseph Addison. Addison remained a close friend, and he appointed Tickell his literary executor and biographer. When he died in 1719, Tickell was at his bedside.

Thomas Tickell's coming to Ireland

In 1724, Tickell found favour with the Lord Carteret, the newly-appointed Lord Lieutenant of Ireland, who appointed him Secretary to the Lords Justices. He landed in Dublin on 1st of June 1724. A stranger to Ireland, he was fortunate in being able to renew his acquaintanceship with his old friends Swift and Delany Thomas Tickell was a minor poet, and one of his better-known poems is "Colin and Lucy" which was published in Dublin in 1725.

In 1726, he married Clotilda, daughter of Sir Maurice Eustace of Harristown, County Kildare, and thereby became a property owner in Carnalway in County Kildare .The Tickells had four children. In 1736 the family moved to Glasnevin to reside in a house, with the land formerly known as "The Great Meadow", demised to him by John Putland. This property would later form the nucleus of the Botanic Gardens, and the house, happily still standing, was to become the residence of its Director. Records show that this house was built before Tickell's arrival.

Thomas Tickell did not enjoy his new house and lands for long. He died in Bath in 1740, and his remains were brought back to Glasnevin where he was buried in the Churchyard of St. Mobhi's. Inside the church is a memorial plaque with the words:

"Sacred to the memory of Thomas Tickell Esq. He was sometime Under Secretary in England, and afterwards for many years, Secretary to the Lords Justices of Ireland, but his highest honour was that of having been the friend of Addison".

The property was eventually sold to the Dublin Society for its new Botanic Garden in 1795.

References: Oxford Literary Companion,
Ehrenpreise's Biography of Jonathan Swift.

Figure 18: Former Thomas Tickell's house, Botanic Gardens

Chapter 22:

JAMES BELCHER, PATRON OF THE ARTS, AND ARDMORE

James Belcher

Up to 1963 in Glasnevin Village there stood a house of the Jacobean or Queen Anne style at the top of the hill and opposite Beechmount. Located close to the roadway, it had a quaint appearance with its narrow doorway and windows and a small lunette window in the top storey. At some time probably in the 19th century, it acquired the name "Ardmore".
This was one of the houses built around 1710 by Sir John Rogerson, and first demised to a Richard Audley in that year.

Perhaps one of its best-known occupants in the 18th century was James Belcher, patron of the arts who held a high position in Dublin Castle as Keeper of the King's Printing press and First Pursuivant at Arms. He came to live in Glasnevin sometime in the late 1730s.
He was one of the literary circle in Dublin at that time, but, as far as is known, he was not a writer. He was interested in literature, including ancient Roman and Greek literature and mythology which was fashionable among literati at the time.

In the large garden at the rear, was a well which he called Helicon (after the home of the Muses on Parnassus), surrounded by trees which he named after the Muses. He is remembered as a patron of two minor poets- John Winstanley, and Henry Jones, who called him "Apollo". He died in 1761, having disinherited his son Frederick John who had "forfeited his affection by his independent conduct", and was buried in the churchyard nearby.

Of the two poets, Winstanley is the better known. A Dubliner and sometime student of Trinity College, he was over fifty years old when he became a protégé of James Belcher, in whose house he stayed from about 1735. Winstanley eulogises his patron in his poem "Doctor Winstanley's ghost to his friend at Glasnevin" as "that friendly bounteous heart that me and mine preserved alive". One little poetic gem by him entitled "Verses addressed by a gentleman of the Church of England to a Roman Catholic Lady" has a concluding verse

> *"I see perfection on her throne,*
> *my errors I'll no more pursue;*
> *Infallibility I own*
> *- infallibility – in you!*

He died in 1750, and is buried in the nearby St. Mobhi's churchyard. His works were published posthumously by his son in 1755.

The next resident of note was the eminent Doctor Constantine Barber, a brother of Rupert Barber Junior, who is recorded as the occupant in 1773.

The Marrable Family

From about 1805 to 1910, Ardmore was the residence of the William Marrable, who is listed in the Vestry Book of 1815 as a church-warden. His son, the Reverend William Marrable, who was born there in 1821, was a scholar of some distinction who became Treasurer of Christ Church. He lived here until his death in 1903. His widow remained there until her death in 1910.

Ardmore in the 1900s

During the "Troubles" the garden was used for training purposes by the local members of the George Rex Association, a type of voluntary Unionist Home Guard.

The property was later acquired by Johnny Hart who converted the building into flats. The house gradually deteriorated, became derelict and was demolished in 1963 to make way for the commercial motor car business owned by Denis Mahony.

Figure 19: Ardmore, Glasnevin Village 1950

Chapter 23:
THE LARGER LANDOWNERS IN GLASNEVIN 1700 – 1840

Changes of ownership

Two major landowners in Glasnevin at the end of the 1600s were Daniel Hutchinson and Thomas Twigg. Hutchinson was succeeded by his grandson John Weaver, whose property (the Deane's Farm) was demised to Thomas Twigg in 1705. In 1719, their leases were surrendered to the Dean of Christ Church and demised to Ursula, Dowager Lady Altham.

Ursula, Dowager Lady Altham was a major landowner for a short period in 1719 when she assigned her property to Anne Rowe for £800 (Deed 20/298). Anne Rowe, widow of John Rowe, gradually took over most of the larger leases as well as Lady Althams, the Deane's Farm, the Great Farm and Gough's Farm. In 1730, Anne Rowe demised her property to Jane Putland, widow of Thomas Putland (Deed 64/340).

The Putland family

The Putland family came from London early in the 18th century to seek their fortune.The Putland name crops up in many of the property transfer leases all over Glasnevin in the 1700s, when they became the biggest landlords. For example, the 1799 deed map for Glasnevin Demesne shows the ground landlord as George Putland.

The eldest son John (1709-1773) graduated from Trinity College with an arts degree and a divinity degree in 1734. In 1735, following his mother's example, John decided to invest in property in Glasnevin, and he borrowed fifteen hundred pounds from Dean Swift for the purpose. He took up his country residence in the former home of Sir John Rogerson (now the Holy Faith Convent). The Putlands owned a town residence in Great Britain Street (today Parnell Street) which would become the head office of Williams and Wood in the twentieth century.

William Henry Gore

For a brief period of a few years after the Putlands, the major landlord in Glasnevin was a Colonel the Hon. William John Gore, agent for Lord

Forbes. He held about 350 acres in 1807. Parish and records indicate that he lived at Roseville around this time.

Glasnevin Demesne (The Mitchell Estate)

The original Glasnevin House was built by Sir John Rogerson in the first decade of the 1700s and it was occupied by the Rogerson family until about 1735 when it was demised to John Putland who later leased it to William Bogan.

In 1760, Henry Mitchell, M.P. for Bannow, took over possession of Glasnevin House. and its lands from John Putland. Henry Mitchell was a wealthy man, banker, merchant and ship owner. He was well-connected with the higher levels of Dublin society, and he entertained many noble visitors at his home.

Glasnevin House

Henry Mitchell built a new house that incorporated part of the original house built by Rogerson, a practice that apparently was common in the 18th and early 19th centuries. A major part of the house, with its ornate plasterwork on walls and ceilings, has been preserved to this day as a residence for the Holy Faith Sisters.

Figure 20: The original Glasnevin House (Holy Faith Convent)

The staircase with its mahogany handrail leads from the hall to the upper storey. The walls and ceiling of the stair area are richly embellished with delicate stucco work, spiralling in intricate trailing designs. On the first floor is the splendid reception room with its elaborate plasterwork in graceful leaf and flower motif. There is a magnificent white - and - rose-hued marble fireplace with two white pillars supporting the pediment and a centrepiece sculpted in high relief. Adjoining is a smaller reception room with an ornamental squared ceiling and a marble fireplace.

The original main entrance facing the roadway was demolished when the convent was built, but the ornate hall ceiling has been preserved. Parts of Rogerson's original house are still to be seen on the ground floor and in the cellars with their barrel-vaulted ceilings.

Figure 21: The original Glasnevin House interior c. 1930

Henry Mitchell died in 1768, and his widow remained in Glasnevin until her death in 1779, when she was succeeded by her son Hugh Henry Mitchell who later demised it to Charles Costello.

The next owner of Glasnevin House was the Bishop of Kildare, the Honourable Charles Dalrymple Lindsay, who came to Glasnevin in 1806. The Lindsay Family would remain the principal and most powerful family in Glasnevin for the next hundred years.

The Turrets

One of the more distinctive dwellings in Glasnevin built by Sir John Rogerson, in or about 1710 in the prevailing Jacobean style, was called "The Turrets" The Turrets was described as "a very interesting 18th century house with a tower-like central block of two storeys flanked by single storey wings" over underground cellars. Of particular note was the set of outside steps with its curved marble balustrade leading to the simple architrave doorway. It incorporated a few small circular towers (hence the name) and contained what was thought to be a "Priest's Hole", although this seems unlikely in view of the history of the house and its occupants. Entry was by Claremont Avenue.

Its first occupant was Isaac Ambrose, Secretary to the Irish Parliament, and, later, Isaac Ambrose Eccles. In 1829 or thereabouts it was acquired by Bishop Lindsay for his family. Some years later, his son built a new house adjoining the Turrets, and renamed the combined residence "Glasnevin House" after their previous residence which had now become a convent.

Figure 22: The Turrets, (Glasnevin House) c.1920

Figure 23: Glasnevin House rear view, 1981

Figure 24: Glasnevin House front view, 1981

Subsequently, the name "The Turrets" was no longer used, although it appears in the Dublin Directory and on the old maps up to 1870. The building was demolished in February 1982. The picture of the Turrets shown here was taken in the 1920s or 1930s.

Bishop Lindsay and the Lindsay family

Charles Dalrymple Lindsay (1760 – 1846) was the fifth son of the Earl of Crawford and Belcarris, of a noble Scottish family known affectionately as "the lithesome Lindsays". He studied at Balliol College Oxford where he took holy orders. He came to Ireland in 1801 as Private Secretary to the Lord Lieutenant Earl Hardwicke. He was created Bishop of Killaloe and Kilfenora in 1803, and in 1805 he was transferred to the positions of Bishop of Kildare and Dean of Christ Church. In 1806, he acquired Glasnevin House and Demesne, and a very large area of Glasnevin which he took over from William Gore.

Bishop Lindsay is recorded a being of "a benign and venerable aspect, a good scholar of refined taste, greatly proficient in music", and that "he much enjoyed the pleasures of society". His portrait in the Chapter House of Christ Church Cathedral shows him as a tall, handsome and vigorous man. He decorated his house in lavish mode, and he entertained in style.

He took an active part in the affairs of Glasnevin Parish, and appears to have been a benevolent landlord. During the cholera epidemic of 1829 he set up a temporary hospital in his grounds. He set up a dairy farm where he introduced the most up-to-date methods as well as bringing in dairymen from Scotland. Unfortunately, the local milkmen saw this as unfair competition and he incurred some unpopularity with those people who nicknamed him "The Buttermilk Bishop".

A sensational incident occurred on a narrow local road (possibly Johnstown Lane, now called Ballygall Road East). The Bishop was proceeding in his carriage when he met a local man with a horse and cart, who refused to yield the right of way. The result was a fist-fight between the two men, which was reported in a Dublin newspaper under the headline "The Boxing Bishop". Bishop Lindsay died in 1846, and he is entombed in the nave of Christ Church Cathedral, the last cleric to be interred there.

His son Captain (later Colonel) Henry Gore Lindsay and his widow Catherine survived him.
Colonel Lindsay, a veteran of the Crimean War, and a magistrate, became the most influential man in Glasnevin. Over the years, he gradually sold off most of the land, which originally comprised more than 300 acres. In 1878, Colonel Lindsay became one of the first Commissioners of the Township of Drumcondra, Glasnevin and Clonliffe. He died in 1911.

During the "Troubles", the house was occupied by the Commander-in-Chief of the British forces in Ireland. The remaining family members left shortly after the establishment of the new Irish Free State in 1922. The family grave is in St. Mobhi's churchyard by the eastern wall, beside the grave of Dr. Patrick Delany.

Chapter 24:

GENTLEMEN AND THEIR VILLAS FROM 1700 ONWARDS

The smaller estates and their residents

Apart from the large landowners, there were many gentlemen residing in Glasnevin in the 1700s and 1800s having villas with grounds or small estates. Some have been mentioned previously such as Dean Delany, Rupert Barber, Thomas Tickell and James Belcher, but there are a few others of note that merit mention. In many cases, the occupiers are tenants and not the owners or leaseholders as can be seen from the applottment lists for the Parish.
The period from 1950 onwards saw the demolition of most of the eighteenth century houses, and very few remain today.

Roseville

One of the more attractive Georgian houses in Glasnevin was Roseville, which was a red-brick building situated directly opposite the gateway of the Holy Faith Convent, on the site of the former semi-state agency called Enterprise Ireland (among other designations allocated to it over time). Colonel William Henry Gore, the major landholder in the area, owned, and lived for a while in, Roseville from about 1800 to 1820.

Figure 25: Roseville, Old Finglas Rd. c.1980

The Lindsay family used Roseville for their visiting relations and guests. Thom's Directory for 1903 gives the Hon. Viscount Ikerrin as the occupier. On one occasion, the village was decorated with bunting, presumably celebrating his marriage to a wealthy heiress from Waterford.

It was let in apartments from 1950 to 1970, following which it was restored and refurbished by the IIRS for use as offices. Along with Glasnevin House and the Turrets, it was demolished in February 1982 to make way for new offices.

Beechmount

Looking up Glasnevin Hill today we can see the imposing residence called Beechmount, a Jacobean –style house. The house dates from about 1710, and its first residents were Hugo Batho and his family who were Huguenots. None of the succeeding occupiers is of particular note.

Two ancillary buildings, a small lodge to the left and a slightly larger dwelling on the right which eventually became a butcher's shop, formed part of the property. The butcher's shop (Montgomery's) was possibly built as a dairy, with accommodation upstairs for workmen. It was demolished in 1998.

From about 1850 to 1870 the house was a post office, grocery and drapery occupied by the Cantrell family, and from 1870 to 1900 by Moses McClelland and his family. In 1900 it was purchased by Andrew Ryan, a prominent local publican and business man, and occupied by his brother Timothy. In the 1920s it was occupied by Patrick Byrne, followed by the Boland family from the 1930s to the 1950s.

In the 1990s, the house was entirely reconstructed as an apartment building, and the façade was rebuilt as a reproduction of the original.

Figure 26: Beechmount,(restored) Glasnevin Village 2009

Church Hill House

Another of the very few eighteenth-century houses in Glasnevin to last until the twenty-first century, Church Hill House (or Churchill House as it became known later) stands on Ballymun Road, prominent amid the red-brick Victorian terraces. In the late 1700s it was a modest two-storey dwelling, the residence of Doctor William Harvey M.D., and in the early nineteenth century it was occupied by Dean Batson.

From about 1815 to 1833, the occupant was the Reverend Robert Walsh, Rector of Finglas and noted Dublin historian. The house appears to consist of two buildings, an older 18th century house at the rear and a newer house built on in front. The Wyatt front windows, unusual in Glasnevin, indicate that the latter was built in the 1830s.

About 1870, it was taken over by Alex Campbell who established Church Hill Nursery there. He was previously Curator of the National Model Gardens of the National Commissioners for Education, and the Campbell family remained in the nursery business until the 1920s. The Craigie brothers Robert and John, dairy farmers from Scotland, lived at Merville next door, until they left in 1925. They subsequently set up their Merville Dairy on the Finglas Road.

In 1918, a farming family from County Wexford, the Nolans, bought the house and land and started a dairy business which they called the Wexford Dairy. The family remained in possession until the year 2005 when the property was sold.

Figure 27: Church Hill House, Ballymun Rd. 1995

Greenmount

Perhaps the least- known of the big houses in Glasnevin, Greenmount with its small estate, was hidden from the roadway, and access thereto was by an avenue with a lodge situated at the entrance on the south side of Botanic Avenue. The original house, built by Sir John Rogerson with its estate was demised to James King Davis and Rowland Parker, City Adjutant, in 1709. (Part of the estate was demised William Thwaites in 1729 - see below).

The new house was built in or about 1834 and named Greenmount. It was quite large, having four reception rooms, six bedrooms, a dining room, a nursery, and a large kitchen and dairy in the basement. An imposing set of granite steps with wrought-iron railings led to the front door.

The last family to live there were the Nugents when Michael Nugent took up residence there in the 1920s. It was demolished in the 1950s and the site is now occupied by Botanic Square and Botanic Park. Botanic Park was the site of Rowland Parker's quarry, which was a popular playing area for the local children until about 1950.

Fairfield, Swift and the dancing ghosts

In 1928, the people of Glasnevin witnessed the demolition of Fairfield, a fine example of a Jacobean house, to make way for the new branch of the Bank of Ireland and the houses on the new Fairfield Road. It was in this house that Dean Swift is purported to have scratched this message on the window pane to a servant- maid:

> *Mary Kirkpatrick, very young*
> *Ugly face and pleasant tongue.*

This incident has been alleged to be the inspiration for W.B. Yeats play *"Words upon the window pane"*.

In 1729, Rowland Parker demised to William Thwaites "a dwelling-house messuage or tenement with the pleasure garden, kitchen garden stable and coach house and gardens containing three acres (Irish Plantation Measure)". The house was given the name Fairfield at some time later. According to the applottment list for 1776, a Thomas Hutton lived there, and later the Reverend Joseph Hutton (1880).

In the early 1900s, the house was occupied for a time by the Power family, one of whom, Arthur, a writer, wrote about the "dancing ghosts" that he claimed haunted the place. According to his account, sounds of dancing began around 10 o'clock at night in a large attic room at the top of the house, but the Powers could hear no accompanying music. Sometimes the sound was just gentle tapping noises, but the tempo was always exact and perfect. Now and again, the family could hear the rustle of ladies' dresses as they moved about overhead. "We would leave our beds and stand on the landing in our night attire, sometimes shivering as we listened to the ghostly revelry", he wrote, (reminiscent of Sir Roderick Murgatroyd's song "The spectres' holiday" in Sullivan's "Ruddigore").

The next occupier was Doctor Henry Gogarty, whose son Oliver St. John Gogarty (1878 - 1957) would become famous as a surgeon, a writer, a Senator in the first Free State Senate, and a noted wit. His life has been well chronicled, and has been the subject of more than one biography. Gogarty writes of his boyhood in Fairfield, fishing for pinkeens in the River Tolka among other activities and he describes its garden and orchard which were profuse with fruit and wild flowers. At the east end of the estate lay a "Curious Well" - the Deane's Well, dating from medieval times (Chapter 1).

Later, as a student, James Joyce visited there several times, and Oliver St. John Gogarty is immortalised by him as the flamboyant Buck Mulligan in "Ulysses". As is well known, their friendship did not last. Oliver's son Oliver Duane was born here.
In 1927.it was compulsorily acquired by Dublin Corporation, and demolished soon afterwards. The Corporation, as a gesture, decided to preserve two tall pine trees that had stood in the garden, and were located just outside the Bank of Ireland. Today, only one of those trees remains, the last reminder of Fairfield.

Figure 28: Fairfield, Glasnevin c.1900

Glasnevin Lodge

Adjoining Addison Lodge and behind a high wall, hidden from view of all save the passengers on the upper decks of buses, stood a neat Georgian villa called Glasnevin Lodge. Not much is known about its origins or early history, and it is not until the nineteenth century that we find clear records of the residents.

Hampstead

In the north of Glasnevin we find the area known as Hampstead. Hampstead is divided into Hampstead North, Hampstead South and Hampstead Hill. Hampstead Avenue (formerly Lane) is shown, unnamed, in the 1640 Survey Map of Glasnevin. Hampstead South is justly famous as the location of the Hospital that has been in the possession of the Eustace family since 1819.

The lands of Hampstead, with the Wad, formed the greater part of The Great Farm, the largest holding in Glasnevin, and they subsequently formed part of the extensive property in Glasnevin acquired by Sir John Rogerson in 1703. One of the buildings thereon was Hampstead Castle, a Tower House dating from the 15th Century and demolished in 1875.

The earliest occupant was Captain John Davis, who is recorded as being in Glasnevin in 1706, and it is a conjecture that he named the area after Hampstead in London because of some perceived resemblance between the two. His son Charles succeeded him. Charles died in 1769 and was buried in St. Michan's. Another recorded occupant was J. Hewetson, Counsellor-at law, in 1736.

Part of the property, Hampstead South, was demised in 1769 to Sir Richard Steele Bart., of Bettyville in Co. Carlow, and M.P. for Mullingar. The Steele family was to remain in possession for the next hundred years. Sir Richard Steele and his heirs gradually enlarged his estate by purchasing or leasing more land in the vicinity from the Lindsay family. (Deed Map 51/88). Sir Richard died in 1784 and was succeeded by his son Parker Steele, and grandson Sir Robert Smith Steele. About 1820, Hampstead Castle and part of Hampstead South were sold by Sir Robert to Doctor Isaac Ryall. Dr. Ryall formed a partnership with Dr. Richard Grattan and Dr. John Eustace to set up an establishment for the mentally - ill which would later become Hampstead Hospital.

The lands of Hampstead South were sold off in stages to the Eustace family between 1869 and 1879, after which the Steele-Graves (as they had become) relinquished their interest. In 1875, the ruined Hampstead

Castle was demolished to make way for Elmhurst, the present convalescent home.

Hampstead House and Hampstead North saw a succession of owners and tenants. They included Judge Parsons and Richard O'Gorman. In 1838, the newly-established Commissioners of National Education acquired Hampstead House and its lands and set up the Glasnevin Institute there. The house was renamed Albert College in 1853, and it was again renamed in the 1920s as Cuilin House (see "Colleges and schools of the Commissioners of National Education").

Clonmel Cottage

Clonmel Cottage or House, a late Georgian building, probably dated from the early 1800s. The occupiers are given in successive census' as William Connolly, John Reilly (1901) Pat. Derham (1905) A.J. Healy (1916). The last owners were the Duff Family. It was demolished in the 1950s to make way for a new housing estate, and the name Clonmel was retained in the names of some of the modern roads there.

Wadelai, the Wad River and the Wad

The Wad River forms the northern and eastern boundaries of Glasnevin, and at one time flowed under the old Wad Bridge on Ballymun Road. The Wad is a large townland whose area was the northernmost part of the Great Farm, lying between Hampstead North and the Parish of Santry. The name may come from Wadd's Farm, another name for Draycott's Farm.

A house called Wadelai lay at the end of a long avenue off the west side of Ballymun Road until it was knocked down about 1950. It was located on the boundary between the modern townlands of Walnut Grove and Ballygall. This was a comparatively modern building dating from around 1900, and its name seems to have been derived from Wad and the Ellis Family that lived here. This name was given to the present Wadelai housing estate which occupies the townland of Walnut Grove. The Wadelai area was originally a part of the Great Farm, and is named "Cullinagh" in the Survey of 1640.

West Park

On the present Ballygall Road East (formerly Johnstown Lane), half-hidden behind an untidy hedge and a solid gate, stands an old Georgian house called West Park, its gable-end facing the road. It is not recorded in the applottment of 1772 and probably dates from the late1700s or even the early 1800s. The land forms part of the Claremont Estate and part of the lands purchased by Sir John Rogerson in 1703, its earliest proprietor was Richard Audley, of "Ardmore" in Glasnevin Village in the early 1700s. Still standing, its present owners are the Fitzmaurice family, solicitors.

Some confusion has arisen about the name West Park because it was adopted for other properties. West Park House was located behind the present Cremore Drive and on the present Griffith Avenue. The last owners were the Doyle family who ran a small dairy and shop that survived into the 1960s when it was demolished to make way for the extension to Griffith Avenue.

Figure 29: West Park Farm, Ballygall Rd. c. 1950

West Park Farm (formerly known as West Park Cottage) with a house dating from the mid 1800s, on the opposite side of Ballygall Road, was occupied by the Coyle family until 1952. It was demolished in 1952 when the Ballygall Road was being widened. The site was occupied by a motor-car company (Joe Duffy) until 2002, and by a small apartment building since then.

Another house, Claremont Cottage (an old house on the site of the present Ballygall shopping centre) changed its name to West Park House in the 1850s. At one time, around the 1900s, the adjoining part of the present Ballygall Road East was designated "West Park Road".

References:
Register of Deeds
Thoms Directories

Chapter 25:
GLASNEVIN IN THE 19TH CENTURY

Glasnevin in the early 19th century: "Departed prosperity and splendour"

After the modest prosperity of the 18th century, Glasnevin Village suffered a decline in population in the early 19th century. At a time when the national population was increasing by huge numbers, the population of the Village fell from 559 in 1831 to 370 in 1841. Whether this was a result of people leaving or dying, or lack of new residents, is not obvious. It could not have been confined to the poorer classes, seeing that the drop in numbers was twice the number of labourers in the parish (98).

The only productive activity was in the agricultural and dairy farms in the area, and with the village tradesmen – for example blacksmiths, cobblers and shopkeepers that served the community. There was a substantial sailcloth factory owned by Terence Murray of Claremont Villa, which is described by D'Alton as "having six looms, and located on the Dublin side of the village". Griffith's Valuation 1847 describes Terence Murray as owning a house, offices a factory and five acres of land in Drishoge, that is, the Cory Lane (Botanic Avenue) area, where the River Tolka provided ample supplies of water for most of the year.

D'Alton's *History of County Dublin 1836* describes the "classical village of Glasnevin" as follows:

"The village may be considered as divided into the old and the new, both sweetly situated, but the former, though once recommended and frequented for the salubrity (sic) of its air, is, with the exception of four to five houses, a range of ruins. The River Tolka over which there is a fine bridge, divides them; the new being on the Dublin and improving side; the great objects of interest are, however, in the old village".

He apparently overlooked the thatched mud-cabins that remained a feature of the "Dublin and improving side" of the river for many years afterwards. His description of the road approaching Glasnevin as "a melancholy lane" conveys to the reader the depressing state of the area. He gives a detailed description of the flora and topography of Glasnevin at that time, which, unfortunately, is of little relevance today, and he mentions the typical black calp limestone that was quarried in this part of County Dublin, and which can still be seen in many old masonry walls.

Population 1831-1851

The *Parliamentary Gazetteer* for 1844-45 describes Glasnevin as follows:

"It luxuriates amidst a profusion of such ornaments as are contributed, not alone by mansions and villas, but by great public institutions. The Village of Glasnevin crowns a rising ground which declines gently to the Tolka.
Several ornamental mansions in Glasnevin are still inhabited by persons of distinction and great respectability, but others and numerous domestic dwellings, some in a state of ruin, present a scene of desolation, which forcibly directs attention back to times of departed prosperity and splendour".

It gives the following statistical information:

Glasnevin: Length: 2 miles, breadth:1 mile, area: 995 acres

Population: 1001 in 1831 and 1226 in 1841

Village: Area: 21 acres, houses: 60

Population: 559 in 1831 and 370 in 1841

In 1834 the religious populations in the parish were as follows:

Church of Ireland:	348
Roman Catholic:	585
Presbyterian	15
Others:	16

The 1851 Census returns gives the total population of Glasnevin as 1162. Houses were classified and counted as follows:

First class: 35 (Superior houses)
Second class: 100 (good farm or town houses)
Third class: 17 (better class mud houses with 2 – 4 rooms
Fourth class: 2 (Mud cabins).

Glasnevin village: recovery

After 1841, the Village began to recover, as may be gathered from an entry in the Dublin Directory of 1847:

"The Village occupies elevated ground, rising gradually from the river, and containing sixty houses, several of which are handsome buildings. The church is a small edifice. There is a Carmelite Convent, a Widows' Alms House, a dispensary, a private lunatic asylum, and several schools of which one is the Model Training School of the National Board.
"The mail from Dublin arrives at 30 minutes past 8 a.m., and is despatched at 35 minutes past 12 and 15 minutes past 2 p.m."

The 1837 O.S. Map shows the location of Glasnevin's first Post Office on Vincent Terrace, a few doors up from Tolka House.

The Cross Guns area

The Cross Guns, Glasnevin's other village acquired some new houses, notably Bengal Terrace on the Finglas Road, which is shown on the 1837 O.S map, followed by a succession of small terraces on what is now Botanic road.

The year 1832 saw the opening of Prospect Cemetery, which brought some business to the public houses in the area of Cross Guns despite the opposition of the cemetery committee. The new Cemetery Lane, now called Prospect Avenue, eventually contained at least twelve small public houses during the period that the old gateway was in use.

Schools and institutions

A distinguishing feature of Glasnevin in the latter half of the 19th century was the proliferation of schools and institutions throughout the area. At the time, for a number of reasons, Glasnevin did not attract building developers. The existence of turnpikes (not to mention bad roads) and the opposition of local landowners proved a sufficient deterrent. Institutions of the educational sort, and the Cemetery, were tolerated, probably because they did not intrude unduly on the "pastoral nature" of Glasnevin cherished by the better-off residents.

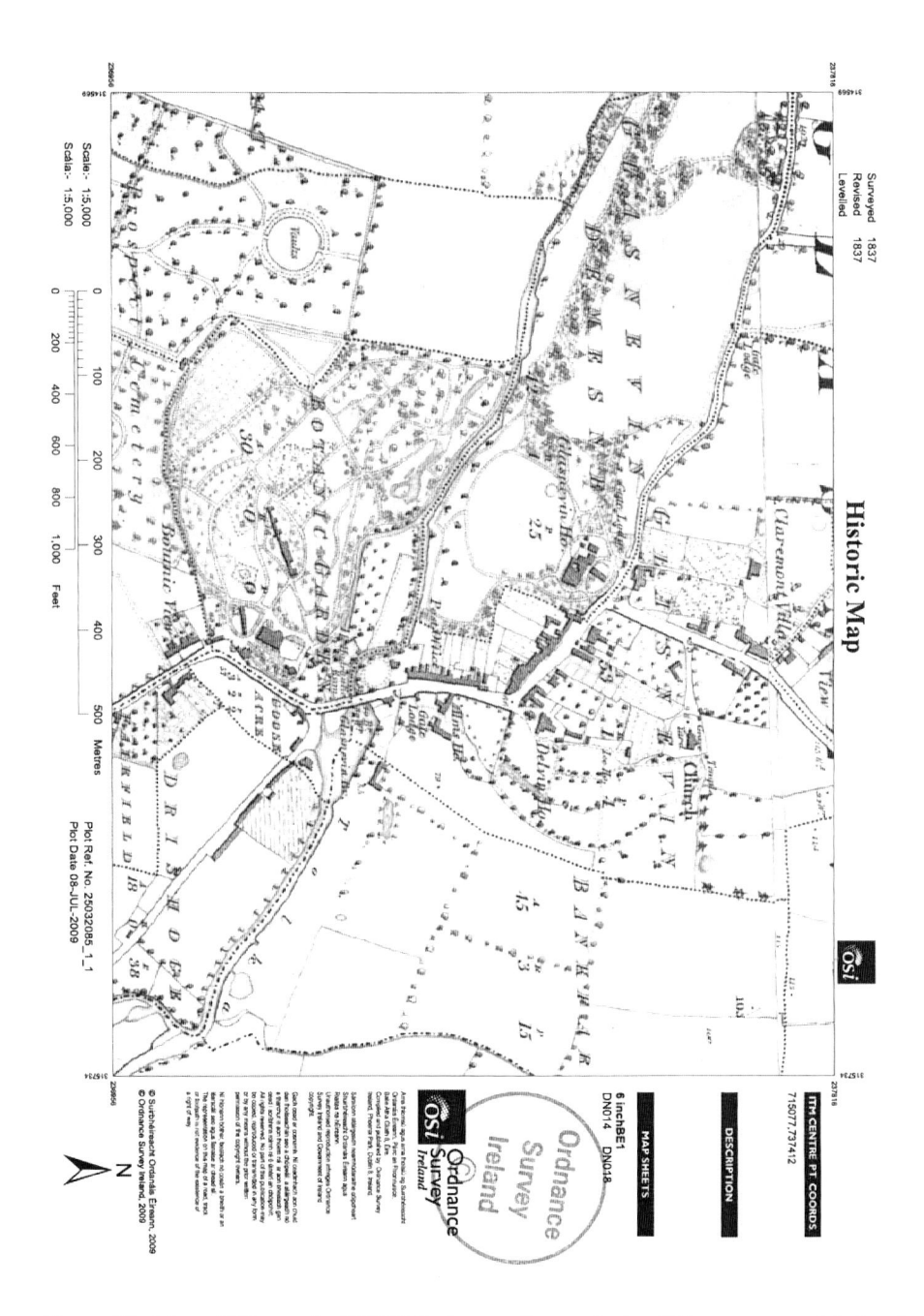

Figure 30: Map of Glasnevin 1837 ©Ordnance Survey Ireland/Government of Ireland copyright permit No. MP 001411.

Chapter 26:

FAMINE AND PESTILENCE: RELIEF MEASURES

Bad weather and famine

The year 1816 has been called "The Year with no Summer". On 10th April 1815, Mount Tambora, a volcano in Indonesia, erupted with such ferocity that the debris was sent 50 km into the sky, eventually spreading over the entire northern hemisphere; even the normally sunny Mediterranean regions did not escape the gloom. The sun's light was dimmed and temperatures dropped so low that there was no summer in 1816. There was incessant rain, crops failed, grass did not grow, and winter lasted for the entire year. The next few years were not much better, and the prolonged and bitter cold, combined with the lack of food and fuel, took its toll everywhere. Disease, including typhus, became rampant.

Relief measures for the poor people of Glasnevin

Since the beginning of the eighteenth century, the care of the poor and destitute in Glasnevin had been the responsibility of the Parish, and it seems to have been just adequate by the standards of the time.

On 19th November 1816, the "Year with no Summer", the Parish Vestry decided that *"timely precautions against impending dearth of provisions should be used to alleviate as much as possible the distress of the labouring class of people residing in the Parish"*. It was decided that, in principle, the provision of regular work for "industrious persons" in the first instance was preferable to opening a subscription for their relief.

Relief work for the labourers

Under this scheme, the number of labourers would be ascertained, distinguishing between those permanently employed and those that depended on "precarious" (sic) work. For any redundant labourers, it was deemed expedient to open a subscription for the purpose. The labourers, totalling 98 in number, were divided into three classes:

1   Persons commonly employed by public bodies or individuals: 61
2   Persons making a "pretty constant livelihood" jobbing for two or more individuals: 4
3   Persons in "precarious" employment: 33.

The Vestry decided that some of the unemployed labourers should be employed in making "permanent and beneficial improvements" throughout the Parish, including the making of footpaths at the sides of the highways. In addition, it was decided to write to John Bucknall McCarthy, Secretary of the Royal Dublin Society, requesting aid for improving the road to the Society's Botanic Gardens, and also to write to the Directors of the Turnpike Road from Dublin through the Village of Glasnevin to Knocksedan, with a similar request.

The Vestry in 1816 decided that a subscription would be raised to provide coal and meal for the unemployed labourers and poor people.

The poor were divided into two classes:

1   The poor relieved from absolute want who were "in the shelter of the Alms House", a total of ten, of whom eight were in the Alms House

2   Those that could manage partly by themselves and partly depended on their charitable neighbours or their families.

In 1830, the spectres of poverty and hunger loomed once again, and the Vestry took steps to organize work for the unemployed, again in improving the footpaths. This occurred again in 1836, when it was decided that the unemployed labourers of the Parish should be profitably set to work repairing the pathway on the Naul Road from Claremont Lane to the Wad Bridge on the Parish Boundary.

Relief for the poor: Glasnevin Charitable Committee

In January 1830, the Vestry set up "The Glasnevin Charitable Committee" to raise money in order to relieve the numerous poor women and children of the Parish "found almost in a state of destitution". Funds were provided for two tons of coal, one ton of potatoes, two cwt of meal and coffins for the poor.

These measures continued for some years, and in 1838, those in receipt of relief out of the church fund were obliged to attend after Service every Sunday in order to receive their allowances (presumably having attended Service).

Sickness and health care: Government measures

Poverty and starvation left the less fortunate prone to sickness and disease, in particular the dreaded cholera which remained a threat for most of the century. In 1820, the Lord Lieutenant set up the General (or Central) Board of Health for the purpose of advising on the institution of local health boards. In the same year, under an Act of Parliament (59th Geo 3rd Chapter 40), regulations "for preventing contagious diseases in Ireland" were issued. Following the outbreak of cholera in the year 1832, the Board was renamed the Cholera Board.

The new Board set up local health boards, health-officer positions, dispensaries, small hospitals and the notorious workhouses. It was overwhelmed by the demands caused by the Great Famine, and it handed over its responsibilities to the various poor law unions. In 1872, the Local Government Board took over those function.

Sickness and health care in Glasnevin

In April 1822, in response to the new regulations, the Glasnevin Parish Vestry appointed two Officers of Health: Col. W. Gore and Marmaduke Smith. Those local worthies did not receive a salary for their posts, but they were paid expenses.

Some years later, cholera broke out, with devastating effects on the people of Dublin and its surroundings. In the winter of 1827, Bishop Lindsay set up a temporary fever hospital in his grounds at Glasnevin House (the present Holy Faith Convent), for which he provided money and furnishings. This scheme seems to have been remarkably successful.

The Parish was fortunate in having a number of medical doctors resident, notably those in the Eustace's hospital in Hampstead. In May 1828, from the Alms House funds, the Parish paid £1-18s to Dr. Gibson for his expenditure on medicine for Mary Meehan.

The thanks of the Parish are recorded as follows:

"Thanks to Isaac Ryall M.D. for his constant attention to the sick poor, and on his successful attendance on a Temporary Hospital prepared for their reception during the late contagious and dangerous fever, when all their cases terminated favourably, and our families through his remitting care were prevented from a spreading evil which carried off great numbers of persons of all ranks and circumstances in the neighbouring metropolis".

Isaac Ryall had been a surgeon in the Royal Navy with the rank of Commander. He became a famous eye surgeon, and he was the founder of what eventually became the Royal Victoria Eye and Ear Hospital in Dublin. In 1825, he formed a partnership with Dr. John Eustace and Dr. Richard Grattan for the purpose of establishing a hospital for the mentally-ill. He retired to live in Devon.

Coffins for the poor

The Parish records show that over this period, a large number of coffins and shrouds were provided for the poor, at prices from ten shillings upwards.

Famine relief

In 1847, a relief committee was set up in Glasnevin Parish for the impoverished. Captain Lindsay wrote to Sir Randolph Routh in Dublin Castle informing him of this and of the amount £38.3s. 6d. collected from thirty three parishioners. The relief committee made a "respectful application" to the authorities for a subsidy in proportion to the amount collected.

Chapter 27:

FROM PASTORAL AREA TO TOWNSHIP

Local government and rates

The Church Temporalities Act of 1833 revoked the right of churchwardens to levy parish cess, and effectively ended the civil role of the parish vestry. Following this, each parish was levied by the Finance Committee of County Dublin. For example, in 1849, Patrick Magrane, Collector, Barony of Coolock, directed that £207-7s-5d be levied on the Parish of Glasnevin.

The latter half of the nineteenth century saw a radical re-organization of local government in Ireland which culminated in the Local Government (Ireland) Act (1898. This provided for county councils, district councils and rural district councils which took over the administrative and fiscal duties of the Grand Juries.

The coming of the townships

The development of the suburbs of Dublin began with the establishment of "townships", as they were styled, the first of which was Rathmines in 1847. These were areas outside the Dublin City boundary which were marked down for development by powerful vested interests comprising businessmen and politicians, who managed to maintain control over the local administration. Townships were invariably based on existing villages or other population centres.

For a number of reasons, mainly the type of land ownership, development mushroomed on Dublin's south side, as the middle classes moved out of the "smoky city" to the new airy suburbs. Dublin Corporation saw the new townships as a threat to its finances, and lobbied for their annexation. Such was the general opposition to this move, that, with rates at 2s 9d in Drumcondra, and 6s 10d in the city, and the lack of sympathy from the Castle authorities, the matter was left in abeyance for another twenty years.

Dublin's north-side development: the problems

Development, in the modern sense of the word, took place more slowly, and over a relatively smaller area, on Dublin's north side. The delay was caused within the city by a lengthy law-suit concerning the will of the Earl of Blessington, and outside the city by local vested interests along with the restrictions of toll-gates or turnpikes of which there were nine. These latter were officially abolished in 1855, but by then south-side development was well under way.

The greatest problems with nineteenth century development in Dublin were those of water supply and drainage or sewerage. In rural areas, people had ready access to local wells and rivers, but in no way would this system be adequate for the mass housing that was to come.

The developers

In the nineteenth century, the principal developers and entrepreneurs on the north side were Nationalist politicians and business men Edward McMahon M.P., Maurice Butterly, builder, and J.F. Lombard, a director of Arnotts drapery company.

Starting in 1870, they developed areas north of the city centre as far as the Royal Canal, which was the city boundary at the time. Their motives were not only commercial, but political and, to some extent, religious.

Obstacles and frustrations

The developers next decided to extend their activities to the Drumcondra area. There, the greatest obstacle to development was the absence of public services.

The environment in Drumcondra had been steadily deteriorating due to problems with water pollution, cesspools and bad and dirty roads. Sewage was emptied directly into the river Tolka, which became a health hazard, and by the time it reached Ballybough and Fairview its waters were heavily polluted.

Dissatisfaction with the lack of public services was growing among both residents and developers, and they came to realise that the Grand Jury that ruled County Dublin had neither the will nor the resources to solve the problems. They decided to take action. Attempts to obtain water from the county were unsuccessful, and a proposed drainage scheme was turned down by the local government board. They then sent deputations to Dublin Corporation and the North Dublin Sanitary Board with proposals, which, alas, were also rejected.

The solution: a new township

The developers and residents decided that the only way to change matters was to establish a township. In addition to their political clout, in this venture they had the support of Cardinal Cullen, Catholic Archbishop of Dublin, and Lord James Butler the major landowner in Drumcondra. The area of Drumcondra was too small for a viable township, and the proposers sought to include Glasnevin, an area still largely undeveloped. In 1877, a bill establishing a township consisting of Clonliffe, Drumcondra and Glasnevin was introduced to parliament.

Unsuccessful opposition

The old gentry of Glasnevin led by Colonel Henry Gore Lindsay, with Henry J. Gogarty and William V. Barre, created strong opposition to the bill, arguing that Glasnevin was a "pastoral area" and quite unsuitable for urban development. A more cogent objection was not only that the new rates for providing public services would cost them money in any event, but worse, they would be paying taxes for the improvement of other areas.

Support for the township, however, came from another Glasnevin resident, Sir Patrick Keenan of Delville, a Commissioner of the National Education Board. The opposing representations were of no avail, and on 2nd of September 1878, the bill setting up a township of Drumcondra, Clonliffe and Glasnevin became law.

The township of Drumcondra, Clonliffe and Glasnevin

The township was divided into three wards. Glasnevin Ward was allocated four commissioners drawn mainly from the middle- and upper-class residents and landowners. The other two wards had five commissioners each, who represented property developers, builders and small householders. There was, understandably, some hostility between the two groupings.

The Commissioners

Elections were held on 15th October 1881 and fourteen commissioners were elected to serve for a term of three years. The franchise was confined to occupiers of property with a valuation of £5 or more, and owners of property with a valuation of £50 or more. The qualification for a candidature as a commissioner was restricted to resident males owning property with a valuation of £25 or more and owners of property valued at £50 or more.

The Township Commissioners did not enjoy the luxury of a town hall, the expenditure on which was limited to £1000. Their first premises was in No.1 Burnett Place (now named St. Anne's Road) beside the location of the present Drumcondra Railway Station. In 1882, they moved to Hollybank House, and finally, in 1885 to No. 36 Lower Drumcondra Rd. beside the former Sacred Heart Home. The Minutes of the meetings of Commissioners are irretrievably lost, so we have to rely on newspaper reports and *The Irish Builder* for information on their activities.

The Commissioners of Glasnevin Ward

The first commissioners for Glasnevin were Colonel H.G. Lindsay, (Glasnevin House), Henry J. Gogarty (Fairfield) (father of Oliver St. John), William Barre (Hillside, Glasnevin Hill) and Stephen McCarthy (Daneswell House, the Lynch Estate). These four held office until 1889. Later Commissioners included Michael Scally, the landlord of Brian Boru House. In 1895, the Commissioners were: Colonel Lindsay, Thomas Connelly (builder), John Thornton, and Blayney Mitchell J.P. of Greenmount.

The end of the township

In spite of the formation of the township, the problem of poor roads and services remained. Finances were in a bad way, but the commissioners, mainly concerned with keeping the rates at their low level, did not see their way to improving matters.

In the *Evening Mail* on 9th July 1880 there is a letter from Mr. Barre' opposing the removal of mud-heaps and the asphalting of pathways. In it he complains " *Our poor township cannot afford the extravagant and injudicious outlay, spending 4s-6d per yard on asphalting choice corners and leaving the rest of the roads worse than those of Connemara, when other townships are satisfied (as we should be) with well-gravelled paths*".

However, the real problem was that the resources were inadequate, because the new township, with its existing population, was still too small to be viable.

The 1898 Local Government Act gave Town Commissioners the status of Urban Councils, but they were to enjoy their new status only briefly.

Meantime, Dublin Corporation had been biding its time. In 1898 it moved to extend its boundaries northwards, and it contrived to have a bill for this submitted to parliament.

Again, there was mounting opposition to this bill, and in the local elections of 1899, its leading opponent, Colonel Lindsay, headed the poll. In 1898, government auditors were sent in and they found that, despite the low expenditure and poor services, the finances were in bad way and the situation was therefore untenable.

It gradually became obvious to all that a take-over by the Corporation was inevitable. The Dublin Boundaries Bill became law on 6th August 1900, and on 1st January 1901, the greater part of Glasnevin, with Drumcondra and Clonliffe, followed by Clontarf, became part of Dublin City.

References:
Drumcondra, Clonliffe and Glasnevin Township 1878-1900, by Patrick Kelly
Dublin the Deposed Capital, by Mary E. Daly
The Irish Builder, Vol.. XXI No. 462, Vol. XVIII No.407, Vol. XX No. 435.

Chapter 28:

POPULATION AND HOUSING 1850 - 1900

A slow start

Few houses, if any, were built in Glasnevin village between 1800 and 1850.
The year 1850 saw the commencement of building in the Cross Guns village area. These included Keegan's Buildings with the Brian Boru Public House on the present Prospect Road, Bengal Terrace on the Finglas Road, and Mount St .Michael and Brighton Terrace on the present Botanic Road. (See "Glossary of place-names").

Following the setting up of the township in 1878, there was no mass-development in Glasnevin on the scale of that in Drumcondra, while the gentry held on to their lands. In fact, the census returns for that period show a fall in population and house numbers. Building of new houses remained on a modest scale, and it was not until the Corporation took control in 1901 that developers got their opportunity.

Ballymun (Naul) Road: 19th century houses

The short row of cottages on Church Avenue (or "Lane" as it was then) dates only from the 1860s, except for the low-lying dwelling nearest the Church which dates from the early 1700s and was very likely the house of the Parish Clerk at one time.

On the west side of Ballymun Road was a cluster of four houses dating from the early 1800s: Ivy Cottage, Church View (both demolished before 1920), Melville and the adjoining Newton House (formerly Newtown Cottage), Church View appears to have been assigned the name "Caperlough" in Thom's Directory for 1910. It and Ivy Cottage were knocked down before 1920.

Newton House was occupied by the Cunningham family from 1882 to 2004, when it was demolished. Melville was the Church of Ireland Rectory for Glasnevin, the last incumbent being the Rev. Henry G. Carroll. The present house appears to be on the site of a much older building, and the Survey by Richard Francis in 1640 shows a substantial house here owned by Edward Wickham.

Redbrick development: Thomas Conolly, Master Builder

The first master builder in Glasnevin was Thomas Conolly, who preceded Alexander Strain. He built St. David's Terrace (behind the Met Office) and St. Thomas's Terrace on Glasnevin Hill around 1878. He built many of the older terraces on Botanic Road before and after 1900, including Addison Terrace (as it was known) opposite the Botanic Gardens. Both he and Alexander Strain built houses in the Iona area (see Chapter 40), but his most prestigious achievement was the building of Iona Church in 1905. He lived in Fernville, the last house in St. David's Terrace. One of his daughters married Mr. Patrick McGilligan, Minister for Finance in the Free State Government, and later, the Interparty Government in 1948.

Population and housing 1881-1891.

The population of Glasnevin Ward during this period is recorded as follows:

1881: Population: 1714, houses: 280.
1891: Population: 1644, houses: 264.

The figures require explanation, seeing that there had been some building in progress. It is possible that the reductions were caused by the demolition of the old mud cabins, mostly in the Botanic Avenue area, and the dispersal of their inhabitants elsewhere.

Water supply.

Dublin's first public water supply, the Vartry Water was made available to a few major Catholic institutions in Drumcondra in 1871 at their own expense, and it was extended to the Botanic Gardens and Glasnevin Village in 1878. It was extended to Claremont Institute in 1885.

Reference: Irish Builder Vol. XXI No. 462 (1879)

Chapter 29:
PUBLIC HOUSES IN GLASNEVIN

The Cross Guns

The earliest record of the name "The Cross Guns" is found in the Vestry Book for 1721 and it comes from the former public house. This establishment obviously dated from some time in the late 1600s, following the building of the new Road to Finglas around 1600, which branched off at this point. The name "The Cross Guns" was not unique, and another tavern of this name existed in Thomas Street in the Liberties at this time ("Pue's Occurrences" 1703). (A public house on Phibsborough Road - proprietor Mathias Bushe - bore the same name up to the year 2000).
The village there became known as The Cross Guns, and the name appears on many old maps. Between 1830 and 1922, the building served as a police station, after which it became Hart's Newsagents (owned by the eponymous Johnny Hart) which lasted until the 1970s. It eventually became a bridal shop.

The Brian Boru: a new type of public house

With the increase in funerals going to the Cemetery, it became clear that a suitable hostelry for the needs of the better-class mourner was needed. When a builder named Keegan built the row of houses named Keegan's Buildings in 1850, it included a public house of a superior type which soon became one of the best-known hostelries in Dublin north of the Liffey.

Figure 31: The Brian Boru, Prospect Rd. c.1950

The public house was acquired in 1850 by Denis Scally, who named it the *Brian Boru,* after Ireland's most famous monarch who, allegedly, was killed nearby in 1014 A.D. towards the end of the Battle of Clontarf. His tent is thought by historians to have been pitched in the general area of what is now modern Phibsborough.

Denis Scally was a vintner in Mayor St. who remarried in 1850 and moved house to a tavern in Ballymun whilst awaiting the completion of his new public house. The Scallys were a well-known and prosperous family with other properties and interests such as quarries, sculptor yards, cattle lairages, the adjoining family residence "Mononia" and another public house called Botanic House on Botanic Road. Denis was succeeded by his son Michael in 1870. After the township of Drumcondra, Clonliffe and Glasnevin was established in 1878, Michael Scally became a Town Commissioner for a year.

The Beer Garden "Carriges"

The style and strategic location of the Brian Boru drew the patronage of a great many people, in particular those "better off". In those days, and indeed for most of the next one hundred years, most women, and especially ladies, would not venture inside a public house, and those more fortunate could remain outside in their carriages.

In the mid-1850s, the enterprising Denis Scally set up the first German-style Beer Garden at the rear of the premises, where ladies could sit and obtain refreshments without having to cross the threshold of the public house. The ladies were accommodated in a number of little timber huts thatched with straw, with open fronts and sides, and containing timber benches. The huts were styled "Drinking Carriges" (sic) for reasons that we can only guess. Each "Carrige" was decorated inside with a painting of one of Ireland's scenic spots. The Beer Garden itself attracted a great many patrons from all over Dublin. Sunday afternoons were especially popular and the Beer Garden became a tourist attraction in its own right, whither the jarveys conducted their fares.

A painting over the front door of the building by a famous church artist called Nagle depicted King Brian Boru mounted on his horse, holding up a crucifix in front of his army. This painting was replaced some time in the 1950s.

The clientele

The Brian Boru was the main "port-of-call" for mourners, rich and poor, going to and returning from the Cemetery until the latter part of the 20th century, and family tradition tells of the poor bearing their dead on a handcart, the men inside taking their refreshment and the women waiting patiently outside with the coffin.

Scally family tradition also tells of the jarvey James "Skin-the-goat" Fitz Harris who was involved in the notorious "Phoenix Park Murders" when, on the 6th of May 1882, he carried members of "The Invincibles" to Phoenix Park where they assassinated Lord Frederick Cavendish, newly-appointed Chief Secretary, and Thomas Burke, Under-Secretary. That morning, Fitz Harris had been in the Brian Boru. He subsequently served sixteen years imprisonment for his alleged involvement.

In James Joyce's "Ulysses", Daedalus, Bloom and their friends drive past the "Brian Boroimhe", behind the hearse bearing the coffin of Paddy Dignam to Prospect Cemetery.

New owners

In 1892, the Brian Boru was taken over by Ignatius Conroy, and subsequently by a Mr. J. Ryan. In 1904, Mr. Patrick Hedigan from Limerick acquired the public house and it has remained in the possession of the Hedigan Family ever since. In 1911, Patrick Hedigan began modernising the premises with the removal of the Beer Garden, and it remains largely unchanged since then. In the 1970s, the adjoining residence Mononia was demolished, and a new annex constructed at the rear, with a car park. The building has since been refurbished.

Kavanaghs in Prospect Square ("The Gravediggers")

The village of Cross Guns in the 19th century appears to have had an almost inordinate number of public houses, following the opening of Prospect Cemetery in 1832. On Prospect Avenue (formerly Cemetery Lane, the approach to the original cemetery gateway), there were at least thirteen establishments, including one styling itself "The Cottage of Contentment". Many were probably little more than shebeens that did not last very long after the gates in Prospect Square were closed and two new Cemetery gates opened on the Finglas Road.

Figure 32: John Kavanagh's, Prospect Square 2010

Only Kavanaghs public house now remains tucked away in Prospect Square, beside the old gateway to the Cemetery. This is an establishment that has been in the possession of the Kavanagh Family since 1833 and it retains its old-style form, although with a modern annex at the rear. Originally established by John Sheehan from Tipperary in 1832 when the Cemetery was opened, it was taken over in 1833 by John Kavanagh from County Meath, the first of the Kavanaghs and a former employee.

It suffered a set-back in 1849 when the new gates to the Cemetery on Finglas Road were opened in 1849, but it managed to survive. Due to its proximity to the old Cemetery gateway, it became known as "The Gravediggers" from the activities of some of its patrons.

As a result of its retaining an old-style format and atmosphere, it became popular in the 1970s and later with film-makers, and it was the scene of many films and TV features, for example, *Angela's Ashes, Agnes Brown, Strumpet City.*

Tolka House (formerly "The Bull's Head")

Not as well-known as the Brian Boru or Kavanaghs, Tolka House is situated in Glasnevin Village at the bottom of the Hill and beside the bridge. Notwithstanding its comparative lack of fame, it is one of the oldest public houses in County Dublin. It existed at the beginning of the 18th century when it was called "The Bull's Head", and its location is such that it may very well have been the site of the local ale-house in medieval times when its one-time landlady, Mariotta Daweney, supplied ale to the Prior of the Holy Trinity during his stays in the Castle (or Manor Hall) nearby (Chapter 7).

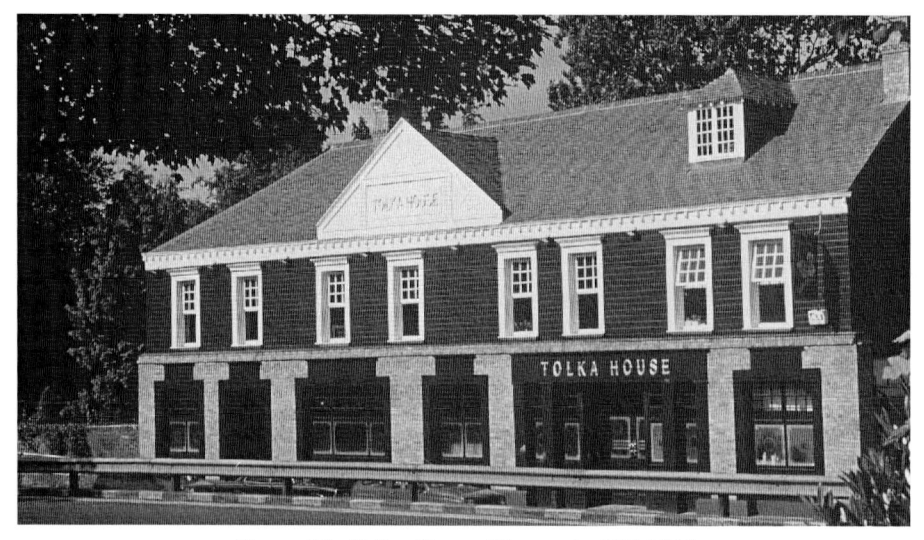

Figure 33: Tolka House Glasnevin Hill 2010

There seems to be no information about this inn before 1700. It was almost certainly rebuilt early in the 18th century and according to the Vestry Book for 1707, its first recorded landlord was William Wolfenden. "The Bull's Head" is mentioned by name in the Dublin Directory for 1738 as facing "Florence Court" (later renamed Carlingford House).

By the middle of the century, Glasnevin, (with Drumcondra), had become a popular venue for the city dwellers that flocked there on Sundays to find welcome rest and refreshment at the Bull's Head. The following advertisement appeared in the *Dublin Journal* in 1761:

"Lancelot Donnelly of the Bull's Head in Glasnevin begs leave to acquaint his friends and the public that he has fitted up said house in a genteel manner and has laid in a choice stock of wines and other liquors and is determined to have a larder well furnished with provisions in season.
"He will sell best claret at 20 pence per bottle and will furnish tea, coffee and the best of hot cake.
"Dining is bespoke, and a good ordinary on Sundays at 3 o'clock.

N.B. Said Donnelly has a meal house, well furnished in said town of Glasnevin to let with convenience of stabling, and coach house if required, and a neat garden to walk in."

Lancelot Donnelly lived until 1806, and was buried in the churchyard of St. Mobhi's nearby.

The next recorded landlord was Thomas White who acquired its first licence in 1848. It appears that he was succeeded by his widow Mary

White. In 1883, the new owner Hubert Briscoe renamed the premises "Tolka House". In 1890, it was taken over by Joseph Camac, and in 1895, it became the property of Andrew Ryan, a prominent Glasnevin businessman. In the 1930s, the landlord was John Spillane. A male preserve, it displayed a notice stating "ladies not catered for" until well into the 1960s.

Mary White is recorded as the proprietor of another and smaller public house "Garden House" on Corey Lane (Botanic Avenue) between 1865 and 1890. It was then taken over by Thomas Ryan, a brother of Andrew Ryan. It was destroyed in 1912 by a fire which had broken out in the adjoining butcher's shop and had set the thatched roofs ablaze.

Tolka House passed through a succession of owners until it was acquired by the O'Malley chain of public houses. In the 1990s, it was completely refurbished and its exterior changed so as to be virtually unrecognisable from its previous more modest appearance.

Other public houses

The fine red-brick **Botanic House** dating from 1913 was built on the site of an older establishment dating from the mid 1800s. The first owner is shown as Bridget Devine, followed by Hugh Temple. In 1903, the proprietor was Joseph Camac, followed by the Kelly family who were proprietors for the first half of the 20th century. It underwent a number of changes of owner and name until 2003 when the new owner, Mr. J. Fitzsimons, restored its original name.

Figure 34: Botanic House (Fitzsimons) Botanic Road 2010

Old 19th century maps and Thom's Directory show a now-defunct establishment called "**The Dollar**" on the Finglas Road, opposite the cemetery entrance.

Sunnybank Hotel was originally a maternity hospital, surviving as such until the late 1940s. Around 1960, it became a licensed hotel, while retaining the name Sunnybank.

Addison Lodge, opposite the Botanic Gardens, and dating from 1850 was originally a gentleman's residence. In the early part of the 20th century, it was the home of Walter McNally, a celebrated operatic baritone with the Moody Manners Opera Company, and his family. In 1953, it became a public house under the ownership of the Freyne Family for over fifty years. It was sold in 2006.

Two modern public houses are Quarry House (its present name) on Ballygall Road East, and "The Cremore" on Fitzmaurice Road.

Chapter 30:
THE MILL OF GLASNEVIN

The origin of the watermill

Watermills were invented in Asia Minor in the first century B.C., and they spread rapidly throughout Europe and the East. They were eventually brought to Ireland by the early Christian missionaries from the Near East. Their antiquity may be judged from the remains of a horizontal watermill discovered in Little Island in Cork which have been dated to about 630 A.D. In 1848 an ancient horizontal watermill dating from this period or later was excavated in Milverton near Skerries.

The type of mill found in ancient Ireland was the Greek type which consisted of a horizontal water- wheel with two paddles attached, located directly in the water or in a wooden channel or duct. The wheel drove the horizontal millstone by means of a vertical shaft. The vertical water wheel that used gearing to drive a horizontal millstone was invented by the Romans towards the end of the first century B.C. Two heritage sites (Bunratty and Ferrycarrig), each contain a reconstruction of a horizontal water mill.

The location of the Mill of Glasnevin

A watermill existed in Glasnevin probably for one thousand years. It was situated on the south bank of the River Tolka, just west of the Bridge, in an area now forming part of the Botanic Gardens.
It may safely be assumed that it belonged to the ancient monastery of Glasnevin, since it was part of church property in 1179 when the lands of Glasnevin were transferred to the Priory of the Holy Trinity.

The former Mill House and mill pond were located beside the watermill. The tail-race waters flowed under the bridge, through the site of the present Catholic church, and joined the river beyond. The millrace could be diverted directly into the river when required, for example when flooding was imminent, and the weir gate and channel for this can be seen today. The Mill was used for grinding corn until the late 1600s In the 1700s, it was used as a paper-manufactory.

The millrace today forms a feature of the Botanic Gardens, and the island formed by the millrace and the river was, and still is, known as the Mill Field. The area today contains the rhododendron and heather collections.

The Middle ages

In 1189, following the arrival of the Normans, re-organization of the Dublin archdiocese was ordered by Archbishop Laurence O'Toole. The lands of Glasnevin were transferred from the Abbey of Finglas to the Priory of the Holy Trinity (Christ Church), and a decree of Pope Urban IV confirming this arrangement mentions "Glasnevin with its mill" ("Glasnevin cum Molendino") (Crede mihi). A major reconstruction probably took place under the Normans.

The sub-precentor and sacrist of the Priory enjoyed the benefice of the watermill of Glasnevin and the Mill Field adjoining. The Mill was a source of considerable income, since all tenants were obliged to bring their corn there for milling. In addition, the Mill Field was probably used as a trading area under licence, with the Ale House close by, and the levies from the traders would have been another source of revenue.
In 1504, Archbishop Walter confirmed to the Priory the town of Glasnevin with its church, tithes and mill.   (CC Deed 318).

In 1540 following the break by King Henry VIII with the Pope, the Priory was changed to a secular Chapter under a Dean. The Treasurer (his new title) was allocated the Water Mill of Glasnevin with the small piece of land adjoining.

The Mill of Glasnevin from 1540 to 1700

In 1540, the new Dean and Chapter decided that they would no longer manage the mill directly, and from that time onwards it was leased to a succession of tenants. The first lease was granted to Alderman Oliver Stephyns (with his wife Alison and son Oliver) of the Mill of Glasnevin with its "tacht and watercourse thereof". (The word "tacht" could be a version of the Gaelic "teacht" meaning an approach, i.e. a mill race or "head race"). In 1542, it formed part of a new lease to Alderman Stephyns for 31 years, excluding the Mill Field. In 1647, The Treasurer granted Richard Kennedy a lease of "the House and Watermill of Glasnevin, with all the pond water and water courses, and all the profits and commodities thereto appertaining, for 41 years for £4 sterling at Michaelmas and Easter, the said Richard to repair the buildings". In 1660, the lease passed to John Serjant, merchant, and in 1661, to Richard Fyan, and in 1661 to John Langour for 21 years.

In 1668, a lease was granted to Anthony Hollingsworth of "the ruined house and watermill of Glasnevin, with all land, water and watercourses for 21 years with 19s for the first seven years, 40s for the second seven years and £4 for the last part. By the end of the century, the Mill had fallen into ruin, along with the church and most of the Village.

TONY O'DOHERTY

The Mill of Glasnevin from 1700 to 1830: A family concern

Paper manufacturing did not exist in Ireland before 1700 when the Irish Company of White Papers was set up with government assistance. The industry was supported by the Dublin Society (later the Royal Dublin Society) and a number of paper mills were established in the Dublin and Cork areas as the printing industry expanded to meet the growing demand for books and newspapers.

Andrew Macklewraith (to give one of the spelling variations of the name), a paper maker from Dundonald in Belfast, was given a lease of the old mill premises in Glasnevin where he built a paper-mill. The mill remained with the family until the end of the century. The name Andrew Macklewrath first appears in the Vestry Book for 1719, and the same name (obviously his son) appears for the years 1739 and 1741. In 1770, Andrew Macklewraith (probably a grandson) was awarded a prize for making "paste board" by the Dublin Society, as reported by Faulkner's Journal on 9th June 1770. In 1771, Andrew Macklewraith renewed his lease. In 1772, his sister Mary married another papermaker - Robert Randall - who lived in the locality.

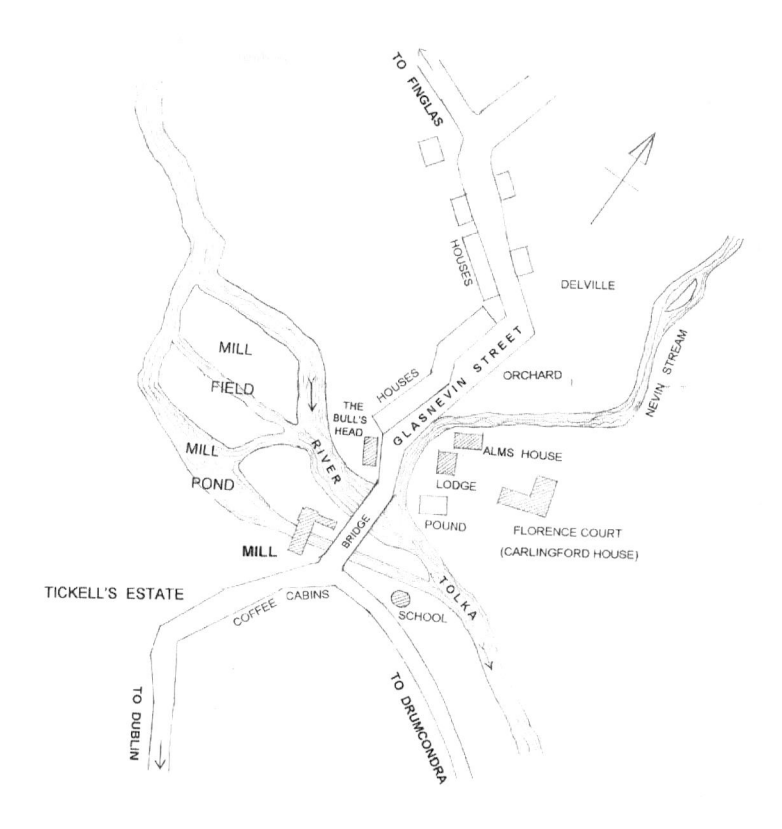

Figure 35 The Mill of Glasnevin location c, 1750

The landlords

During the eighteenth century, the mill was leased to a succession of landlords. In 1709, James Croft obtained a lease of the house and watermill for 21 years at a yearly rent of £3 and a £5 fine to the treasurer. In 1722, William Croft obtained a lease of "the watermill place at Glasnevin whereupon a paper mill is erected". The lease was renewed in 1737. In 1764 the mill was leased by Dr. John Jebb, Treasurer, to his son David Jebb of Chichester in Surrey, merchant, and later, in 1765, 1770 and 1785, to Alderman John Jebb of Drogheda for £5 sterling yearly. It was renewed once more in 1799.

The last years of the mill

The paper manufacturing industry in Ireland experienced difficulties towards the end of the 18th century, mainly caused by the shortage of rags and the fall in demand for paper. This would have had a damaging effect on the Glasnevin enterprise, but worse was to come. The Hibernian Journal of 5th January 1784 reported on the flood damage at the time: *"Every hour brings accounts of damages caused…by the floods…The Paper Mill belonging to Mrs. Mackleraith near Glasnevin is partly swept away"*. The result must have been devastating, and very likely caused the end of paper-manufacturing here. Almost one hundred years after the coming of the Macklewraiths to Glasnevin, the last of the family, Mrs. Macklewraith, died in 1803, and was buried in the local churchyard.

In 1807, the site of the now-ruined watermill was demised to the Dublin Society for £5 per year. The price of the mill and the mill field was £625. The lease was renewed in 1812 when the Society added this property to the Botanic Gardens. The Society spent £1,184 in restoring the mill for the purpose of demonstrating methods of dressing hemp and making cement, but the project proved too costly. In 1817, the mill was leased to a John Hill.

In 1830, the house and mill were levelled, despite some protests, and that was the end of them. The name the "Mill Field" still in use today, and the mill race with its weirs, are the only reminders of this historic artefact. Two other watermills on the River Tolka are worthy of mention here, namely the pin mill near Finglas Bridge, and the Drumcondra Textile Manufactory.

References:
Deed map 51/98: Mill and mill-dam (National Library of Ireland)
Christ Church deeds
Correspondence with Mr. Ron Mackleworth
The Brightest Jewel, By Charles Nelson and Eileen McCracken
Article on paper-making, An Irishman's Diary Brian McCarthy Irish Times 15th July 1996

Chapter 31:

COLLEGES AND SCHOOLS OF THE COMMISSIONERS OF EDUCATION IN GLASNEVIN

The national school system in Ireland

The Commissioners of Education were established in 1806, and they set up a national system of education in which children of all religions were to be educated together. However, by 1873, control of the national schools had been taken over by the two main churches, a situation that has lasted until the present day.

In 1830 the Commissioners acquired a substantial house in Glasnevin Village near the corner with Ballymun Road (or The Naul Road, as it was known then), which served as an administrative centre during the early years. This would become "Marlborough House" in 1912. Their second acquisition was the large estate comprising the townlands of Hampstead North and Wad.

The Model School

The house in Glasnevin Village possessed a rear garden comprising one acre, which stretched as far as Church Lane (now "Avenue"). It was on this site in 1847 that the Commissioners built their first Model School. The school catered for boys and girls, both Protestant and Catholic, and they were taught the usual subjects, namely, the "Three Rs", and in addition, horticulture for the boys and needlework for the girls.

Figure 36: The Model School, Glasnevin c.2000

The adjoining garden became the National School Model Gardens which were used for instructing the boys from the school and from other establishments. Its first Curator was P.J. McCarthy, followed by Alex Campbell who remained in charge until 1873, when the land was sold. St. David's Terrace now occupies the site. Campbell subsequently acquired Church Hill House where he established a Plant Nursery.

Horticultural instruction was taken over subsequently by the Albert College. The Headmaster up to 1895 was a Terence O'Donnell.

Matthew Fitzpatrick, scholar, athlete and patriot

Matthew Fitzpatrick was a native of Hilltown in Co. Down, and in 1884 he entered the old Marlborough Street Teacher Training School. He later graduated from the Royal University of Ireland, and subsequently held positions in the Inchicore Model School and Marlborough Street School. In 1895, he was appointed Headmaster of Glasnevin Model School, a position he was to hold for the next forty years. Matthew was a noted mathematician and an examiner in mathematics for the Intermediate Education Board. He also published a number of text books on mathematics. He was very active in other fields, notably Gaelic athletics and the revival of the Irish language. He was a member of the Council of the Society for the preservation of the Irish language, and an active supporter of the movement for Irish independence. He served as a member of Dublin Corporation, and was a member of the group that helped with the building of Iona church.

He was succeeded as Headmaster by Brian O'Carroll, who resided in Cremore Park, and who later became a well-known broadcaster ("Peadar O'Connor") on Radio Eireann with his series of talks on "Making and Mending".

The Model School: changes in ownership

The Model School continued nominally as a non-denominational school until about 1935, when its name was changed to the "Sacred Heart National School", with the word "Buachailli" in large Gaelic script painted on the front wall. From the mid 1950s, it went through a number of changes in ownership and control. Its small size meant that was not really suitable for a modern suburban school, and it was used for various special educational purposes.

It became Scoil Ciarain, a temporary school for children with learning difficulties, and afterwards an all-Irish-speaking school called Scoil na tSeachta Laoicht. From 1984 to 2002, it housed the new North Dublin National School Project which in 2003 transferred its premises to a new site on the former lands of Claremont, off Ballymun Road, beside Glasnevin Tennis Club. It is now The Educate Together School, an interdenominational project. The wheel had come full circle.

The Albert College: The Model Farm

In 1838, the Commissioners of Education acquired the estate and townland of Hampstead North, with its Georgian residence, and the townland of the Wad to the north. They founded the Glasnevin Institute there "to qualify elementary schoolmasters to instruct their pupils in the theory of agricultural science". The students resided in the house for their short period of training. The house later became known as Cuilin House.

Prince Albert, Queen Victoria's consort, visited the college in 1853 where he was so impressed that he sent one of the men from his Osborne Estate on the Isle of Wight to Glasnevin. Following the visit, the college was renamed the "Albert Agricultural College". It became the chief centre for the training of farmers and land stewards (or farm managers as they are styled these days).

In 1900, it passed under the control of the newly-established Department of Agriculture and Technical Instruction for Ireland. This was followed by considerable improvements and expansion of buildings with new classrooms and laboratories. The range of subjects taught was expanded including agricultural chemistry and biology. At this time, there were about sixty students in residence undergoing a one year's course of instruction. Some would become roving instructors in agriculture and horticulture.

Following the establishment of the Irish Free State in 1922, the Albert College was taken over again, this time by University College Dublin (UCD). Over the next five years, courses were given for the sons of farmers in milk testing and other farming crafts. Subsequently, the college became part of the Faculty of Agricultural Science.

In 1934, the new Government under Fianna Fail decreed that instruction in agricultural science in rural national schools be replaced by lessons in the Irish language.

The college continued to be called colloquially "The Albert College" until it was closed down in 1960, when a substantial part of the lands to the north was sold to Dublin Corporation for housing, and forty acres were laid out as a public park, named "Albert College Park". Cuilin House became the "Glasnevin North" (sic) Community Centre and the Ballymun Comprehensive School was built on the site beside Ballymun Road. The College buildings were then taken over by the National Institute for Higher Education, to form the nucleus of the future Dublin City University.

Teacher-Training

One of the responsibilities of the Commissioners of National Education was the training of teachers. In 1834, they founded their Teacher Training College in Marlborough St. in central Dublin as a non-denominational institution. It was associated with the Model School in Glasnevin and other schools in various parts of the country.

Most of the 133 students were Presbyterians, who had no college of their own, with the remainder evenly divided between Roman Catholic and Church of Ireland adherents. The college in Marlborough St. was the only teacher-training college in Ireland until 1884 when the denominational training colleges of the Roman Catholic St. Patrick's in Drumcondra and the Church of Ireland Training College in Kildare Place were established. This development had an adverse effect on the number of students entering the college.

The area around Marlborough St. was dingy, close to the notorious "Monto" area, and in the Report of 1903-1904, it was deemed to pose a risk to the health of the students. For this reason, the Commissioners looked for a new site in a "healthful" locality, and they acquired such a one in the townland of Bank Farm in Glasnevin, on the north side of the River Tolka. This consisted of twenty-seven acres of land which were purchased from Colonel H.G. Lindsay, the major landowner in Glasnevin.

Chapter 32:
MARLBOROUGH HALL AND MARLBOROUGH HOUSE.

James F. Fuller, architect. (1835-1924)

The design of the new building was consigned to James Franklin Fuller, a Fellow of the Royal Institute of British Architects and of the Royal Institute of Architects of Ireland, an outstandingly gifted architect who specialised in ecclesiastical buildings. He was architect to the Representative Church Body (RCB).

Fuller was very much a practitioner of the "Victorian Gothic" style of architecture, which he implemented in the many notable buildings he designed. They include Ashford Castle, Kylemore Castle (now Abbey) and the Great Southern Hotels in Kenmare and Parknasilla. He designed many churches, schools and bank buildings in various parts of Ireland. He was also an antiquary, a genealogist and even a novelist.

The new college and residence

Fuller's design for a new residence for male students was in typical style, built with Wicklow granite, with gables, and turrets and a clock-tower. Despite its Gothic façade, this was a building that was to be "state of the art", and ahead of its time. It used fire-proof materials in its construction, and it had a most elaborate fire-fighting installation with hydrants in every corridor. Electric lighting was installed, supplied by two 40 HP d.c. dynamos powered by suction-gas engines. An electric pump was provided to pump water from the river.

Work commenced by the builders, Mc Laverty and Son, in the autumn of 1907, and proceeded at a rapid rate. It was completed by the end of 1908. During early stages of building, a number of rusted artefacts such as swords and shields were unearthed, which may have there since the Battle of Clontarf. The entrance gates of the College were beside Glasnevin Bridge, opening to the avenue to the College, which would later become St. Mobhi Drive when the entrance was relocated to its present position on St. Mobhi Road, beside the new bridge.

Figure 37: Marlborough Hall (Colaiste Caoimhin)

The college was officially opened on 24th August 1908 by the Lady Aberdeen, the consort of the Lord Lieutenant at that time. The standard of accommodation was higher than that in many of the expensive boarding schools. However, lack of money continued to be a problem, and the planned residence on this site for female students was abandoned.

A doomed project

Despite the provision of a very fine building in a salubrious location, the college was not a success. The number of students did not come up to expectations, their numbers continued to drop, and by 1914 "the writing was on the wall" for the college. The situation was aggravated by the outbreak of the First World War (or "Great War"), and the college was finally closed down in January 1917.

There were two principal causes for the failure of Marlborough Hall as a teacher - training college. The first cause was the setting-up of separate Roman Catholic and Church of Ireland training- colleges. Denominational schools, which were in the majority, were reluctant to engage teachers from a non-denominational college. The second cause was that fewer men than women were taking up teaching as a career, probably on account of the low initial salary that was being paid.

The Irish Counties War Hospital: The Bluecoats

In April 1917, the buildings were transferred to the War Department for use by the Irish Counties War Hospital Committee as a convalescent home for wounded British soldiers, who were transferred there from King George V Military Hospital (the present St. Bricin's Hospital). Nursing was provided by the Voluntary Auxiliary Detachments (VADs). The Hospital was officially opened by Vicereine Lady Wimburne on 14th July 1917, with great festivity.

The patients, known as "Bluecoats", wore a distinctive blue tunic, and they did not associate with the local denizens in the Village nearby. During the "Troubles", British Army personnel continued to be treated there until the Truce in 1921.

Refugees from the North

Following the "pogroms" in East Belfast in 1922, many of the displaced Catholic people fled south, most of them on foot and with no possessions. The authorities did not want them in the City, and they were conveniently accommodated in Marlborough Hall for the period before they gradually drifted back home or elsewhere.

The Free State Army Medical Service

After the departure of the British forces, the new government installed the newly-formed Free State Army Medical Corps in Marlborough Hall, and the building continued in use as a convalescent home, this time for the troops and Civic Guards of the Irish Free State during the Civil War. After the end of the Civil War, the building lay empty for the next few years. It appears that a domestic-science college was located there for a very brief period in 1925.

Colaiste Caoimhin and the Irish language- revival movement

The Department decided to establish a number of preparatory colleges at secondary level to teach Irish to prospective teachers prior to their proceeding to the formal training colleges. The first of these was set up in Marlborough Hall, which was renamed Colaiste Caoimhin (or St.Kevin's College, as it appears in some records).

The Roman Catholic Archbishop of Dublin was appointed Manager, and the running of the college was entrusted to the Irish Christian Brothers. Some lay teachers were also employed. Special entry examinations based on the National School curriculum were held, and the College opened in September 1926 with the admission of sixty scholars between the ages of fourteen and sixteen.

The Principal for the twelve years of its existence was Brother Donal Lucius Hurley from Bandon, a noted Irish language enthusiast. The curriculum covered a broad range of subjects, all to be taught through Irish (except for English and other languages), as well as Gaelic sports and physical education.

By 1938, after almost 500 students had passed through its portals, it was decided to close the college which by then had achieved its aim, and moreover, there was now a surplus of teachers. In 1939 the doors were closed.

The Department of Defence

Following the outbreak of the Second World War on 3rd September 1939, the Department of Defence was expanded to cope with the vastly enlarged Defence Forces. The Finance branch was transferred to Marlborough Hall, or "The Colaiste" as it continued to be known, and it was to remain there for almost fifty years. In 1989, the Branch was moved to Renmore in Co. Galway.

Education and sport once again

The grounds of the college now contain two schools - Scoil Mobhi and the Dominican Scoil Chaitriona which moved there from Eccles Street. They also contain the clubhouse and playing fields of Na Fianna GAA club.

Marlborough House

This property, on the corner of the village and the Naul Road, was included in the extensive lands leased by Maurice Berkeley in 1667, which were demised by his widow Dorothy to Sir John Rogerson in 1703. The house was almost certainly rebuilt during the 1700s, judging by its Georgian style. Its last owner, before it was acquired by the Commissioners in 1830, was Maurice Peppard Warren.

The Commissioners designated the premises the "National Education Model Training Establishment". Part of the ground was used for the Model School and the National School Model Garden (see above). In

1870, approximately half of the land was sold for housing, and St. David's Terrace and St Thomas's Terrace were built thereon in the mid-1870s. The ground to the west by Ballymun Road (or The Naul Road as it was then called) remained with the house.

Shortly afterwards, the building was leased and divided into two residences which were named respectively, The Villa and Rose View. Rose View was occupied in the 1890s by the local Roman Catholic curates.

Accommodation for the women students of the Marlborough St. Teacher Training College in Talbot House nearby gradually became a problem as their numbers increased, apart from the unsuitability of the area. After 1900, the Commissioners took back their building and converted it for use as a women- students' residence. A Miss Emmeline Cantillon was appointed Superintendent.

They renamed the building "Marlborough House" so as to proclaim its connection with Marlborough Street and Marlborough Hall. A neighbouring shopkeeper, a Mr. McClelland, was appointed curator. In 1914, the building was extended with a large new wing to the rear. During the digging of the foundations, some eight or nine early Christian slab graves were discovered (Chapter 3).

Figure 38: Marlborough House Glasnevin Village, c. 1940

Colaiste Einde

Marlborough House was used both as a residence and as a training college long after the closing of Marlborough Hall in 1917. After the Treaty of 1922, the Lindsay Family vacated their home in Glasnevin House which was subsequently acquired for a residential annex to Marlborough House, and renamed Colaiste Einde. Both were closed down in 1938. Colaiste Einde was acquired by the Emergency Research Bureau in 1947, and became the offices for the Institute for Industrial Research and Standards in 1961.

The remand home

From 1944 to 1971 Marlborough House was used as a remand-home for "juvenile delinquents", as they were termed in those days. Untrained lay staff was employed, and standards were low, even for that time. The regime was harsh and brutal, with emphasis on punishment, The periods of detention usually comprised a few weeks, and neither educational nor recreational facilities were provided.

Up to fifty boys could be accommodated, and it was a regular and somewhat heart-rending experience to see groups of small boys being herded to Mass in the Wooden Chapel on Sunday mornings by burly officials. The treatment they received gave them a foretaste of the fate that lay ahead for them in the industrial schools. In 1969, the Kennedy Report recommended closing Marlborough House, but it was two years later before this was done. In 1971, a group of the boys went on a rampage of damage to the premises, and shortly afterwards the institution was closed. Many years later, the Ryan Report in 2009 revealed a history of physical and sexual abuse of the inmates that had occurred there over three decades.

The end of Marlborough House

After 1972 the building gradually fell out of use until it became derelict and was knocked down. The site remained vacant until the spectacular new Met Eireann Office was built there in 1979.

Reference:
Booklet "Colaiste Caoimhin (1908-1988) A history, by J.A. Foley

Chapter 33:
Claremont Institution and St. Clares

Claremont: The stately house

The stately house called Clermont or Claremont was built between 1760 and 1770 by William Purdon otherwise Lord Clermont, the Irish Post-Master General at the time. In 1768, Purdon leased the property to Alderman Benjamin Geale, a banker who was also Treasurer of Dublin Corporation. Geale is mentioned as the occupier in 1771 and as a member of Vestry in 1772.

The succeeding occupiers are recorded as Edward Croker, William Andy who died in 1796, and a Mr. Butler in 1799. A deed map dated 1807 shows that Claremont belonged to a Mr. Howey. The last private owner was a Mr. Robert Hayes.

The education of the "Deaf-and Dumb"

The first organised attempt in Ireland to provide for the education of deaf-and-dumb children was the "Deaf School" which was set up in 1816 in the Penitentiary for Young Male Criminals under the charge of the House of Industry in Smithfield through the pioneering efforts of Dr. Charles Orpen.

In May 1816 the National Institution for the Education of the Indigent Deaf and Dumb in Ireland was established. The following year, the inmates were obliged to leave because of the lack of space and the general unsuitability of the accommodation. The Committee acquired a temporary residence at No.6 in Brunswick St. to which the inmates were transferred. Meantime there was an increasing number of applications for admission, including some from wealthy families. Clearly, a bigger premises was needed, and in a more salubrious area. In 1819, the Committee succeeded in acquiring Clermont in Glasnevin from Robert Hayes, who demised the property for a fine of £1000 and a rent of £220 10s 9d to William Caldwell Hogan representing the Committee.

Figure 39: St. Clare's, formerly Claremont Institution for Deaf

The Claremont Institution

Following its acquisition by the Committee, the new premises became the home of the Claremont Institution for Deaf and Dumb Children when they moved in on 31st July 1819. It was placed under the patronage of Queen Caroline and the Duke of Gloucester. Its first Principal was Joseph Humphries who was given a house rent-free, but he had to accommodate the pupils from rich families.

It was open to children between eight and sixteen years of age, regardless of religion. The normal fee was 25 guineas per annum, but many were supported by private charities. Children were bound to the Institution for a period of up to five years before they could be taken away.

Some poor children were accepted without having to pay a fee, but they were confined to separate classrooms, eating rooms and playgrounds. It depended to some extent on charitable donations from the public, the most munificent of which was a sum of £70,000 bequeathed by Dr. Jacky Barrett, Vice-Provost of Trinity College, who died in 1821 and is buried in St. Mobhi's churchyard. Unfortunately, as with many bequests, litigation by Dr. Barret's family delayed payment for several years..

Extension

In 1823, the house was extended to provide classrooms and dormitories for 160 pupils. A special printing press was installed for the purposes of training pupils and printing books for the deaf and dumb. In 1829, further extensions were constructed to provide accommodation for teachers. Many of the pupils prospered in later life thanks to their education.

Protestant and Roman Catholic institutions

Claremont Institution was open to Protestants and Roman Catholics equally, but, having the support and patronage of the Established Church of Ireland, (the Institution described itself as being "Church of England in its character"), it was perceived by the Catholic clergy as a proselytising body. Consequently, accounts exist of interference by Catholic clergy preventing, or trying to prevent, children from going there. The expressed emphasis in Claremont on the teaching of Scripture and the history of England would seem to have fuelled their misgivings. Otherwise, the education of the pupils was praiseworthy by all accounts.

The situation was to change radically when the Committee for the Catholic Institution for the Deaf and Dumb opened St. Mary's School for Deaf Girls in Cabra in 1846 and St. Joseph's Monastery in Prospect took over the care of deaf boys in 1849.

Decreasing numbers

By 1834, the number of pupils had reached 100, requiring further extensions to the premises, and by 1844 the number was 136.

Following the setting-up of the Catholic school in Cabra, there occurred a steep decline in pupil-numbers in Claremont, and from 136 in 1844 they fell to fewer than 60 in 1857. Amongst other matters, this had an adverse effect on revenue.

From that time onwards, the numbers continued to decrease, and by 1921 there were only 18 pupils. The buildings were now clearly too big, but no attempt was made to move to smaller premises.

The Headmasters

Claremont was served by seven headmasters from 1819 to 1928. The first, Joseph Humphries, was followed by Rev. J. Martin (1840), James Cook (1843), and James Foulston (1847). Edward J. Chidley was Headmaster from 1856 until his death in 1881. He was succeeded by his son Edward William Chidley then aged 23. He resigned in 1887, apparently in frustration at the lack of resources for his attempted improvements. Father and son are buried in St. Mobhi's churchyard nearby, and there is a memorial plaque inside the church to his son, John Chidley a medical student who died of fever.

The next and last Headmaster was George Taylor who resigned in 1928. Thereafter, only one teacher was required for Claremont. By this time, the number of pupils was only seven.

The end for Claremont

From 1928 to 1943, the staff consisted of a single female teacher – a Miss Deacon- with from six to ten pupils. By 1940, the Claremont Institution had become virtually redundant and in 1943 a Local Government Order bought the property for £3,400 to be used for sick children following an outbreak of gastro-enteritis and tuberculosis. The Claremont Institution and its remaining pupils were thereupon transferred to Carrick Manor in Monkstown in Co. Dublin, which eventually closed in 1978.

St. Clares

In 1972, Claremont was taken over by the Eastern Health Board for the care of the elderly and re-named St. Clares. Many improvements have been effected since. Residential- and day-care are provided, along with social amenities for groups of senior citizens.

In the 1970s, the new Griffith Avenue Extension took a considerable area of Claremont land, cutting across the old approach avenue from Ballymun Rd. A new entrance was built on Griffith Avenue Extension. The old bridge remains over the Nevin Stream on the approach to the house, a relic of earlier times.

In 2000, the Health Board sold most of the land to DCU for playing fields, except for a 2.5 acre site which was sold to the North Dublin National School Project.

References:
Private accessions 1123 in the National Archive,
The Avenue; A History of the Claremont Institution, by Rachel Pollard, Denzille Press.

Chapter 34:
THE EUSTACE FAMILY AND HAMPSTEAD HOSPITAL

The first John Eustace

John Eustace was born in 1791, the son of a Cork Quaker merchant, Benjamin Eustace. Before qualifying as a doctor in Trinity College in 1815, he had worked in Bloomfield Hospital, and he then obtained the position of visiting physician there. This where the newly-qualified Dr. Eustace embraced the idea of "Moral Treatment", as distinct from medication, for the mentally-afflicted.

Hampstead Hospital

John Eustace wished to set up his own hospital, and in 1825 he formed a partnership with two other doctors, Dr. Isaac Ryall (a former Commodore in the Royal Navy), and Dr. Richard Grattan. Dr. Ryall had already bought the land at Hampstead South, which included Hampstead House. The new establishment at Hampstead was named "The Asylum and House of Recovery for Persons affected with Disorders of the Mind".

Dr. Ryall left the partnership in 1826, and Dr. Grattan left in 1830, leaving John Eustace in sole possession of Hampstead. He proceeded to enlarge the estate by acquiring an adjoining 23 acres which contained Hampstead Lodge, now "Hillside". In 1844, he built The New House, Hampstead Cottage and Hopetoun Cottage.

John Eustace's sons, John II and his brother Marcus, took over from their father in 1853. The brothers embarked on the enlargement and development of the estate. First, they leased neighbouring Highfield on the far side of the Swords Road, and ten acres of land. By 1892, the Eustace estate comprised 150 acres of land, stretching from the Naul Road to the lands of Clonturk and Highfield on the east side of the Swords Road.

Of Dr. John II's four sons, three became doctors- John Neilson Eustace, Henry Marcus Eustace, and William Neilson Eustace, and the fourth, Benjamin Fawcett Eustace, took on the farm. William outlived his brothers, dying in 1948. It was William that began the family tradition of service in the British Army, and several Eustaces served therein during both world wars and afterwards.

Cousins William Desmond Eustace and Henry Jocelyn Eustace both qualified as doctors and took over the running of the hospital from the late 1940s until the late1980s. Dr. Jocelyn became eminent in the field of psychiatry. He lectured in TCD and was a consultant in several Dublin hospitals which included the Royal Victoria Eye and Ear, Sir Patrick Duns and the Rotunda. He met even men such as Freud and Jung during his career. William's brother Terence took over the running of the farm.

This was a time of great change in the treatment of mental illness, with the introduction of new drugs. This was so successful that it reduced the length-of-stay from months and even years to weeks.

Elmhurst

Elmhurst, the present convalescent home, was built in 1869, using the materials from the site of the ruined Hampstead Castle. This was originally built with money from a wealthy patient who insisted on having Dr. Marcus live there with him. It remained a private residence until 1924 when it was registered as a hospital. Lisronagh was built in 1908 by Dr. William Neilson, and in 1912, Shournagh was built as a family residence. The Badminton Hall was built in 1927.

Figure 40: Elmhurst, Hampstead Hospital, Glasnevin

The new generation: great changes

In the 1980s, William Desmond's two sons Denis, a qualified psychiatrist and Michael, who worked in industry, were persuaded to return home in order to preserve the hospital which was beginning to suffer difficulties, not least of which was great reduction in admission levels due to modern medication and treatment. The two brothers commenced making far-reaching changes to suit present-day requirements, in both the organization and the buildings. For one thing, they would have to cater for out-patients, who were now in the majority.

In 1984, Elmhurst was closed and the patients were transferred to Highfield on the Swords Road. Elmhurst was then completely refurbished and in 1985 it was opened as a high-standard convalescent home.

Care of the old: The Alzeimer Centre

With the increasing longevity of the population, the problems of old age grew greater, notably the onset of dementia and Alzeimer's Disease. In 1991, the first purpose-built Alzeimer Care Centre with 135 beds was opened in Highfield, the first new hospital since Elmhurst in 1869, The four hitherto separate hospitals became the Highfield Hospital Group. In 1996, a 22-bed extension to the Care Centre was opened.

The Farm

The Hampstead property in 1825 consisted of 23 acres, and by1888, 63 acres. By 1900,it had extended to 150 acres after the acquisition of the land between Hampstead and the Swords Road. It is now much reduced in area for several reasons. Apart from death duties which became increasingly onerous over the decades, compulsory acquisition by Dublin Corporation of land for building the new suburb comprising The Rise and Griffith Avenue made large inroads into the Eustace property. Three acres were sold in 1923 for the building of Corpus Christi Church. The 15 acres beside the Swords Road eventually became the location of Plunkett School and Home Farm playing fields. In the 1990s, death duties resulted in the sale of another 13 acres north of Griffith Avenue.

Reference: Booklet:
In the Care of Friends (The Alzeimer Centre).

Chapter 35:
The Convent of the Holy Faith Sisters in Glasnevin

Glasnevin House and Demesne

Part of the residence of the Holy Faith Sisters in Glasnevin includes a Georgian house situated between a red-brick Victorian building and a late 20th Century building. This house was built by Hugh Henry Mitchell in or around 1765, on the site of an older house occupied by Sir John Rogerson from 1709 to 1724.

The Carmelite Brothers

Despite the repressive Penal Laws, the Catholic Church managed to survive, and the religious orders, in particular flourished as the enforcement of those laws began to ease. In 1807, the Carmelite Tertiaries established a community in Clondalkin. Some years afterwards, they established a branch in Fairview under James Young, a former merchant from the area. This consisted of a house and chapel, (on the future site of the now defunct Fairview Cinema), which was consecrated by Archbishop Troy in 1819.

For many years up to this period, relations in Dublin between the Catholic Regular clergy and parish secular clergy had been acrimonious, and Fairview was no exception. By 1829, friction between the Carmelites and the parochial clergy had become so acute that the brothers felt obliged to close their chapel and monastery, and they departed from Fairview.

By a seemingly ironic turn of fate, they were given accommodation by the Protestant Bishop of Kildare, Charles Lindsay, in Glasnevin House around this time, where they remained until 1849. The reasons for this arrangement are not known, and it may very well have been informal since neither deeds nor memorials exist. One can only speculate on a possible connection with the temporary hospital set up by Bishop Lindsay during the cholera epidemic from 1827 to 1830, when their services would have been very welcome. In 1849, the Carmelite Brothers moved to their present location on Grace Park Road where they ran a school for the blind. With the numbers dwindling, the school was later taken over by the Rosminians.

The Sisters of the Sacred Heart

The Roman Catholic authorities, in particular Archbishop Cullen, were anxious to have the premises remain in their domain, and he invited a recently-arrived order of French nuns, the Sisters of the Sacred Heart, to set up a school there. The house with its extensive lands of about 40 acres was purchased on their behalf by a Mr. Hugh Scully from Captain (later Colonel) H.G. Lindsay, son of the late Bishop.

The Society of the Sacred Heart was founded by Madeleine Sophie Barat in France, with the objective of providing education for Catholic children, especially those from rich or aristocratic families. Mlle. Barat had first to contend with some reaction to her principle that the women-religious should not be cloistered, but the Roman Catholic Church was in the process of restoration and reform after the Revolution, and her initiative was welcomed. By the time of her death in 1865, the new order had spread throughout Europe and the Americas. The Sisters came to Ireland in 1841 and they opened their first house in Roscrea.

On 7th October 1853, the Sisters of the Sacred Heart under Madame Louise Dumont took up residence in their new home in Glasnevin. They were clearly delighted, and Madame Dumont wrote in their Journal : *C'est une demeure charmante …pres du jardin botanique …elle est belle mais pas assez grande. Tout le monde a'accorde a dire que c'est un des plus jolies sites des environs de Dublin".*

The Sisters opened a school for the poor children of the area, which was subsequently taken over by the Sisters of the Holy Faith.

Some members of the community fell into poor health, which was blamed on the presence of Prospect Cemetery across the river, although this was never proved. They decided that they needed a larger house, and in 1863 they left Glasnevin for Mount Anville on the south side of Dublin.

Cardinal Cullen once again took steps to ensure that the property remained in Catholic hands, and in this he was fortunate when, at his instigation, the property was purchased in 1865 by Margaret Aylward, a Catholic lady who had set up a fosterage scheme for orphans and deserted children.

Margaret Aylward

Margaret Aylward was born in Waterford City in 1810, the daughter of William Aylward, a wealthy Catholic merchant with strong nationalist sympathies (he was a close friend of Thomas Francis Meagher). She had a comfortable upbringing, and she received the best education available. She was very much aware of the poverty of her fellow-citizens, which was to be her inspiration in adult life.

The Ladies of Charity

Margaret suffered from a spinal ailment, and she was sent to Dublin for medical treatment. Staying with her brother John in Clontarf, she soon came to realise that the poverty in Dublin was, if anything, far worse than that she had seen in Waterford, and on a more massive scale.

Margaret joined the Ladies of Charity, a branch of the Society of St. Vincent de Paul in the inner city, and immersed herself in charitable work with the poor and the sick. She formed a new branch to help children, which received the blessing of Archbishop Cullen.

The Irish Church Mission to Roman Catholics

During the 18th century, the Established Church was content to rest on its laurels, and no serious attempt was made to proselytise Roman Catholics. The coming of the evangelical movement from England changed this delicate balance when it commenced its missionary activity among the Irish Catholic population. It was well funded and able to exploit the terrible circumstances of poverty and famine for its ends. The main organization was the Irish Church Mission to Roman Catholics which was set up in 1847 by a Mr. Dallas. The Mission was particularly active in Connaught and Dublin City, and it established schools and orphanages all over Ireland. Practically all orphans and deserted children were of Catholic parents, so that the schools and orphanages were in effect proselytising institutions. Furthermore, it had the backing of the Establishment, Church and State, until Disestablishment in 1869.

Margaret Aylward was to devote much time and effort to countering these institutions, even to the point where she would suffer imprisonment.

The Daughters of St. Brigid and St. Brigid's Orphanage

Margaret Aylward decided that the care of orphaned children would be her aim in life, and she sought help and advice from lay and clerical people, including Cardinal Cullen. One, a Fr. John Gowan C.M., was to become her life-long friend and helper.

In January 1857 a meeting was held of the Ladies of Charity and other concerned people, and a decision was taken to set up St. Brigid's Orphanage. An office was opened at 6 Berkeley St. that year, but shortly afterwards it was moved to 46 Eccles St. By June, more than seventy children had been placed in suitable homes. The Ladies of Charity on the whole concentrated their efforts on the poor generally, and a small group with Margaret Aylward formed themselves into a religious society which, at the suggestion of Fr. Gowan, they called "Daughters of St. Brigid" for the care of orphans.

Margaret Aylward's trial and prison sentence

In one of the most infamous and extraordinary travesties of justice in Ireland, Margaret Aylward was to spend six months in a penitentiary as a result of her work in fosterage. Little Mary Matthews was the daughter of Henry Matthews, a Catholic, and his wife Maria, a Protestant. The marriage had been short-lived and Maria ran away to the Bahamas, deserting her husband and the two children, a boy and a girl. Henry was in bad health, and he died in 1858. Before his death, he was informed officially by the Governor of the Bahamas that his wife was to be deported because of "her own misconduct". He entrusted his son to a Catholic orphanage, and his four-year old daughter Mary to St. Brigid's Orphanage, from which she was placed in fosterage to a Mrs. Kenny in Saggart.

Mary's mother Maria, now widowed, came to Dublin to claim the children, and for this she received substantial support from the Smyly Home in Kingstown. She eventually traced Mary to St. Brigid's and she sent a legal writ to Miss Aylward to produce the child. Unknown to Miss Aylward, the child had been taken away for safe-keeping by a friend of her late father's, a Mr. Heffernan, who used the subterfuge of a forged letter purporting to be from Miss Aylward. He was obliged to take the child out of the country, and after a series of adventures on the continent, he eventually succeeded in placing her in a convent in Belgium. Mary Matthews eventually entered the novitiate of the Sisters that had cared for her.

Unfortunately, Margaret's inability to produce the child led to a Court summons. During a lengthy case lasting from May 1958 to November 1860, all the evidence would have seemed to have favoured Margaret - affidavits, documentation, and even the letter from the Governor of the Bahamas concerning the character of Mary's mother. Margaret was subjected to an intense and hostile interrogation by the Prosecution for five long days in a separate room. The trial concluded on 5th November 1860.

Chief Justice Thomas Lefroy rejected the evidence, but, despite this, he was unable to convict Miss Aylward. Instead he committed her to six months imprisonment in Grangegorman Penitentiary for contempt of Court. There, she was locked in a small cell and treated by the Matron with vindictiveness and harshness. Her health rapidly deteriorated and was not helped by the denial of medical attention. A recommendation by the Prison Medical Officer that she be released was ignored, and she was obliged to serve her full sentence.

The case of Margaret Aylward became a "cause celebre" throughout Ireland. Pope Pius IX in February 1861 sent her a gift of a cameo depicting the head of St. Peter, cut in precious stone and set in gold. In 1864, she visited Rome where she was granted an audience with Pope Pius IX, who called her a "Confessor of Faith".

Her case would come to form a part of the chain of events that led eventually to the Disestablishment of the Church of Ireland in 1869. The case back-fired on the Establishment when the habeas corpus precedent set entitled any parent to claim back his or her child that had been placed in an orphanage of any persuasion.

What may be of interest concerning Chief Justice Lefroy (1776 – 1869) is the revelation that he had a brief dalliance with Jane Austin in 1796, and was very likely the inspiration for the character of Mr. Darcy in the novel "Pride and Prejudice". Coming from a Limerick Huguenot family, he studied law in Lincoln's Inn in London, and subsequently met Jane in Hampshire. He opposed Catholic Emancipation in 1829. He was appointed Chief Justice in 1852, despite the reservations of some about his age and suitability for the position. At the time of the trial of Margaret Aylward, he was well into his eighties.

(From an article) "Clues to Darcy's character" by Edmund Honohan in the Irish Times 10.03.2007, and the film "Becoming Jane" (2007), also Wikepedia).

The Sisters of the Holy Faith

Margaret realised that a permanent system or organization was needed to look after the orphans, and only a religious order could ensure this. With the encouragement of the Cardinal Archbishop and Fr. Gowan, Margaret and her companion, the Daughters of St. Brigid, became the Sisters of the Holy Faith and became a Religious Congregation in 1867. Margaret took the name Mary Agatha. The recently- purchased house in Glasnevin became the Mother House.

Glasnevin: A new home for the Sisters and their pupils

The Sisters took possession of the house and lands on 10th October 1865. Mother Agatha wrote
"Glasnevin is a paradise on earth. Too lovely for us, I was never a poetess, but Glasnevin makes me one".

In 1869, the first Sisters were publicly professed in the little oratory. They kept the school in operation, which they renamed St. Brigid's Catholic School.
With the expanding affluent Catholic middle class after the middle of the century, the need for more Catholic secondary schools became pressing, and Cardinal Cullen wrote to Margaret Aylward, now Mother Agatha, urging her to open a secondary school for the daughters of the middle-class families *"Business and professional classes need a Catholic education even more than the poor"*, he wrote. The Sisters responded and the new boarding school for young ladies was opened in 1873.

In 1874, the enlargement of the house and the building of the convent proper and novitiate began. Part of the old house was demolished, including the main entrance, but the remainder with its magnificent mahogany staircase and ornate walls and ceilings was retained and has been preserved to the present day. The new chapel was built in 1899 by the renowned builder Alexander Strain.

The death of Margaret Aylward, Mother Agatha

Margaret was in great physical pain for the latter part of her life, which she bore with fortitude, and she spent the last two years of her life as an invalid confined to a wheelchair. On the morning of 11th of October 1889, Margaret Aylward, Mother Agatha died. She is buried in the sisters' cemetery in the grounds.

No photographs exist of her, as she refused to be photographed. A story is told of a young novice who tried to photograph her with a box camera, but the negative was subsequently found to be blank.

Her friend and mentor Fr. Gowan died in January 1891, and his remains were buried in the Sisters' cemetery, a mark of the esteem in which he was held.

Margaret Aylward: Her successors

After the death of the Foundress, Sister M. Agnes Vickers became Mother-

General. She founded five more convents in locations around Dublin, including Clontarf and Finglas. In 1899, a day Pension School for the better-off pupils, St. Mary's, was opened, and in 1903, a new secondary and boarding school.

The Holy Faith Convent in the 20th Century

The Order expanded during the time of Mother Regis who took over in 1910. Two new primary schools were founded in the area: St Columba's on Iona Road in 1922 and Corpus Christi on Home Farm Road. The existing boarding school was no longer adequate for the number of pupils, and Mother Regis commenced the building of a new boarding school in Glasnevin. Unfortunately, she did not live to see its completion and she died on 23rd February 1939.

On 8th December 1939, the new boarding school building was opened, in the presence of a distinguished gathering of personages from church and state. The building is an imposing if plain edifice, with a facing of red brick with granite corner stones, still the largest single building in Glasnevin, and with room for 120 boarders.

With the advent of free secondary education in 1967, the numbers of pupils increased. St. Anne's extension was built in 1970, and later, a science laboratory and art room. In 1985, a new Gym Hall was opened.

By 1980, with the growing numbers of day schools in rural Ireland, boarding schools were no longer as necessary as they had been, and in 1982, the boarding school in Glasnevin was closed down and converted into a day school for the burgeoning secondary school numbers.

Figure 41: The Holy Faith Convent Glasnevin

The grounds of the Holy Faith Convent

The extensive grounds of Glasnevin Demesne were at one time noted for their ornamental gardens, but by the time the Sisters arrived they were in a state of neglect. The Sisters landscaped the grounds and used the fields as a farm with tillage and grazing.

In 1877, Captain Lindsay was disposing of more of the family estate to the Dublin Cemeteries Committee, and he suggested to Margaret Aylward that she purchase a small plot of ground on the other side of the river, opposite the convent grounds. This plot was duly acquired, and a new bridge thereto was then built across the river, close to the grotto and Shrine to St. Joseph.

In 1970, the land forming the Violet Hill end of the grounds was sold off for building, and in 2000, another part, including he field across the river, was sold for the building of an extensive apartment complex named "Addison Park". The land still remaining in the 21st century gives an uninterrupted view from the convent windows, with, in the distance, the famous centuries-old Cedar of Lebanon.

The Convent Cemetery

The burial place of the Sisters of the Holy Faith is located at the eastern end of the grounds. Two men are buried here: Father Gowan and John Steiner, a German convert who gave his life to helping the St, Brigid's Orphanages, particularly with the raising of funds.

Convent Cottages

Up to the 1950s, a row of cottages, called "Convent Cottages", was located at the west end of the grounds. These had been built on the site of a former gate lodge, facing the Old Finglas Road. and were provided for men that worked for the Convent. They were demolished when the road was widened. The last tenant, Paddy Kerr, continued to tend the grounds for many years afterwards.

References:
The Life of Margaret Aylward by Margaret Gibbons (Sands & Co.London)
The Parish of Fairview by Rev. John Kingston (Dundealgan Press)
Cornelius Nary, by Patrick Fagan (Royal Irish Academy)
Madeleine Sophie Barat: A life. By Phil Conroy, Cork University Press

Chapter 36:
St. Vincent de Paul Male Orphanage, St. Joseph's School and St. Vincent's School

St. Joseph's School (Prospect Monastery)

Although the Claremont Institute for Deaf and Dumb was open to those of any religion, nevertheless its patronage and prevailing ethos were predominantly Protestant. Two prominent Catholic clergymen, Monsignor William Yore, P.P Arran Quay, and Rev. Thomas McNamara, Phibsborough (St. Peter's), undertook a campaign for Catholic schools for the deaf. In 1846, a diocesan committee under the Archbishop of Dublin acquired a house on Prospect Lane (now Avenue) for a rent of £15 per annum. With the title of St. Joseph's Monastery, it was opened on 2nd February 1849 under the care of the Carmelite Order with four pupils. By 1853, the numbers had increased to seventy, and more room became necessary.

An advertisement in W.J. Battersby's Complete Catholic Registry and Directory for 1849 contains the following:
"Boarding and day school, Prospect Glasnevin: Religious Brothers of the Carmelite Convent. Boarders: 24 gns per year".

A new and much larger school for the deaf was built on the Navan Road, near the junction with Old Cabra Road, and it opened in October 1857, under the control of the Christian Brothers. St. Joseph's, as it was named, flourished and expanded to become the largest institution of its kind in Ireland today.

The care of orphans in Dublin

The care of orphaned children became a matter of concern for the Catholic hierarchy and clergy in the early 1800s when proselytising by the Irish Church Mission to Roman Catholics and other agencies, became widespread. After the Crimean War (1856) and the later Indian Mutiny, the orphaned children of dead Irish soldiers became numerous, and many were taken into care by the British authorities. Some were sent to London, some were sent to the Royal Hibernian Military Academy in Phoenix Park (now St. Mary's Hospital) and others were placed in various Protestant institutions. Only ten per cent were in Catholic institutions.

The Society of St. Vincent de Paul: The first orphanage

The society of St.Vincent de Paul was founded in France in 1833 by Frederic Ozanam, and it was introduced to Ireland in 1844 by Rev. Dr. Woodlock of All Hallows College. In 1856, the Society's Orphanage Committee acquired No. 6 Mount Brown for their purposes. It was intended for boys between seven and eleven years, and it opened on 14th December 1856. The Committee succeeded in persuading the Patriotic Fund and the Indian Mutiny Fund in London to give their support on the grounds that Catholic children had a right to a Catholic education. With the approval of the War Office, ten children were transferred from the Military Academy. By 1858, the house at Mount Brown was full, and the Committee had to find new and larger premises.

Figure 42: St.Vincent de Paul Male Orphanage Glasnevin c.1970

St. Vincent de Paul Male Orphanage, Prospect, Glasnevin

In 1858, the Committee purchased six Irish Acres from Captain (later Lt. Col.) H.G. Lindsay at Cross Guns in the Prospect townland adjoining the Brian Boru Public House. On 8th September 1858 the foundation stone of the new orphanage was laid and the new orphanage was formally opened on 21st September 1860 by Archbishop (later Cardinal) Paul Cullen. It could house 120 boys, and 55 were transferred there from Mount Brown.

Donations were obtained from many sources, private and institutional, lay and religious, at home and overseas. These included the Viceroy, the Lord Mayor, Bishops, prominent business men, the Patriotic Fund and the Indian Mutiny Fund, and the funds of the Franciscan Orphan Society which were transferred to the new orphanage.

The care of the Orphanage

The Committee first entrusted the care of the pupils to the Fathers of the Congregation of the Holy Ghost, a French order. Unfortunately, the Fathers (and Brothers) were unable to cope and they withdrew at the end of October 1863. The Orphanage was thereupon entrusted to the Christian Brothers under their new Superior, Bro. T.A. Hoope who stayed until 1870, and was succeeded by Bro. O'Neill.

Development

In 1865, there were 75 boys, and with more admissions subsequently a new wing was opened in 1879, to accommodate the increased numbers. In 1894, a new Science Room was opened, and the Memorial Chapel in 1896.
In 1890, pupils took the new Intermediate Examination ("The Inter") and gained good marks.

The day school

In 1926, it was decided to admit day pupils, and a strong lobby from Iona Parish which included the Parish Priest Fr. Wall, persuaded the school to admit boys from the locality. By 1930, the numbers exceeded 300, about half of whom were day-pupils. More space was now needed, and a new Primary day school was opened in January 1939. This left more space in the old building for the secondary school pupils.

Following a fire in February 1943 which destroyed the recreation hall, a new recreation hall was opened in 1945. In the late 1960s, the school opened its new swimming pool to the public.

The end of the orphanage

From 1960 onwards, the position of orphans changed radically with the provision of widows' and orphans' allowances and a decrease in the mortality rate of mothers. It was decided to close the Orphanage, and in 1973 the building and grounds were sold to the Irish Transport and General Workers' Union which planned to set up a training school and conference centre for its members, along with living accommodation.
This project proved unviable, and the building and lands were sold for residential development. Dalcassian Downs, Clareville and Claremont Lawns now stand on the site.

Reference: St. Vincent's Glasnevin Centenary Record 1856 – 1956.

Chapter 37:
GLASNEVIN (PROSPECT) CEMETERY

"The Dead Centre"

Glasnevin Cemetery, as Prospect Cemetery is now known, is the largest in Ireland, occupying 124 acres in the western part of Glasnevin and fronting to the Finglas Road (now the N2). Much has been written about it by various authors, and it even gets a mention in Joyce's "Ulysses". A local history such as this can give only a summary description, and the reader will find details in other publications.

So many famous Irishmen and women are interred there that the Cemetery can be said to be a shrine to resurgent Irish nationalism and Catholicism. The lives of those people constitute the history of Ireland over two centuries. Here, leaders of Church and State lie alongside the many patriots, poets and writers, and the ordinary people of Dublin. One of the most famous Irishmen, Daniel O'Connell, is commemorated by the impressive O'Connell Monument - an oversize replica of a round tower, visible from afar.
It is a part of Glasnevin that belongs to Dublin and the nation, and to national history rather than local history.

Burial places

The traditional burial places throughout Ireland have been the churchyards belonging to ancient churches, ruined abbeys and monasteries, all of which became the property of the Established Church following the Reformation and King Henry VIII's break with Rome. Protestant and Catholic alike were buried in these burial places, but under the Penal Laws Catholic burials had to be conducted without religious ceremonies. With the passage of time, the severity of the Penal Laws eased and Catholic burial rites became customary. However, bigotry and intolerance were still prevalent, and some sextons resented, and tried to prevent, the Catholic burial service. This led to occasional altercations and general resentment in the populace.

In Dublin, the Protestant Archbishop Magee was reputed to be particularly obdurate on the matter, and an incident occurred in 1823 which set in train the events that would ultimately lead to the establishment of Prospect Cemetery. A number of incidents that occurred (notably one in St.Kevin's graveyard) gave rise to indignation and resentment in the body of Dublin's Catholics, who determined to do something about the matter. They approached Daniel O'Connell, the famous Irish patriot and lawyer for a legal opinion. Declaring the ban illegal, he brought the matter before the newly- established Irish Catholic Association, where he advocated the establishment of a Catholic cemetery that would be open to all denominations regardless.

Goldenbridge Cemetery

In 1824, the Westminster Parliament passed the Easement of Burials Act which improved matters somewhat. In 1829, the Catholic Association purchased land at Goldenbridge for use as a Catholic burial ground. It became clear shortly afterwards that the site was inadequate, and that a much larger area was needed.

Prospect Cemetery

The Association's cemeteries committee looked for a bigger site, and in September 1831, it purchased nine acres in an area in Glasnevin called Prospect, from Capt. George Lindsay of Glasnevin House.
The project was enthusiastically welcomed and supported by Daniel O'Connell.

The first problem was where to have the entrance. Toll- gates still existed at the junction of Finglas Road and Glasnevin (now Botanic) Road, but O'Connell, who boasted that he could "drive a coach and horses through an Act of Parliament", solved the problem by suggesting a new road between the two toll roads, going directly to the entrance in what is now Prospect Square. This new road was at first called Cemetery Lane and, later, Prospect Avenue.

The new cemetery

Prospect Cemetery (the name comes from the townland), popularly called Glasnevin Cemetery, was consecrated on 21st February 1832 by Rev. William Yore, P.P. of St. Pauls Arran Quay. On the following day, the cemetery received its first burial, that of four-year old Michael Carey of Francis St. in the area afterwards known as the Curran Section.

The original entrance gateway in Prospect Square is still in use, but for pedestrian access only. The original mortuary chapel just inside the gate no longer stands.

Figure 43: Glasnevin Cemetery: Old entrance

The first trustees were Archbishop Daniel Murray, Dr. Coleman V.G.P.P., Dean Lube P.P., Daniel O'Connell M.P., Nicholas Mahon and Christopher Fitzsimons. In 1837, Henry Grattan Curran, son of the famed John Philpot Curran, was elected a member.

The concept that burial grounds could exist outside the consecrated grounds of churchyards was a new one, a fashion that began in France as part of secular and anti-clerical sentiment. This was the subject of a decree by Napoleon Bonaparte in 1804 prohibiting interments in churchyards and one of the consequences was the founding of the famous Pere La Chaise cemetery in Paris.

The compelling reasons for the new cemetery were different in Ireland, but the increase in population in Ireland, with the ensuing deaths from cholera and starvation, and the already overcrowded churchyards (e.g. St. Mobhi's), meant that new and much larger areas would be needed to cope with the burials.
The new cemeteries were intended to be gardens wherein mourners and visitors could walk and feel close to nature. Prospect Cemetery was laid out in this style with trees and shrubs and little pathways.

Burials in the first years

At the time of the opening of the Cemetery, burial space in Dublin had already become overcrowded, with the increase in population and a succession of outbreaks of cholera. Within two months, the death rate was so high that the cemetery had to be left open for twenty-four hours each day. Protestant and other funerals and the officiating clergymen were freely admitted.

A HISTORY OF GLASNEVIN

John Philpot Curran, father of Sarah Curran, the famous lawyer and patriot, who defended Wolfe Tone, was buried, or rather re-buried, here. He had died in London in 1817, and his remains were transferred from thence to Glasnevin on 19th February 1837. He is interred in a highly ornate sarcophagus near the old entrance gate.

Perhaps the most famous burial of all was that of the founder, Daniel O'Connell in 1847, his funeral being one of the largest ever in Dublin. His remains were interred in a vault in the original O'Connell Circle (later the Old Chapel Circle), where they remained until they were transferred to the impressive O'Connell Monument in 1869.

Enlargement

The cemetery was first extended in 1836, and again in 1838, when another plot of land was added, which would be known as the New Ground. With the acquisition of St. Brigid's Section and St. Patrick's Section, by 1878, the cemetery area exceeded fifty-eight acres, containing the remains of about a quarter of a million people. By the end of the century, over 620,000 people had been buried there.
A plot comprising over fifty acres and known as St. Paul's was acquired on the other side of Finglas Road bringing the area to a total of 124 acres.

Figure 44: Glasnevin Cemetery main entrance

The entrances

The first entrance to the cemetery was the fine gateway on Prospect Square, with the original chapel nearby. These and some of the older buildings were designed by the Dublin architect Patrick Byrne (1783-1864). It being the only entrance, the traffic could become chaotic there with funeral carriages trying to enter and leave simultaneously. A minor entrance was provided on the Finglas Road in 1838 to facilitate burials for the poor in the New Ground recently acquired, but funerals would have to pass through the toll-gates which were still in operation, an additional expense for poor people. The cemeteries committee solved this problem by providing workmen who used a "shoulder hearse" to convey the coffin to the cemetery. Following the abolition of toll-gates in 1849, this facility was no longer needed.

The beneficial outcome was that there was no longer any obstacle to having an entrance on the Finglas Road. The matter was discussed at length for over twenty-five years until a new entrance became an urgent necessity. Apart from the traffic problems at the old gates, the centre had shifted westwards with the acquisition of more ground. Furthermore, the cemetery committee had become concerned about the number of public houses and shebeens that had come into existence, as many as twelve, on the new road. The present two gates on the Finglas Road were erected in 1878, along with the adjoining offices. The two gates provided the solution to the traffic problems and closer access to what had become the new centre of the cemetery, some distance removed from the old entrance and its adjacent array of public houses.

The O'Connell Monument

The round tower in the cemetery commemorating the Liberator Daniel O'Connell is one of the highest landmarks north of the River Liffey. Some time after the interment of the Liberator in a vault in the O'Connell Circle, the O'Connell Monument Committee was set up to erect a suitable memorial. It was originally planned to build a chapel and a Round Tower, but the tower at a height of 168 feet was on too large a scale to render the other building feasible. On 14th May 1869, the remains of Daniel O'Connell were transferred to an altar tomb in the crypt at the base of the tower. The O'Connell Monument Circle around the Monument contains 42 vaults for the privileged few, families and individuals.

The watch-towers and the body-snatchers

In the first half of the nineteenth century, burials were at risk from the activities of grave robbers, or "sack-em-ups" as they were called, and in a large cemetery elaborate measures were needed to foil the depredators. High walls with watch- towers were built around the cemetery, and a system of patrols with watchmen and bloodhounds was set up, with stationary watchmen positioned in the towers. By 1844, eight watch towers had been built, including the Finglas Road Tower built in 1841.

The activities of the "sack-em-ups" or Resurrectionists had expanded with the increase in the numbers of medical students, and no burial place was safe from their depredations. Even the ancient churchyard of St. Mobhi was the subject of at least one attempted grave-robbery. However, the security measures in the Cemetery proved successful against the body-snatchers.

The religious

Many religious orders have dedicated areas for their deceased. Secular clergy lie in their separate graves, and two of the Archbishops Dublin, Cardinal Paul Cullen and William Walsh, are interred beneath very imposing monuments which are clearly visible from the Finglas Road.

James Joyce's "Ulysses"

No account of Prospect (or Glasnevin) Cemetery would be complete without a reference to the fictitious funeral of Paddy Dignam in James Joyce's "Ulysses", the "Hades" chapter. The story is based on the real-life funeral of a Matthew Kane who was drowned on 10th July 1904.

New burials

Families having existing graves are permitted burials, but the cemetery was closed to new interments, which are accommodated in the new cemetery in Dardistown near Dublin Airport. In 2006, work commenced on extending the burials area northward towards the River Tolka.

The Heritage Centre

In April 2010, the elaborate Heritage Centre was opened, which gives substantial information on the Cemetery and those interred there.

Chapter 38:
THE BOTANIC GARDENS GLASNEVIN: THE BRIGHTEST JEWEL

Introduction

The material in this chapter is drawn mainly from the publication "The Brightest Jewel: A History of the National Botanic Gardens Glasnevin, Dublin", by E. Charles Nelson and Eileen McCracken, published by Boethius Press, Kilkenny Ireland. This chapter, forming part of a general history of Glasnevin, is confined to giving an outline of what is of local historical, rather than botanical, interest. It deals mainly with the origins, buildings and the social aspects.

Figure 45: Botanic Gardens entrance 1910
(Courtesy of The National Library of Ireland)

The first Botanical Gardens

The earliest known botanical garden in Dublin was laid down in Trinity College during 1688 as "The Physic Garden", for teaching purposes. In 1731, the Dublin Society (later the Royal Dublin Society) was set up with the objective of the advancement of the country's economy by promoting skills and technology, particularly in agriculture. As part of its programme, in 1733 it commenced by acquiring a one-acre plot at Summer

Hill to be used for research and experimental purposes. The project was relocated to a four-acre site at Martin's Lane (later renamed Gloucester Street). This site was found to be unsuitable because of the soil conditions and it was abandoned in 1740.

In 1749, the Society received a Royal Charter of incorporation as "The Dublin Society for promoting Husbandry and other useful Arts". The proposal for a botanical garden continued to occupy the minds and energies of some of the worthies of the College of Physicians and of Trinity College, and intensive lobbying of the political leaders took place over many years for the provision of the necessary funds.

Legislation

On 9th February 1790, Dr. Walter Wade, a physician and surgeon who was also a lecturer in botany, tabled a petition to the Irish Parliament for the establishment of a "Publick Botanical Garden in the City or its environs". The previous lobbying now paid off, and the petition received widespread support, notably from the Speaker, John Foster, who was also Chancellor of the Exchequer and a scion of a prominent land-owning family in Collon in County Louth.. A member of the Dublin Society, he was keenly interested in the application of modern science to agriculture and farm management, and his family estate contained a fine garden.

The outcome of all this was an insertion into the Dublin Society Bill of 1790 granting three hundred pounds "towards providing and maintaining a botanic garden". This seems to have taken the Society by surprise (Wade was not yet a member) and they were quite unprepared for the task assigned to them. Progress was slow as a result.
In 1793, Dr. Wade submitted his *Statement of the Progress which has been made for the purpose of instituting a Public Botanic Garden* to both Houses of Parliament. Wade suggested a plot that was in the Harold's Cross area. On 26th May 1791, Parliament voted another three hundred pounds for the project.

Acquiring a site

In 1793, the Society set up a committee for the purpose of acquiring a suitable ground. Shortly after this, Parliament granted another three hundred pounds to the Society. The head of the Committee was John Foster, but the moving force this time seems to have been Andrew Caldwell, a well-known patron of the arts and resident of Glasnevin. He persuaded the Committee to proceed to acquire Delville, the residence of the late Dr. Patrick Delany. They proceeded with negotiations which lasted twelve months but ultimately failed because the lease included a clause prohibiting the breaking of ground and the felling of trees.

In February 1795, John Kernan, lessee of the former Tickell property situated immediately south of the River Tolka, offered the sixteen Irish acres, or twenty-seven statute acres, to the Dublin Society for a down-payment of twelve hundred pounds, or one hundred and twenty pounds immediately and one hundred and twenty pounds each year for the rest of his life and that of his wife. The offer was accepted and the Dublin Society took full possession on 25th March 1795.

The beginning of the Gardens

The land may be described as "gently hilly", sloping to the north where it is bounded by the River Tolka. The soil at the time consisted of a thin loam overlying gravel, and containing lime. The trees there included an avenue of yews, which survives to the present day and is named Addison's Walk, after Joseph Addison who was friend of Thomas Tickell (its previous occupier). It is surmised that Tickell may have planted the trees in memory of Addison. In the grounds was the millstream with the derelict mill situated beside Glasnevin Bridge.

With a total of £2,200 provided by the Irish Parliament, work began. The Gardens were intended primarily for promoting scientific knowledge of agriculture rather than as a purely scientific institution. This was in keeping with the objectives of the Dublin Society, which were practical rather than academic. One of the final acts passed by the Irish Parliament on 2nd August 1800 provided a grant of fifteen hundred pounds for the Botanic Gardens.

The early days

The man behind the project from the beginning was Dr. Walter Wade, and he was the only possible choice for the position of head of the new Botanic Gardens. However, the driving force for a considerable period before and after the formation of the Gardens was Speaker John Foster. Foster remained in full control until his death. Dr. Wade proceeded to lay out the grounds and to organize the collection of plants from various locations such as Cork, Wicklow and London. A request to the Royal Garden at Kew for plants seems to have been unsuccessful.

In 1798, John Underwood from Brompton Middlesex was appointed head gardener at a salary of sixty-eight pounds per year, with a furnished gate-house at the entrance. His experience and background enabled him to procure a good selection of plants and seeds from English sources, including exotic specimens originating in Australia and southern Africa.

The first buildings and glasshouses

The original Tickell residence was retained and survives to this day, albeit substantially enlarged and modified. It is described at the time as having two storeys and a basement, with its main entrance facing the main road, and with steps leading to a walled garden. A major extension was carried out in 1876 when the new main entrance was placed at the rear of the original house.

The first glasshouses were designed by architect Edward Parke in 1799. They were located beside, and linked to, the house, and were approximately on the site of the present Sensory Garden. A heating system with coal-fire furnaces was provided, but there were problems from the beginning: The design and location were poor, the glasshouses were aligned east-west, they were too close together and they were difficult to heat and maintain. In 1808 an additional and larger glasshouse, the "Epiphyte House" was built between the gate and the house.

By 1817, the original glasshouses were in such a bad state that a new glasshouse - the Long Range - was built near the site of the present Palm House. The addition was found to be inadequate for its larger trees. A larger building was needed and in 1819 the Octagon House, the precursor of the present Palm House, was built on the site of the present Fern House. It was forty feet high, and it had a diameter of thirty feet.

Lodges for the gardeners and a new boundary wall on the main road were built before 1800. The original entrance to the estate included a pair of Doric cottages, and in 1815, they were replaced by a pair of gate lodges on either side of a pair of gates. The cost of £600 was borne by Thomas Pleasants, a member of the Dublin Society. Originally single-storey buildings, in 1891 they were extended to form the present two-storey buildings.

Figure 46: Botanic Gardens entrance 2000

Leases and acquisitions

In 1804, the Dublin Society decided that it should acquire direct possession of the grounds, and to that end it purchased part of the leasing rights from the Tickell Family in that year, and the remainder from the Putland Family in 1806. In 1807, it acquired the Mill Field, an island consisting of a meadow and a small garden, and the ruins of a paper mill, for £625. In 1879, the gardens were extended to take in a nine-acre field beside its western boundary. This new acquisition was used for a new arboretum, and designated The Far Grounds.

The final land acquisition was the South Field which was added in 1899 and has since been used as a nursery plot. It facilitated the providing of a separate goods entrance at the end of the cul-de-sac named Botanic Villas. This brought the total area to forty-seven statute acres.

Water supply

The supply of water was a problem and mains water was not to be available until the latter end of the century, when Vartry water was laid on in 1880. In 1833, a hydraulic ram, the first in Ireland, was installed beside the mill stream for the purpose of pumping water from the river to a reservoir near the Long Range It was replaced by a modern pump in 1903. The old ram-house remains to this day, partly below path level, at the eastern end of the millstream.

The Curvilinear Range

By 1840, all the glasshouses, except the Octagon House, had deteriorated to a condition beyond repair, and their replacement was urgently needed. In 1842, it was decided to proceed with the building of the Curvilinear Range, a structure that would last for one hundred and fifty years before needing restoration.

A bid from a William Clancy, a man of limited experience, was accepted with unfortunate results. The cost overran the tender price and Clancy barely completed the first stage, the east wing, almost bankrupting himself in the process.

Richard Turner, an ironmaster, who had achieved success elsewhere, notably with the construction of the Great Palm House at Kew Garden, obtained the contract for the completion of the Curvilinear Range and the heating system. This consisted of the west wing, an east wing, and a central palm-house, forty feet high, of rectangular plan, connecting the two wings. The work was completed by January 1848, except for the heating system which had to be postponed until an additional government grant was obtained in 1850.

Figure 47: Botanic Gardens curvilinear range

The Victoria Regia or Aquatic House.

In 1854, the Victoria Regia House was built containing a circular heated pool to accommodate the giant lily called Victoria Amazonica. It was situated on the west side of the old Octagon House, and was kept in service until 2004 when the deterioration of the structure and that of the adjoining Succulent (or Cactus) House forced their closure.

The Fern House

In 1886, the Octagon House was demolished. A new Fern House was erected on the site and linked to the Victoria Regia (or Aquatic) House by a glazed passageway. This was a structure of simple elegance with a thirty-two-foot square base surmounted by a square curved dome. It was to last for more than a century when, in 1966, it was replaced by the present wedge-shaped structure.

The Succulent (Cactus) House

The range was completed with the erection of the Succulent (or Cactus) house linked to the west side of the Victoria Regia House. This was closed down in 2004 due to its deteriorating condition.

The first great Palm House

The old Long Range had deteriorated by 1852, and it was decided to replace it with a new building which would be tall enough to contain large palms. The new building, consisting of a central palm house sixty feet high with two low flanking wings, was completed in 1860. It was of "astonishing ugliness" with a large gable at each end of the central part. The structural design was so defective that the building swayed in high winds. Major repairs and reinforcement of the structure were carried out in 1871, and more in 1873. In the following year, the woodwork at the front was found to be rotten. It was so badly damaged by the winter storms of 1883 and 1884 that it was now deemed unsafe, and had to be demolished.

The second Great Palm House

A design for a new palm house was prepared by the Keeper Frederick Moore, and built by James Boyd of Paisley, Scotland commencing in March 1884 and reaching completion by October of that year. The new glasshouse was sixty-five feet high, eighty feet wide and one hundred feet from front to rear. The two original side wings were retained, one for orchids and the other for camellias. This glasshouse gave good service, and it lasted for more than a century before it was restored in 2005.

The Director's Residence

The Director's residence(or Curator's residence as it was called previously) dates from the early 18th century (see Chapter 21), the oldest building in the Gardens. In the late 1860s, the building was restored with some alterations which included reversing the back and front to place the front door on the west side.

Visitors

The Botanic Gardens in Glasnevin have always attracted a wide range of visitors from the City and outside, from abroad, but especially from the immediate vicinity where the local people have always had a particular regard for this amenity. Entry to the public has always been free-of - charge, apart from a brief experimental charge in 1854 and 1855.

From 1800, the gardens were open to the public on Tuesdays and Fridays, but visitors required a pass and they had to be accompanied by a staff member. By 1852, the public was admitted on weekdays only and a pass was no longer required. In 1857, the gardens were opened to the public on Saturdays. The Royal Dublin Society showed reluctance towards Sunday- opening, partly on religious grounds and partly on grounds of additional expense. In 1861, pressure came from the government to allow Sunday opening, culminating with a threat to withhold the annual grant. The Society capitulated, and Sunday- opening commenced on 18th August 1861. The government, as a gesture of goodwill, provided a sergeant and six constables every Sunday free of charge. In 1869, an extra grant of thirty-five pounds yearly was granted as a form of compensation.

By this time, the Sunday visitors were coming in their thousands, and seemingly were, on the whole, well behaved. It was in 1861 that the well-known rectangular cast-iron notices reading *Keep off the grass edgings* were installed throughout the gardens. Surprisingly, vandalism and pilfering of plants has never been a major problem up to the present day, even in the mid-1800s when many visitors on Sundays came from the poorer areas of the inner city, north and south.

Amenities for visitors

From the beginning, amenities for the public were not a priority (in fact even amenities for the staff were very basic). The first toilets were installed in the waiting rooms in 1898, and a cast-iron enclosed "earth-closet" was erected at the furthest point on the riverbank in 1910. Modern toilets were built in the Far Grounds in 1944, and the old earth closet removed. These, unfortunately, had to be closed some decades later for safety reasons. They were re-opened in 2010 for the World Congress of Botanic Gardens.

For a long time, there were no shelters from the rain, the conservatories being kept locked for most of the time. In 1894, two shelters were erected, one at the entrance gate, and the other- an ornate hexagonal-plan gazebo –at the opposite end in the Far Grounds. They still exist.

For a brief period from 1908 to 1911 refreshments were sold in a tearoom outside the gates on the left-hand side, but visitors had to wait until almost 2000 before a proper and adequate café/restaurant was built.

Royal Visitors

On 6th August 1849, the Botanic Gardens received an unexpected visit by Queen Victoria, accompanied by her Consort Prince Albert and their children, with an array of the top nobility, which included the Duke of Leinster and the Lord Lieutenant the Earl of Clarendon. The Royal couple were brought on a tour of the Gardens, and it was particularly appreciated by Prince Albert who had a keen interest in science and agriculture. The honours were performed by the Curator David Moore supported by a large gathering of members of the Royal Dublin Society.

In 1877, Dom Pedro II, Emperor of Brazil, paid a brief visit to the Gardens during his two-day stay Ireland.

Restoration

By 1990, almost all the glasshouses were visibly deteriorating. Metal structures were corroding, timber was rotting and glass panes were beginning to crack and fall out. A government grant of six million pounds was obtained to fund the restoration of the Curvilinear Range. A decision was made to re-use as much of the original material as possible, and 85% of the iron window bars were manufactured in this way. The remainder of the necessary material was obtained from Kew Gardens in Surrey, where there was now scrap available following replacement of window bars with aluminium. The restored glasshouses are a faithful restoration of the original, except for the heating system. Even the paintwork replicates the original pale cream colour.

By the year 2000, the Great Palm House had deteriorated to a dangerous extent, and access had to be restricted. The structure was found to be coming away from the main supporting rear wall, and most of the timber was now rotten. Fortunately, a government grant of ten million pounds for its replacement became available. In the year 2004, the new Palm House was completed, an exact replica in appearance, but now structurally sound, thanks to modern construction techniques and materials.

New buildings

Most of the buildings were erected in the nineteenth century, and the accommodation for staff, artefacts and antiquarian exhibits was quite inadequate by modern standards. Around the year 2000, two new large modern buildings were erected. One, near the gateway, contains public restaurant, lecture rooms and an exhibition hall. The other building, a short distance away, contains the museum and the National Herbarium. Both buildings are in the shape of a leaf in plan view, with long panoramic windows at one side overlooking the gardens. Around this time, the little building on the left-hand side of the gate lodge, the location of the former tea-rooms, was demolished.

In 2008, a new fruit and vegetable walled garden was opened which contains a vinery that had come from the former Brennanstown Nurseries belonging to a Mr. H. Baker in Cabinteely.

Filming

The Botanic Gardens have always been popular for wedding photography and commercial photography. In July 1964, they provided the Edwardian background for a scene in the film comedy "Rocket to the Moon", which was based very loosely on the book by Jules Verne. Kenure House in Lusk was also used for this film.

Chapter 39:

The 20th century

The end of the Victorian era

In the latter half of the 19th century, the prospering middle-classes gradually moved from the city into the developing southern suburbs of Dublin, as the city boundaries extended southward. As a result, much of the old city centre, which had begun to begun to deteriorate after the Act of Union, deteriorated into slums that would become the worst in Europe. Extensive suburban development on the north side did not start until the 20th century, for reasons that are explained below.

Queen Victoria in Glasnevin

The event that, perhaps, best symbolized the end of the Victorian era in Ireland was the visit to Ireland in April 1900 of the aged Queen Victoria, in the last year of her reign. Her Majesty stayed at the Vice-Regal Lodge, and she used to "take the air" in her open carriage, and without any escort. From to-day's point-of-view this seems remarkable, but Ireland was generally peaceful at this time, despite a growing and assertive nationalism, and Queen Victoria had gained much public respect after her long reign.

The author is indebted to the late Doreen Scally for the following anecdote:

In the sleepy little village of Glasnevin one spring morning, eight-year old Arthur Cunningham was sitting on the Round Stones at the end of Ballymun Road when he saw an open carriage slowly wending its way up the hill, in which a little old black-clad lady was sitting, her head nodding in the manner of the elderly. As the carriage drew near, Arthur, being a mannerly boy, stood up and doffed his cap to the lady, who gave him a gracious little wave of her hand as she passed by. The lady was Queen Victoria, as Arthur was to realize afterwards and remember for the rest of his life.

There are two other reports of her presence in Glasnevin at this time: Dr. William Eustace (of Hampstead) saw the Queen while he was cycling up Whitworth Road, and on Glasnevin Hill she was seen by young Freddy Jones who would later tell of the little old lady in black in the open carriage, her eyes closed, her head nodding.

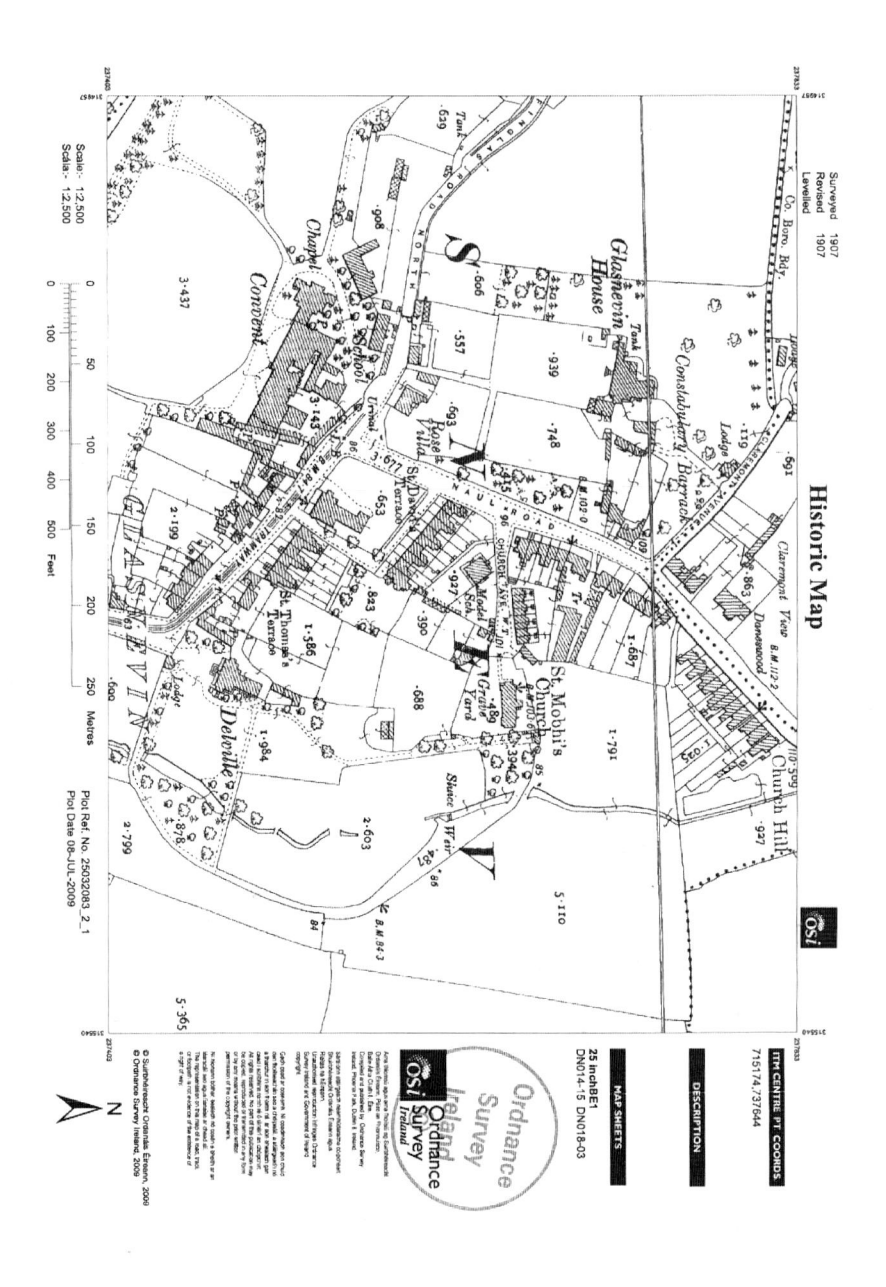

Figure 48: Map of Glasnevin1907 ©Ordnance Survey Ireland/Government of Ireland Copyright Permit No. MP 001411

Figure 49: Prospect Road, 1910

Glasnevin and the city of Dublin

In contrast with Dublin's south- side suburbs which developed rapidly, development on the north side during the late nineteenth century was impeded by a number of factors. Although gas supplies had been extended to Glasnevin and other north-side suburbs, there was no adequate water supply or sewerage scheme. While some blame could be put on the existence of turnpikes in the first half of the nineteenth century, the main factors were the poor state of the roads and the local vested interests in Glasnevin which had opposed setting-up the township in 1878.

Figure 50: Glasnevin Railway Station Whitworth Road c. 1982

At turn of the century there were only two roads linking Glasnevin and Drumcondra, namely the nineteenth century Whitworth Road and the ancient Corey Lane (Botanic Avenue). The one main road ran from Church Street to The Cross Guns where it forked northwest as the Finglas Road, and due north as the Glasnevin Road (now Botanic Road).

After twenty-two years of existence, the Township of Drumcondra, Glasnevin and Clonliffe became part of Dublin City in January 1901. Under Dublin Corporation, resources were now available to provide a modern water supply and sewerage system to these areas, and to deal with the long-standing problem of road surfaces. Builders lost no time in moving northwards across the Royal Canal, and within thirty years many areas had become modern "redbrick" suburbs. Moreover, the advent of new electric trams provided a convenient and efficient means of travel to the city centre. The opening of Glasnevin Railway Station at the top of Whitworth Road in 1908 provided another facility for the residents. It was closed in 1928.

For fifty years afterwards the old village on the Hill remained largely unchanged, a semi-rural place with its Wooden Chapel and its old masonry bridge, still remembered with affection by the older residents.

The roads: new names for old

After the Corporation took over the Township, one of its first acts was the official naming of roads and the numbering of houses. The individual names on the little terraces gradually became obsolete under the new system; nevertheless, even today, some of the original nameplates can still be discerned by the observant passer-by.

Botanic Road (formerly Glasnevin Road), and Botanic Avenue (formerly Corey Lane), received their official names, and the other "lanes" became the more fashionable "avenues" - Church Avenue and Prospect Avenue (formerly Cemetery Lane) are examples.The Naul Road became Ballymun Road, The westward continuation of the village which is designated " Finglas Road North" on the 19th century O.S. maps, was for the most part still outside the new city boundary, and became the "Old Finglas Road".

Chapter 40:
THE NEW SUBURB OF GLASNEVIN
1901 - 1935

The beginning of modern Glasnevin

After the First World War, large-scale building began in Glasnevin. Before that, "development" in the latter half of the nineteenth century had consisted mainly of small groups of houses, mostly in terraces or pairs. These were built mostly on Prospect Road, Finglas Road, Botanic Road, Botanic Avenue and Ballymun Road, and roads and squares adjoining.

Over the first two decades of the century, development in Glasnevin was confined mainly to the area south of the River Tolka. and it was carried out mainly by master builders Thomas Conolly and Alexander Strain.

The first new residential roads were Marguerite Road and de Courcy Square, which were begun in 1902. This was followed by the first major housing development in the area when the "Iona" scheme began. Within ten years, the population of Glasnevin had increased by two-thirds, with more than seven hundred new houses.

After the First World War and the establishment of the Irish Free State, the northern areas of Glasnevin were opened up with the new "by-pass" created by St. Mobhi Road and its bridge, and with the extension from Drumcondra to St Mobhi Road of St. Mary's Road, which was renamed Home Farm Road. The building of Griffith Avenue connecting Glasnevin and Drumcondra to Fairview completed what would be the main road system for the area for the next thirty years.

The first major new building was Marlborough Hall (q.v.), an interdenominational training college for teachers, which was erected on the townland of Bank Farm just north of the Tolka and completed in 1907. Today it belongs to the Department of Defence. The avenue that led to the college is now St. Mobhi Drive, and the entrance gates were situated beside Glasnevin Bridge.

Hart's Corner

The junction of Botanic Road and Finglas Road commonly called Hart's Corner takes its name from the curved row of shops and dwellings designated "Hart's Buildings A.D.1924 -1925" on the plaque overhead, which in turn is named after the eponymous Johnny Hart, businessman, shopkeeper, entrepreneur and extensive property owner in the Glasnevin area. This name has replaced the older area designation "The Cross Guns" which is found on some old maps such as Duncan's Map 1821.

Iona district

The "Iona district" as it is known today, includes areas in both Drumcondra and Glasnevin, but this history is concerned only with the original area in Glasnevin which is associated with two master builders – Alexander Strain and Thomas Conolly. These two gentlemen vied with one another in the building of good quality houses. Conolly – who also built St. Columba's R.C. Church - is now virtually forgotten, but the name of Alexander Strain has passed into history, and even today, the description "Strain-built" is used in advertisements for the sale of houses.

Building began in the early 1900s on the green fields of the Daneswell part of the Lindsay estate with a cul-de-sac named Lindsay Terrace which was shortly afterwards extended to become Lindsay Road, and Crawford Road which later became Iona Road. The first houses were not built by either Strain or Conolly.

Figure 51: Iona Road, Glasnevin

When the new "Iona" church was completed in 1905, there was no direct road access from either end. After negotiations with the Lindsay estate, Crawford Road was extended to St. Alphonsus Road and renamed Iona Road, thus opening a new thoroughfare between Glasnevin and Drumcondra. By 1913, Strain, with another builder Thomas Boyd, had completed the other roads in Iona, namely Iona Park, Iona Crescent, Crescent Villas and Iona Drive and building had been extended into the Carroll estate between Iona Park and Marguerite Road.

The road names in the area were derived from two quite different sources: One source was the Lindsay Family, the principal landowners in Glasnevin, who are commemorated by Lindsay Road, Crawford Avenue, David Road and Claude Road. The other source was the historical lore of the life of St. Colmcille (or Columba) from which came Iona Road, Park and Crescent, Gartan Avenue and St. Columba's Road, for example. One of the roads connecting Iona Road and Lindsay Road has no name, presumably because it has no house frontage.

The houses in Iona are of good quality design and construction in an Edwardian style with bay windows which gave more light than the older Victorian style. Some imposing detached dwellings were built – some here and there on Iona Road – but mostly in Iona Park.
According to local lore, a detached house opposite the new church was raffled in 1902, for which tickets cost a mere 2d. This was afterwards the residence of General Emmet Dalton, close friend and comrade-in-arms of Michael Collins.

Strain's planned scheme of four houses and a row of shops between Lindsay Road and Whitworth Road on the site of the old Daneswell House was not realized until 1925. There was a proposal at one time by builders to provide a linking road from Iona Crescent to Botanic Road, but it ran into difficulties and was eventually abandoned when Players built their factory on the site.

Cliftonville Road

Alex Strain built some houses on Botanic Road and he commenced Cliftonville Road in 1924. The houses on Cliftonville Road are also in Edwardian style but with a brighter appearance, partly due to wider bay windows and partly due to the greater width of road. Unlike the Iona houses, there were no maids rooms or pantries, a sign of the changing times. The name seems to have been taken from a place in the North of Ireland.

Fairfield and Daneswell Roads. Daneswell Villas

Fairfield Road and Daneswell Road were built by a Charles Reddy, solicitor, with builder P. L. O'Brien, on the old Fairfield estate. The Fairfield residence was an old Jacobean house best known, perhaps, as the boyhood home of Oliver St .John Gogarty, where James Joyce was an occasional visitor. The house was demolished in 1928 to make way for a bank premises and an array of semi-detached houses. Fairfield Road was completed in1934.

Daneswell Road, linking Fairfield Road with Botanic Avenue, was named after the townland of that name (which in turn derives its name from the ancient Deane's Well nearby) and it was completed in 1938. (The Irish language equivalent "Bothar na Danarcoille" appears to have been an error in translation). A terrace of houses on Whitworth Road was named Daneswell Villas, and the name plaque may still be seen on an end- house.

Botanic Avenue

Botanic Avenue, formerly Corey Lane (or Gorey Lane on Duncan's map), or "Slut's Alley" (an old local name) and probably the most interesting road in Glasnevin, is a very ancient thoroughfare that contains a great diversity of dwellings and dwelling-types. For long - at least one thousand years - it was the only road between Glasnevin and Drumcondra. Up to 1870 it contained mostly thatched mud cabins dating from the 1700s and a few substantial houses.

Figure 52: Glasnevin National School Botanic Avenue 2010

Figure 53: Players' Houses Botanic Avenue.

Some substantial building was carried out at the Drumcondra end in the late 1800s, but development at the Glasnevin end occurred much later. Some of the very old 18th century buildings were still here in 1900. More dwellings were built on Botanic Avenue between 1920 and 1940, and in 1924 four of the terraced dwellings were demolished to permit the building of St. Mobhi Road.

Beside Glasnevin Bridge stood the Church of the Seven Dolours of Our Lady, colloquially called the "Wooden Chapel", erected in 1881 and enlarged in 1904. Alongside was the historic "Inkbottle" school which was replaced by the present building in 1901. Just beyond the school, the old Maher's Cottages had been levelled to make way for the first of the redbrick terraces.
Opposite were a few thatched dwellings and shops which were destroyed by fire in 1914. According to local lore, the cause was a bonfire lit by the butcher's assistant who had been told to dispose of some rubbish. A small row of modern shops was built on the site in the early 1930s.

A few of the small dwellings in Glasnevin dating from the late 1700s and early 1800s survive to this day as shops and they are distinguished by having their gable-ends facing the street. Two of these face the church: a barber shop with the unique feature of a window under its chimney and a former huckster's shop (Kearneys) which has seen various uses over the years. Also dating from this period is "Tolka Cottage", a modest single-storey dwelling standing between the redbrick terraces.

Behind the Dispensary, half-hidden, is Addison Place, a terrace of plain 19th century two-storey dwellings. Beyond the school, the redbrick terrace houses on Botanic Avenue and its side roads, St. Malachy's, St. Ita's and

St. Michael's, were built in the early 1900s and the 1920s by local builder Daniel Daly. In the early 1920s a builder named Gough built some terraced houses on Botanic Avenue commencing at the corner of Addison Place. These were mostly of red brick with rectangular bay windows.

Around the same time, the Imperial Tobacco Company (Players) built a group of houses for its employees brought over from Nottingham. These houses were purportedly designed by Sir Edward Lutyens, the renowned English architect, in a quasi "English cottage" style".
Known locally as "Players' Houses", they replaced a row of mud cabins called "Sunnyside".

A row of ancient dwellings opposite included Martins - a huckster's shop, a small yellow-washed house and a two-storey house with diamond-pane windows. These lasted until about 1950 when they were demolished, and the field at the rear became part of an enlarged Griffith Park.

Some distance beyond Players' houses, a gate lodge stood at the entrance to an avenue leading to Greenmount, a substantial Georgian house in its own grounds, which was demolished in the 1950s. The north-south boundary of Glasnevin with Drumcondra lies just beyond at a set of steps.

Floods

Botanic Avenue has always been subject to floods from the River Tolka, and the area is indicated on the older Ordnance Survey maps as "liable to flooding". Around 1930, as part of the plan for the new Griffith Park, the Corporation decided to change the course of the river from its curved meandering bed to a new channel going straight through the park. Unfortunately, this did not solve the problem of floods, and very heavy flooding occurred in 1946. Again, on 8th December 1954, the floods caused a near disaster when the river in spate brought down the railway bridge at East Wall. It was not until after another serious river flood on 15th November 2002 that the municipal authority undertook significant measures in Griffith Park and along the river bank to reduce the effects of flooding.

Ballymun Road

Alexander Strain's first venture north of the River Tolka was the building of the row of handsome semi-detached red-brick houses on the west side of Ballymun Road. He usually lived close to or on his building sites, and he lived for a short while in Windermere, the large detached house at the northern end of the row.

St. Mobhi Road area

The main road named after St. Mobhi was originally designated Dean Swift Avenue, apparently because of the slight association of Dean Swift with Glasnevin.

Figure 54: McCann's shop. c.1950

Objections thereto were raised by a number of residents (and not all from that road), the loudest coming from the Parish Priest Canon Dudley, who, according to one account, proposed the name "Corpus Christi Road". Wiser counsels prevailed, and at a meeting of residents called jointly by Canon Dudley and Canon Bond, the Rector, it was unanimously decided that the new road should be called after the local saint.

Figure 55: St. Mobhi Road, northern end

The houses on St. Mobhi Road, Home Farm Road and the neighbouring Griffith Avenue were built by various builders including Alex Strain, as may be deduced from the differing designs of dwellings. In some cases, groups of houses were built by co-operative societies, mainly because increased grants could be claimed in this way.

The principal co- op was the Dublin Commercial Public Utility Society which was responsible for dwellings on upper St. Mobhi Road, and on adjoining Home Farm Road and Griffith Avenue. Alex Strain and his son-in-law George Malcolm Linzell were involved jointly and separately in building houses on St. Mobhi Road and St. Mobhi Drive.

The Rise and Hampstead

Whereas Strain built houses in a conservative style, Linzell's architectural ideas were much more adventurous. He built the scheme called The Rise on Hampstead Hill off Griffith Avenue, which was architecturally unique and well ahead of its time. The design was by a London architect named Harold Greenwood and is of architectural interest even today, with its 1930s "suntrap" houses. The most outstanding example of this architect's work is the detached house on the corner of Hampstead Avenue which is built in a quasi- Cape-Dutch style.

Figure 56: Hampstead Avenue Corner house

Linzell's house Wendon (Balnagowan)

Linzell built for his own use a unique, ultra-modern, "art décor" residence beside the old Cinder Path (now Boithrín Mobhi or Mobhi Boreen) off St. Mobhi Road, which he named Wendon, after his two children Wendy and Don. Designed by Harold Greenwood, it was constructed entirely of reinforced concrete, and in the shape of a quarter circle in order to catch as much of the sunlight as possible. It was subsequently occupied by the Doyle family (of Doyle's Corner fame) and renamed Balnagowan. It was taken over by the Inland Fisheries Board in the 1970s. Opposite, and complementing Balnagowan, stood "Sonnheim", a bungalow of very modern design, on an acre of ground.

Figure 57: Balnagowan, Mobhi Boreen

Cremore

Strain moved his building business to a new site just beyond the village and the tram terminus where he built his final development, which he named Cremore, after the birthplace of his grandfather, Rev. Alexander Strain D.D. in County Armagh. This was, and still is, one of the most attractive small suburban areas in Dublin. The first stage, Cremore Park, was begun in 1927.

Having persuaded the Corporation to extend the sewerage system, he began work on the Old Finglas Road, Cremore Avenue and Cremore Road which was completed by 1934. As building made progress, the design of the houses changed. Most were semi-detached.but the final phase which was Cremore Drive consisted of four rows of terraced houses.

Figure 58: Cremore Road

Alex Strain intended to make Cremore a Presbyterian and Protestant enclave, and he built a detached residence "The Manse" for the Presbyterian Minister on Cremore Park. Nevertheless, the first Catholic family – the O'Carrolls - moved in to No. 2 Cremore Park in 1928, followed by the Monks to No.14 in 1929 and the Barringtons to No.14 Cremore Road in1934.

Alex Strain and his family

Robert Douglas Strain with his son Alex came to Dublin from Markethill in Co. Armagh in or about 1890. Alex established himself as a house-builder just at the time that Dublin Corporation was expanding the City boundaries, and he quickly gained a name for himself of a builder of good quality houses. He usually lived on or near his building projects, which meant that he changed residence each time. His last residence was No. 24, Cremore Park.

He had no sons, but he had four daughters, two of whom lived nearby. One, Mrs. Madge Atock, lived in Cremore House on Cremore Park, and the other in No.2 Cremore Road. One daughter, Kathleen May, married Malcolm Linzell, who came from a family involved in the building industry, and he became an associate of his father-in-law.

Alex Strain was noted for his good works, for the Abbey Presbyterian Church wherein he worshipped, and for secular causes such as the Marrowbone Lane Fund and Drumcondra Hospital, He provided a Christmas party each year for poor children, and he was a popular figure in the locality, until his death on 18th September 1943. He is buried in Deans Grange Cemetery.
His wife Kathleen, who died in 1954, was an aunt of J.M. Synge the famous playwright.

Mrs. Madge Atock was a founder of "The Association of Parents and Friends of Mentally-Handicapped Children" which subsequently established St. Michael's House on Ballymun Road. She died in 1974.

Glasnevin Village

The modernization of Glasnevin Village was a slow process that took a full century. In 1912, a row of old dwellings was replaced by Beechmount Terrace, but apart from this, the Village retained its eighteenth century character and the old 18th century houses on the Hill would last until the 1960s.

Figure 59: Glasnevin Bridge 1910

In 1901, the first modern shops were built between Addison Terrace and Botanic Avenue, in red brick with front gables, which have seen many different uses over the years. The terrace of ancient houses on the Hill (Vincent Terrace) was to remain until the1970s.

Figure 60: Barber shop, Botanic Avenue

Figure 61: Vincent Terrace Glasnevin Hill 1956

Figure 62: Corner House, Glasnevin Hill 1960

Figure 63: The old forge, Glasnevin Village c. 1986

Figure 64: Montgomerys Butcher Shop, Glasnevin village c. 1990

Figure 65: The Village Shop, Glasnevin Village (1942)
(Courtesy of the National Library of Ireland)

New industry

In the 19th century, after the demolition of the paper factory and watermill, Glasnevin had virtually no industry with the exception of Terence Murray's sailcloth factory in the Botanic Avenue area, and the stonemasons' yards close to the Cemetery. The denizens of this "pastoral area" would not have welcomed factories in their midst.

In the 1920s, two large factories were established on Botanic Road. The first belonged to Alex Thom, printers and stationers whose premises in Abbey Street had been destroyed in 1916. The second factory was Players' branch of the Imperial Tobacco Company. This replaced their old factory in Marrowbone Lane."

Brown and Nolan of Richview, Clonskeagh, acquired Thoms in the early 1950s, and replaced the building. Both it and Players were acquired by the Smurfit organization around 1980. In 2006 both factories were demolished to make room for a future residential development. However, the tall chimney and the handsome front offices have been preserved, and in 2008, that building was used for the filming of the BBC television series "Inspector Gently".

Off Botanic Avenue, Meeks "Hydrophast" overcoat factory took over the premises of a former button-factory beside a patch of ground known locally as "The Triangle". It was to last until 1950.

Iona National Airways Ltd.

At the junction of Whitworth Road and Prospect Road, beside the abandoned Glasnevin Railway Station, is a prominent building of somewhat "art décor" style, which is now a restaurant. In the 1920s, this building was a motor garage with showrooms owned by Hugh Cahill, a local resident. Hugh Cahill was one of Ireland's pioneers of aviation who was responsible for establishing Ireland's first commercial airline, Iona National Airways in 1930. It began operations in September 1930 on a temporary basis from Baldonnel Aerodrome, with a fleet of two aeroplanes. The following year it moved its operations to a new site at Kildonan, north of Finglas, where it built a hangar and a club-house. It was officially opened on 8th June 1931.

The administration of the company was carried out in Hugh Cahill's garage, designated "Iona National Airways" in the stained-glass side windows. In 1933, the airline ceased trading when Hugh Cahill left the business. It was subsequently taken over by a new company, Everson Flying Services Ltd.

The premises continued in use as a motor garage until the 1960s, still with the somewhat intriguing name "Iona National Airways". It subsequently saw many uses, a car-showroom, a tool-hire company and a garden centre before eventually being transformed into a restaurant.

Reference: "The Silver Lining": Lady Heath Kildonan – A Golden Age of Flying" by John Haughton published by the Finglas Environmental Heritage Project

Figure 66: Iona National Airways, Prospect Rd. c.1935 (Courtesy John Haughton)

Chapter 41:
THE "GREAT WAR" AND THE TROUBLES

The war and the Rising

War and strife were still a distant matter in Dublin until Easter Monday 1916 when the "Rising" broke out with the seizure of the G.P.O by the Patrick Pearse and the Volunteers. News did not travel very quickly in those days, and in Phibsborough local people there noticed a lone cavalryman – a survivor of the first volley of shots fired by the Volunteers in the GPO at a company of Lancers - galloping on his way to the Vice-Regal Lodge with the news.

The Easter Rising had very little effect on Glasnevin or the other outer suburbs, until food supplies to the shops ran out. The Botanic Gardens drew its usual large attendance all that Easter week. This was the first intimation of the changes and trouble to come. After a week, the Rising was over, but within three years the real "Troubles" of Irish history had begun.

The War for Independence

The War for Independence, as the "Troubles" are now called, broke out in 1918 after most of the elected MPs in Ireland decided to forsake Westminster and instead to set up the first Dail. The rest is history known to us all, and every area in Ireland has its own anecdotes of events that occurred between 1918 and the end of the Civil War in 1924.

The Lindsay family, which had long been a bastion of the British Establishment, left Glasnevin House which was taken over for use as the residence of the Commander-in Chief of the Crown forces in Ireland.

Tales of the "Troubles

The Healy family had come to Glasnevin from the South Circular Road in 1916, and the father set up as a cobbler in a little shop beside Hart's shop in Cross Guns (now a barber shop). A republican supporter during the troubles, his son Tom told of coming to the shop from school one afternoon, when a revolver was placed in his school bag and he was told to go for a walk because word had come of expected "Tan" activity in the neighbourhood. Fortunately, all was clear by the time of Tom's return.

Much more grim is the story of the dead "spy in the lane". A man named Burns posing as a jewelry salesman by the name of Jameson was in fact an undercover agent for the British Secret Service. He succeeded in infiltrating the IRA, promising to supply guns and ammunition. He was eventually exposed, and orders were given for his execution. He was taken to Glasnevin by tram under the pretext of meeting Michael Collins and from thence to Hampstead Avenue where he was shot. His body lay there until it was discovered by a Mr. Naughton, a local milkman, the following morning.

The Good Samaritans

Perhaps the most sensational incident in Glasnevin at this time occurred on the cold wet night of 10th October 1920 and the morning following. Dan Breen, in his book "My fight for Irish freedom" tells the story. He and his equally famous companion Sean Tracy, both "on the run", were accommodated for the night in a "safe house", Fernside, the home of a Professor Carolan on the Upper Drumcondra Road. They lay in bed, half-dressed with their hand- guns at the ready, dozing rather than sleeping, The two men were awakened by the sound of heavy footsteps and the sudden glare of a searchlight. They had been traced by the British Secret Service (the "Murder Gang") and a large contingent of the military had been sent to capture them. In one of the most extraordinary events of The Troubles the pair succeeded in shooting their way out and escaping, leaving thirteen British soldiers and agents dead.

Sean Tracy succeeded in avoiding injury and he eventually reached a safe house in Finglas. Dan Breen, on the other hand, was seriously wounded, having been hit by at least five bullets. Despite his injuries, he managed by an extraordinary effort to escape through the grounds of St. Patrick's College, scaling walls until, barely conscious, he reached the north bank of the River Tolka. Just further up the river lay Marlborough Hall, at that time the Irish Counties War Hospital for British soldiers, which had to be avoided. He continued stumbling along the riverside and eventually waded across the water towards some houses.

Exhausted, bleeding, and tattered, he stumbled to a back door and knocked twice. Mr. and Mrs. Fred Holmes, who lived at No. 13 Botanic Avenue, were awakened by his knocks and on answering, Fred beheld the truly alarming sight of the wounded gunman who fell unconscious at his feet. Fred was persuaded by his wife to give asylum to Dan (her threat to report him to Michael Collins helped him to make up his mind!). These Good Samaritans called Nurse Long from the Dispensary opposite who dressed his wounds. There he lay, in the care of this couple while a message was sent to Dick McKee who arranged to have Dan smuggled to the

Mater Hospital later that morning. Tom Healy told of seeing IRA men on guard near the bridge that day while Dan Breen was being moved.

That Dan Breen led a charmed life there is no doubt. By crossing the river, he later realized that he had broken the scent of the tracker dogs, which probably saved him from capture (or worse).
What was even more extraordinary was the later revelation that in the adjoining houses (numbers 12 and 14) lived an RIC man and a soldier respectively. Dan Breen survived to become a T.D in the Dail and he died at his home in Griffith Avenue in 1969, not far from the scene of his adventure on that fateful night.

The Unionists

On the Unionist side, there was an organization called the "Georgius Rex Association" which was a voluntary Home Guard type of club, comprised mainly of local ex-soldiers, for defending the Union. In Glasnevin, they used to drill and practice shooting in the back garden of Ardmore on the Hill. Their Dublin nickname – the "Gorgeous Wrecks" seems to indicate that they were not taken too seriously by the populace.

The Civil War

The Civil War was of relatively short duration but it was to be the cause of long-lasting bitterness in Ireland. The local people of Glasnevin included sympathizers from both sides, but there is no report of any military action apart from one incident. The Irish Counties War Hospital had been taken over by the new Government for its wounded soldiers, and according to Mrs. O'Brien, the last owner of Delville, on one occasion it was attacked by a party of Republicans (or "Irregulars" as they were termed) who had seized Delville and used it as a firing base.

Despite the differences of opinion that lasted for decades, people in the locality seldom spoke of the events of the Civil War afterwards.

Chapter 42:

BETWEEN THE WARS - A LITTLE LOCAL HISTORY

The new residents

During the 1920s and 1930s Dublin experienced a large influx of people from the provinces, the luckier ones gaining positions in the Civil Service, the teaching professions, the banks and large companies. Many were attracted to Glasnevin where the new houses were bright and airy with gardens to the front and to the rear. These houses were much preferred by the erstwhile country-dwellers to the rather gloomy late Victorian terraces wherein lived the typical Dubliners.

The milkmen

The older residents of Glasnevin soon became a minority in the changed circumstances. One group that welcomed the new dwellers was the local dairy industry, and the many small "milkmen", as they were called, gained new customers. The Martin family had a smallholding behind their shop and another shop named the Evergreen Dairy, on Botanic Avenue. Mick Martin and Molly Martin delivered milk twice a day on foot in the immediate neighbourhood, and they continued their trade until around 1943.

Figure 67: Martin's shop Botanic Avenue c.1930

The best-known name in the dairy business was Craigie. The Craigie Brothers commenced trading around 1900 from a house named Merville, and later Church Hill on Ballymun Road. Their cattle grazed on rented land in Claremont and other locations including the former Church Hill Nurseries. Far-seeing, they realized that the old system of milk delivery could not meet the demands of the huge numbers of new residents and in 1926 they moved to an old factory on the Finglas Road just north of the bridge. Here they set up a milk-bottling plant under the name of the Merville Dairy which grew to become the main milk distributor on the north side of Dublin. Their horse-drawn wagons – green for milk and yellow for buttermilk – became a familiar sight as people chose bottled milk in preference to the milk-can of the local milkman. In 1969, Merville merged with Sutton and Tel-el Kebir Dairies to form Premier Dairies.

Figure 68: The late Ed. Morrison, the last milkman 1995

Despite this development, many households remained faithful to the old-style milkmen, some of whom lasted into the 1950s. In 1918, the Nolan Family from Wexford took possession of Church Hill House and adjoining land in Ballymun Road and set up in business as the Wexford Dairy. The Nolan family remained in possession of the property until the year 2005.

J.J. O'Kelly (Sceilg") (1872-1957)

J.J. O'Kelly, a well-known resident and patriot, originally lived in St. Thomas's Terrace (now No. 59 Glasnevin Hill). He was a committed and uncompromising republican of the old school for his whole life, but unlike many of his compatriots, he eschewed violence. Born in County Kerry, he is (or was) best known to schoolchildren as Sceilg, a writer of short stories in Irish. He was prominent in the activities of the Gaelic League.

In 1918, he stood as a candidate for Sinn Fein in the Westminster elections. He was elected as a Sinn Fein MP, and became Ceann Comhairle of the First Dail in January 1919. He was subsequently appointed first Minister for Education and first Minister for the National Language. He opposed the Treaty, but did not take up arms. When Fianna Fail was founded in 1927, he chose instead to assert his loyalty to the Second Dail, thereby disapproving of Eamonn de Valera's attitude. He would nowadays be termed a "hardliner."

By 1930, the family had moved across the river to 173 Botanic Road (Addison Terrace), opposite the Botanic gardens. He and his wife were both of strikingly handsome appearance, and he could be seen regularly walking around the perimeter of the Gardens, reciting the Rosary (all fifteen mysteries). J.J. O'Kelly lived on in this house until his death in 1957.

A fervent Catholic and Nationalist, he was Irish Editor of the "Freeman's Journal, and Editor of the "Catholic Bulletin" from 1911 to 1922. This latter was a monthly journal or magazine that ran from 1911 to 1939. He was a founding member of the Keating Branch GAA, President of the Gaelic League from 1919 to 1923, and a contributor to Dineen's Irish Dictionary.

Only for his stories in Irish which appeared in a few school text books, Sceilg would have been unknown to the generations that followed. This was remedied to an extent with the establishment of the Sceilg Summer School in Valentia in 1988.

Reference:
History Ireland March-April 2006 p.50
An Irishman's Diary, Irish Times 3rd July 1989

Chapter 43:
THE "EMERGENCY" AND AFTERWARDS: CHILDHOOD RECOLLECTIONS

This chapter consists mainly of a childhood recollection and retrospection of the period known in Ireland as "The Emergency", a euphemism for the Second World War.

Sunday 3rd September 1939: The outbreak of war

On Sunday 3rd of September 1939, in one of the most famous radio broadcasts in history, Neville Chamberlain told the British people that they were now at war with Germany. That afternoon, Dublin was hit by one of its worst thunderstorms, which washed out the All-Ireland hurling final match in Croke Park. An anxious and fearful people wondered about what would come.

"The Emergency"

Although Eire (as it was styled by the 1937 Constitution) was officially neutral, nevertheless the authorities took a number of measures in case of attack. Urban householders were advised to obtain black-out curtains, and the citizens of Dublin (including children) were fitted with gas-masks at local centres. Fuel and food were no longer plentiful, with food rationing, ration books and queuing the order of the day. However, the scarcities were not as severe as in neighbouring Britain, a country now at war.

Farm output was increased and suburban gardens, back and front, were turned into vegetable patches. A large area of publicly-owned land was let out in allotments, for example, "The Plots" in the grounds of Claremont, where men could dig and plant, and children watch and play.

Defending our country; The German bombing of Dublin

Men and some women joined the various security forces: A.R.P ("The Wardens"), L.S.F, L.D.F. (the future FCA), and their distinctive uniforms of grey, blue and brown were a familiar sight in the suburbs. These organizations brought people together, and there was much "socializing" after their regular activities, to the disapproval of the wives.

A familiar feature of the suburban scene in Dublin was the "tank trap", a contraption whereby steel rails could be pulled across the roadway to block or hinder the advance of any invaders. These were traffic hazards, but very few cars were on the roads during the "emergency".

The bombing of Dublin by the Luftwaffe in May 1941 brought the first experience of real war to the citizenry. Glasnevin was spared, although it was well within earshot of the bombing. The following morning, local people saw a German bomber over Dublin being pursued by two fighter planes.

"Up for the Germans": Aiseirghe and its aims

For the first years of the War, apart from the residual IRA faction, many veterans of the old republican movement and their families were openly supportive of the German cause, seeing their "enemy's enemy" as their friend. The main pro-Nazi organization in Ireland was called Aiseirghe, (or, to give it its full title, Craobh na hAiseirghe), whose objective was a repressive Gaelic-speaking dictatorship which they hoped to set up with the help of Nazi Germany. In Glasnevin its local zealots used to meet and train in St. Mobhi Hall, opposite the Wooden Church. According to local lore, their subversive activities were limited to spying on the local Civic Guards. A cobbler's shop off Botanic Avenue hung the following advertisement in its little window: *"Hitler settles the Poles / we settle the soles"*. Aiseirghe had lapsed by 1950.

During the war, No.16 Cremore Avenue was occupied by no less a personage than the Japanese Consul, a Mr. Bepu, much to the disapproval of some residents.

Reference:
History Ireland Sept/Oct 2009 p40

Chapter 44:
POST-WAR GLASNEVIN: 1945 - 1960

Building starts again

The years following the Second World War saw the beginning of a new building boom in the public and private sectors. The Dublin Corporation's slum clearance programme was achieved by the building of large local authority housing schemes on both sides of the River Liffey. In Glasnevin, where private middle-class housing was predominant, virtually all the available building land within the 1901 City boundary had been used up by 1939.

The first new building scheme in Glasnevin commenced in the late 1940s with Iona Villas, on part of the Greenmount Estate, a small development that was in contrasting style to the older Strain-built houses.

Between 1950 and 1960 the farm lands to the north west of the Village beyond the Old Finglas Road and on either side of the narrow winding Ballygall Road eventually fell to the builders. The Glasilawn development and the new Griffith Avenue Extension were built on the Coyle and Doyle farms, but the extension did not link up with the main Griffith Avenue until the 1970s.

The principal builder in the area and up to the Willowpark area around Ballymun Avenue (as it was called then) was Mr. Paddy Byrne, who lived in a prominent detached house on the Old Finglas Road. Ernest Webb, who had been a foreman for Alex Strain, was responsible for the extension of the Cremore area to Cremore Crescent on the other side of Ballygall Road, and the houses downhill on the Old Finglas Road.

The Institute for Industrial Research and Standards

In 1947, the Institute for Industrial Research and Standards (IIRS) moved from its offices in St. Stephen's Green to Glasnevin House. A number of laboratories were built in the grounds for various purposes such as mechanical engineering, chemistry, physics, textiles and building construction. Of architectural note is the modernistic "Butterfly" building facing Ballymun Rd., with its inverted roof sloping towards the centre.

In 1981, the IIRS (later "EOLAS" and "Enterprise Ireland") demolished two 18th century houses – "Roseville" and "Glasnevin House" with "The Turrets". On the site, the front offices were erected in an architectural style known informally as "shoe box". The premises are now largely unoccupied.

The Bon Secours Hospital

In 1944, Delville and its grounds were purchased by the Bon Secours Sisters for the purpose of building a new hospital. The Sisters were founded in Paris 1824 by Josephine Potel, in post-revolution France following a time of turmoil for the Roman Catholic Church. Their object was to provide nursing care for the sick and dying in their own homes, whether rich or poor. During the bloody civil war of 1848 – the "February Days"- the Sisters were called to provide nursing care for the wounded, and their work gained them the respect and admiration of all citizens. The Sisters came to Dublin in 1861 where they established their first foundation outside France. On 6th may 1861, they took up residence in a house in Grenville Place. In 1864, they moved to No. 64, Lower Mount Street, where they were to remain until 1951. Known as "The Nursing Sisters, they continued to provide care for the sick in their own homes. In 1932, they set up St. Bridget's Dinner Hall in Holles Row.

Figure 69: Bon Secours Hospital Glasnevin

With the advances in medical science and hospital facilities, it became clear that home-nursing was no longer practicable for the seriously ill. In 1944, at the request of Archbishop J.C. McQuaid, they acquired Delville from Mrs. O'Brien in Glasnevin for the site of their new hospital. The house became a nursing home during the period 1945 to the end of 1950 whilst the hospital was being built, and it was knocked down in January 1951.

The building was named St. Joseph's Hospital, and it was formally blessed and opened by Archbishop McQuaid on 2nd February 1951. Over the years, the Hospital has developed and improved its facilities to keep up-to- date with advancing medical technology. In 1993, the Bon Secours Sisters set up the Bon Secours Health System, the object of which is to carry on the Mission of Bon Secours ("Good Help").

Management of the Hospitals changed over the years, and today there are Management Teams at local level reporting to the Chief Executive who in turn reports to the Board.

The other Bon Secours Hospitals are in Cork (1867), Tralee (1878), and Galway (2000). In 1966 the Sisters founded the Mission to Peru, which has been flourishing since. It is supported by voluntary donations from local parish sources.

Reference: Milestones on a Faith Journey, compiled by Sister Reginald O'Sullivan, S.B.S

Murder in the Wooden Chapel: A victim's evidence

On the afternoon of the 10th August 1948, an 83-year old lady named Mary Gibbons was attacked and fatally injured by a young married woman named Mary Agnes Daly. Mrs. Daly, who was lodging with her husband at No. 132 Botanic Road, apparently had financial difficulties, and she had borrowed a sum of money the previous week from a local priest. In addition, she was under pressure from her landlady Mrs. Short to move out. On the day of the incident, she had placed a hammer in her handbag and walked the short distance to the Wooden Chapel which she entered and where she saw Mrs. Gibbons, alone, absorbed in prayer in one of the seats. She struck Mrs. Gibbons on the head several times before people, including Mr. Canavan the butcher opposite, came to the rescue and forced their way into the church. Mrs. Gibbons was rushed to the Mater Hospital where she died on 17th August 1948. The subsequent trial during the following November of Mrs. Daly was unusual in that a Deposition had been taken by a District Justice from the murdered woman at her bedside shortly before she died, This was submitted in evidence from the Prosecution and accepted by the Court. Daly's evidence that Mrs. Gibbons had tried to steal her shopping bags was not believed by the Jury.

On 11th November 1948 Mary Agnes Daly was found guilty of murder, but with a recommendation for mercy. She was sentenced to death by hanging. On 16th December, an appeal by the defence was made to the Supreme Court concerning the admissibility of the statement by the deceased. The appeal, on a point of law, was successful whereupon a new trial was ordered.

A new trial took place during the following April and on the 29th, Mary Agnes Daly was found guilty, and sentenced to death. On 4th May the sentence was commuted to life imprisonment. She served only five years in prison before her release in 1953. At the time, moves to ban the death penalty had commenced in Ireland and Britain, notably by a Mrs. Van der

Elst. On the opposing side, a vigorous newspaper letter-writing campaign supporting the death penalty was being waged by a prominent activist, a future judge and future President.

References:
The Irish Times 10th November 1948 and succeeding days and 30th April 1949
Letter to the Irish Times, from John Grundy, September 1996.
Documentary "Idir Mna" TG4

Chapter 45:
GLASNEVIN 1960 TO 2000: RENEWAL

The rebuilding of the Village: a near disaster

The last third of the twentieth century saw the demise of most of the remaining old houses in Glasnevin Village. In the 1970s, a new and tastefully-designed apartment complex called River Gardens was built on each side of the Hill, one part beside the Tolka House, on the site of the early 17th century houses, and the other in the grounds of the demolished Carlingford House. This, with the replacement of the old masonry triple-arch bridge by a modern single-span artifact in 1971 and the widening and re-alignment of Glasnevin Hill, changed the appearance of the Village. On a morning in November 1971, the road builders damaged a gas main at the top of the Hill causing an explosion that wrecked Tom Healy's cobbler's shop and seriously injured members of the Healy Family. They survived nevertheless. No one else was injured.

The Met Eireann Office

The controversial truncated-pyramid building erected on the site of the old Marlborough House, which became the "Met. Service" Headquarters, now styled Met Eireann, has been described with good reason as Glasnevin's "pointless building". Built in 1979, it was designed by a provincial architect named Liam McCormack, an award-winning designer of rural churches, and it was his first urban project. It would be an understatement to say that it overshadows, and clashes with, the Georgian and Victorian redbrick houses of Glasnevin, with its "grim gun-metal façade and its sharp, angled outlines". Inside the building is a large foyer dominated by a metal spiral staircase, with a wall of polished black marble bearing a mural designed by Ruth Brandt.

The reason for the pyramidal shape is not known, possibly to allow some light to David Terrace behind, but from almost the beginning the building was dogged by misfortune. Windows designed for vertical mounting but installed on a sloping surface let in the rain. The cladding panels, of Galway limestone, did not withstand the effects of rain and sun, and most of those facing south became distorted and slid off, fortunately without injuring anybody. The resulting litigation lasted for several years. Eventually, the cladding was replaced with aluminium.

Figure 70: Met Eireann Offices, Glasnevin Village

New housing developments

Following the sale of lands of the Orphanage on the west side of Finglas Road opposite the Cemetery, a number of new houses were built in the 1960s in areas designated "The Willows", Clareville" (after *Clare Villa*, an Edwardian villa) and Claremont Lawn, Court and Crescent.

The two main developments in Glasnevin between 1970 and 2000 were the opening of the Griffith Avenue extension between St. Mobhi Road and Ballymun Road, and the estate called Cremore Lawns, built in the 1970s on land purchased from the Holy Faith Sisters. In 2000, the Sisters sold off more land where the developers built an extensive apartment-block complex which they called Addison Park. In the 1980s, a number of "town houses" as they were styled, were fitted into the garden behind the restored Beechmount on Glasnevin Hill.

Following the demolition of the St Vincent de Paul Orphanage building in 1981, an apartment block complex called "Dalcassian Downs" was built on the site. Around this time, Botanic Park was built on the old Greenmount Estate and the quarry field beside Botanic Avenue.

Chapter 46:
PUBLIC TRANSPORT IN GLASNEVIN

Horse omnibuses: The first public transport

The first recorded horse-drawn buses appeared in France, in the City of Nantes, around 1820, under the name "Omnibus" (meaning "for all" in Latin), and within ten years they had appeared on the streets of London. Around 1860, a limited omnibus service commenced from College Green to Glasnevin, mainly for visitors to the Botanic Gardens.

The omnibus was considerably cheaper than licensed cars and cabs – for example 4d as against one shilling or one-and-sixpence. However, they were very slow – hardly faster than normal walking pace, and their frequency on the Glasnevin route was low. The poor quality of some of the roads at the time, particularly in Glasnevin, made the journey difficult. The primitive braking system of the omnibus depended mainly on the stopping-power of the horses. In one case, this led to a tragic accident elsewhere on the old hump-back Charlemont Bridge when, during icy weather, a heavily-laden bus slithered out of control into the canal lock, resulting in the drowning of all aboard.

The horse-drawn trams

In Ireland, the Tramways (Ireland) Acts of 1860 and 1861 were enacted. In 1867, the City of Dublin Tramways Company commenced the development of a limited tramway system in the inner city area south side of the River Liffey. By mid-1881, Dublin had three tramway companies: The Dublin Tramways Company (DTC), the Dublin Central Tramways Company, and the North Dublin Tramways (NDT). A prominent figure in the tramways business was William L. Barrington, who lived at Glasnevin Lodge, (adjoining Addison Lodge, but no longer extant). He was involved in the management of all three tramways companies in rapid succession but he was obliged to resign in turn from all three for a number of reasons, including bad staff relations and financial irregularities.

Trams on the North Side

The first tram-line on the north side was laid by the DTC in 1873 from Middle Abbey Street to Dollymount, and was called the Clontarf Line. It was followed in 1874 by the North Quays Line which ran from Batchelors

Walk to Parkgate Street, the last line to be built by that company.

William Barrington with the help of some former colleagues, promoted and set up a new company, the North Dublin Street Tramways. The new company succeeded in obtaining an Act of Parliament in 1875 authorizing the construction in 1876 of three tram lines, a total of eight route miles long, to Glasnevin Bridge, Phoenix Park, and Drumcondra Bridge. A line to Inchicore was built some time later. The Phoenix Park and Glasnevin lines ran from Sackville Street via Rutland (now Parnell) Square, Berkeley Road, and North Circular Road where they diverged at Dunphy's (now Doyle's) Corner. These trams served the Mater Hospital and Mountjoy Prison.

Dublin's three tram companies, none of them very large, were in needless mutual competition, a public transport arrangement that was both uneconomic and inefficient. The possible benefits of a merging of the three companies had been raised from time-to-time, and in July 1881, it became a reality with the creation of the Dublin United Tramways Company (DUTC).which would last for nearly seventy years.

The company began with a total of 132 cars. The first trams were both single-and double-deck type. Single-deck types were pulled by one horse and did not have a conductor. Double-deck types were pulled by two horses, and had conductors. Seats upstairs were of the longitudinal "knife board" type. As young ladies began to use the upper deck, screens called "decency boards" were provided at each side. These were used to carry advertisements, and the term "decency board" survived into the twentieth century as a term for the advertisement side- panel, even on the later Dublin buses. The driver's position was open to the weather, as was usual for all vehicle-drivers in those days.

Horse trams ran at an average speed of five miles per hour, which compared very unfavourably with the speeds of steam trains, and they were not perceived as a threat to the railway companies. A team of up to ten horses was required for each tram.

The Glasnevin Horse-Tram 1876-1899

The Glasnevin tramline opened on 10th December 1876. It served Glasnevin Cemetery and the Botanic Gardens, and terminated outside Tolka House at the bottom of Glasnevin Hill (popularly called Washerwoman's Hill). Most of the line at the time consisted of single track, an economic measure that was not justified, since the savings in construction were outweighed by operational problems and increased wear on the single line. The DUTC Timetable for 1897 gives the time for the first tram from

Glasnevin to Nelson Pillar as 8.30 a.m., and the last one from the Pillar as 11.00 p.m. The fare was 2d.

On the dark evening of 29th January 1883, an accident occurred on the Glasnevin Road (Phibsborough Road or Botanic Road) involving a horse-tram. The tram, travelling towards Glasnevin, was struck by a "light vehicle" which had gone out of control. A shaft on the vehicle pierced the breast of one of the horses, causing its death within minutes. The vehicle driver was arrested and charged with drunk-driving.

The photograph shows a horse tram stopped at the terminus outside Tolka House. The gentleman in the driving position appears to be a senior official, or, probably, a director of the company.

Figure 71: Horse-drawn tram outside Tolka House c. 1890

The first electric trams

A major revolution in transport came with the invention of electric traction by Werner von Siemens (founder of the renowned German company) in 1879.

A delegation of top DUTC officials (including William Martin Murphy) went to USA in 1893 where they were favourably impressed by the new electric tramway system. By the end of 1894, a decision had been taken to "go electric". In September 1896, the Southern District Tramways Company was taken over by the DUTC, and the Dublin United Tramways (Electrical Powers) Act of 1897 gave authority for significant expansion of its network.

The first electric trams on Dublin's North Side commenced on 11th November 1897 running between Dollymount and Annesley Bridge. Passengers continuing their journey to Nelson Pillar had to do so by horse tram. Power for 25 trams was provided by a generating station on the site. The following year, the line to Nelson Pillar was completed and the first tram reached there on 19th March 1898.

The Glasnevin Line

Glasnevin had to wait until the following year for its electric tram service, when the track was extended up the hill to a new terminus beside the gates of the Holy Faith Convent. The new electric tram service commenced on 4th December 1899, but ran only as far as Nelson Pillar. It was extended first to Dolphin's Barn and then to Rialto in May 1905, and was allocated the number 7.

The electric trams and their drivers

Like their horse-drawn predecessors, the new trams were double-ended and they could be driven from a complete set of controls at either end. The conductor's bell was operated by a pendant leather strap. For the first two decades, the driver, or the Motorman as he was designated, was exposed to the weather since there was no protection on the operating platform. Unfortunately, the increased speed of the electric tram made bad weather effects far worse than they had been on the horse-drawn trams. Only the healthiest and fittest men could survive such conditions.

Identification and livery

Destination boards were affixed to each side, and destination boxes were mounted at each end. These consisted of back-lit linen blinds or scrolls showing the destinations, with glass in front. In addition, during this period, each tram carried a metal symbol at each end which differed in shape and colour for each route. The Glasnevin Tram bore a brown lozenge (this is included in a description of the symbols by Leopold Bloom in James Joyce's "Ulysses"). Destination scrolls contained the name "Nelson Pillar", but never O'Connell St. or Sackville St., because of the political controversy at that time over these names. It went to Rialto via Dame St. and South Great George's St.

In 1918, it was decided to give each tram route a number based on a radial system. The system began with No.1 Tram to Ringsend, No. 2 to Sandymount Green, successive numbers going in a clockwise direction, and the Glasnevin tram became No.19. The No. 20 tram also served Glasnevin, but it went instead by Nassau St, Dawson St. and Harcourt St. to the South Circular Road where it rejoined the 19 route.

From the beginning until 1928, trams were painted in a dark blue and ivory livery. In 1929, the colours were changed to French grey and off-white, but this change was neither serviceable nor in style and attracted much criticism. In 1936, the colours were changed to green and cream.

Comfort in travelling

The first double-deck trams were open-top, and sitting in an uncovered upper deck in bad weather was not a pleasant experience. By the end of 1903 the DUTC had commenced installing top covers with sliding doors at each end. Initially, the balconies at each end were left completely uncovered, but later they were given some protection by extending the roof. Here, smokers could indulge their habit, removed from others. Unfortunately, providing a closed vestibule for the Motorman's position was not entertained at the time, and this state of affairs lasted until the 1920s on some vehicles. A photograph of the 19 "Balcony" Tram at its Glasnevin Terminus in 1938 shows it with open balconies and closed vestibules. Later versions, e.g. the "Standard", had enclosed balconies.

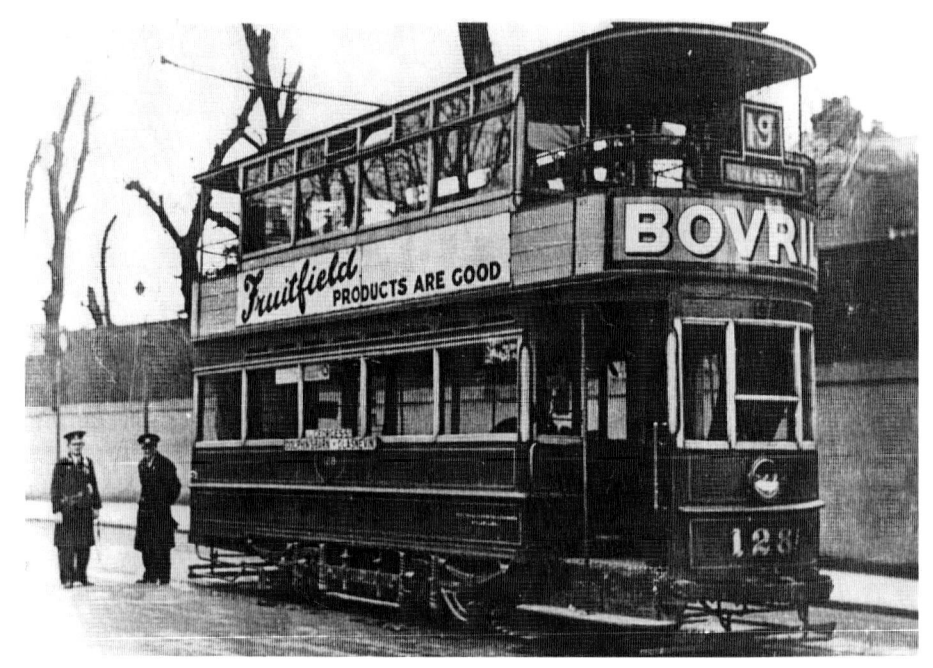

Figure 72: 19 tram at Glasnevin terminus 1939   (Courtesy Michael Corcoran)

The tram crash

One of the best-known events in Glasnevin lore is the story of the "tram crash", which happened on 1st November 1937. At about one o'clock in the day, 19 Tram No. 76, carrying four passengers, left its terminus outside the Holy Faith Convent, picked up speed and ran off the rails just on the bend at the top of the hill. It hit a lamp post and the wall facing, and tumbled over on its side. The driver James Hartnett, the conductor Thomas Scott, and passengers Peggy Hand of Church Avenue, Miss Mc Gory of Lambay Road and Mrs. M. Patterson of Old Finglas Road were taken to hospital. Fortunately, none was seriously injured. A fourth passenger, a young schoolboy, ran off, unidentified and apparently uninjured. The tram, however, was badly damaged, the roof being completely ripped off. It was later righted and towed away, but was never put back into service.

The day was the Feast of All Saints, a Holiday of Obligation for Catholics and a day off for the Catholic schools. A crowd of schoolchildren and others were soon gathered, in time for the Evening Herald press photographer who had arrived on the scene. In the crowd was a little Protestant boy "mitching" from the local school. His escapade was revealed that evening when his father sat down to read the Evening Herald and recognized him in the press photograph. He became another "casualty" of the day!

Reference: Evening Herald 1st November 1937

Figure 73: Glasnevin Tramcar accident 1st. November 1937

The end of the trams

After the First World War, buses and private motor cars began to increase in numbers, and traffic began to increase. Private buses, including the notorious "pirate" buses became numerous on the roads and began to compete with the trams. Eventually, the DUTC invested in buses for some of its new routes from 1925 onwards and it gradually began to substitute buses for trams generally. On 31st March 1938, the DUTC decided to replace its entire tramways network over a four-year period.

On 31st March 1939, the last tram departed from Glasnevin. The swish of the trolley, the clang of the wheels and the loud purr of the motors were now only a memory.
Ten years later on 9th July 1949, the last of the Dublin trams – No. 8 - finished its journey to Dalkey, in a state of total wreckage caused by local vandals and souvenir hunters.

The Arch Company buses

Outside Dublin, road transport consisted mostly of privately - owned buses. These small companies were ultimately absorbed by the two big railway companies GNR and GSR, achieving a virtual monopoly by the mid-1930s. In Dublin City new suburbs were growing beyond the old tram routes, and buses were the only solution. The flexibility of the bus and the lower overheads were an added advantage.

Figure 74: Arch Bus, St Mobhi Road   c. 1930

The building development of the Glasnevin area moved up St. Mobhi Road to Home Farm Road, Griffith Avenue and the Rise, which were not convenient to the tram route. To begin with, the big army of building workers on the site needed transport, followed by the new residents to the area. A private company, the Arch Bus Company operated a service using single-deck buses from the top of St. Mobhi Road via Whitworth Road to Lower Gardiner St. These ran only at certain times, in particular in the mornings and evenings to suit the workers. A dark green in colour, these buses continued in service until 1939. The route was subsequently served by the new 19A bus.

The 11, 19 and 19A buses

The 19 bus route followed that of the tram, but the 19A terminus was at the top of St. Mobhi Road, which was shared with the new number 11. The open rear platform provided an opportunity for athletic latecomers to board the moving vehicle.

These buses served passengers during the war years, and overcrowding was usual at peak times, with some even sitting on the stairs. With the scarcity of buses, bus queues became compulsory, regulated by inspectors in the city centre.

Around 1950, it was found necessary to extend most city bus routes to serve the new suburbs growing around the city. The 19 was first extended to a point some distance up Ballygall Road/Griffith Avenue junction, and later, the 19A, and 11 were extended up Ballymun Rd.

Over the years these services were extended in stages, eventually terminating in Finglas.
The terminus at Rialto remained for many years, and eventually it was changed to Bulfin Rd. (19) and Limekiln Rd. (19A). A major change was from the old tram route through Berkeley Road to the present one through Broadstone and Mountjoy St. to Berkeley St.

The 13 bus

In 1947, a welcome new bus route, the 13, began runnuing from Glasnevin to Beechwood Avenue in Ranelagh via Whitworth Rd. Nassau St. and St. Stephen's Green. It was gradually extended northwards to Wadelai, and eventually to Ballymun town. After 2000, the route was diversified with additional routes 13A, 13B and 13C.

The 34, 134, 83 and 36 buses

In the 1960s, a new bus route numbered 34 was introduced to service the new Ballygall and Finglas areas from the Quays. This became the 134 in the late 1980s. It was replaced in 2003 by the 83 route which was extended southwards to Kimmage. Practically forgotten now is the 36 bus, a single-decker, which ran from Gardiner St. Lower to Tolka Estate, and was called locally "The Jungle Express". It ceased in the mid-sixties when its elderly conductor retired.

References:
"Through streets Broad and Narrow" by Michael Corcoran (Midland Publishing)
"Irish trams" by James Kilroy (Colourpoint Press)

Chapter 47:
ST. MOBHI'S CHURCH OF IRELAND

St. Mobhi's in Glasnevin

Half-hidden at the end of Church Avenue - a cul-de-sac off the old Ballymun Road – and overshadowed by the lofty "pointless" pyramid of the Met Office lies a little stone church with a square tower, enclosed by a high wall. This is St. Mobhi's Church of Ireland in Glasnevin, a place of Christian worship since 530 A.D. when St. Mobhi founded a church and a monastic school here (Chapter 3). The church was rebuilt in 1240 and consecrated to "St. Movus".

The church in Glasnevin after the Reformation

From the time of the Reformation until 1700, there was very little activity evident in the church in Glasnevin. It appears that the Dean and Chapter of Christ Church took little or no action during a period that was not a propitious one generally for the new Established Church.

In 1572, the Curate was entitled to the rent of a house in Glasnevin, but there is no record of any incumbent there at that time. In 1581, the Vicar (of Christ Church) was entitled to the proper rotation of crops in Glasnevin to maintain his tithe.

In 1615, a "Regal Visitation" of the Archdiocese was carried out by Archbishop Jones on the order of King James I. The Report of the Visitation states that Rectory of Glasnevin was impropriate to the Church of the Holy Trinity (Christ Church), and that Richard Wyburn, a Preacher, was Curate, and that the church and chancel were in good repair. Wyburn (or "Wybrans") was curate in other parishes also. The Dean was admonished for not providing a permanent curate. ("Impropriate" here means that the tithe had been assigned to someone other than the local clergyman, e.g. a layman, or in this case, the Dean). The subsequent Archbishop Bulkelely's report on the Diocese in 1630 has no mention of Glasnevin.

Subsequently, and presumably because of the lack of support both spiritual and temporal, the church gradually fell into disrepair. The Parish had fallen into disarray by 1630, when it was combined with Clonturk (Drumcondra) Parish and so it remained until 1700. The Curates in charge of the two parishes were John Allen (d.1639), Laurence Wogan (d.1645), Henry Brereton (d.1646), Michael Clenehan (d.1684 and, Joseph Espin (d.1698).

After 1700, the Rectory of Glasnevin became in equal parts the Corps of the Precentor and Chancellor respectively of Christ church, who presented a Perpetual Curate in return (i.e. one having no endowment or tithe, which was remitted to the Dean and Chapter). (See "Claim for a glebe" below).

A church in ruins

By the end of the 1600s the church was in ruins, although still standing, According to one source, an attempt was made to rebuild it in 1685, which succeeded in restoring only the church tower.

On 13th of May 1706, the Archbishop of Dublin William King visited Glasnevin, and inspected the ruined church. At the request of the parishioners (including Sir John Rogerson, the local property developer), he decided that the church should be repaired, and he appointed a committee for the purpose consisting of Church Wardens Sir John Rogerson and Charles Ryves esq., and two sidesmen (assistants) Mr. James Proby and Mr. Solomon Fairweather (a publisher and friend of Dean Swift).

A new church

The Committee set to work at once and called a vestry which met in the ruined church building on 21st May 1706. The following worthies attended the vestry:

William White, Curate, Sir John Rogerson, Charles Ryves, Ch. Philips, Mich. Teeling, Peter Drelincourt (a Huguenot) Jos. Elsemere, David Thomas, John Hudson, Richard Hovid, Wm. Woolfinden (innkeeper), Thomas Browne (farmer), Solomon Fairweather, James Proby, and John Davis.

A rough plan and specification had been prepared for the new building and this was approved as follows:

"1st that the walls of the said Church being defective ought and shall be pul'd down.

"2nd that the said walls shall with all convenient speed be rebuilt in the following manner, viz, the said walls shall be built 60 foot in length from out to out, and also 30 foot wide from out to out, likewise from the floor to the wall plate 22 foot in height.

"3dly that the walls of the said Church be at the foundation three foot thick, and carried up taper or rush to two foot at the top.

"4thly that the Roof of the said Church be made of good Oak timber proportional to such a Building and covered with the best Welsh Slates and rendered".

5thly that towards defraying the Charges of the said Building the sum of Six pence per acre be forthwith applotted and raised from the said Parish and that the Church Wardens and Mr. Peter Ward be and are hereby appointed overseers to agree with workmen for carrying on the said work and Mr. Fairweather and Mr. Proby and Mr. Teeling or any two of them with the assistance of the Constable of the Parish for the time being be and are hereby appointed assessors to applott the said Sum of Six pence per acre upon the several inhabitants of the said Parish".

It is fairly evident that no architect was involved, and the task was given to local stonemasons and carpenters. Judging by the subsequent maintenance problems, the quality of workmanship and materials left something to be desired.

The church building was completed by the end of November 1707, at a cost of £143 - 7s- 1d, following which the Vestry met on 5th December 1707. Its first acts were to order that a bell be provided, the churchyard cleaned up, all graves to be dug at least 4 foot deep, and to decide on the allocation of pews to the various parishioners.

Figure 75: St. Mobhi's Church c. 1876
(Courtesy Architectural Archive)

Public subscription

As well as the income from parish applotment, two public subscriptions were raised in 1706 from the citizens of Dublin and local businessmen. The lists included the Lord Archbishop of Dublin (£5), Dean Drillincourt (£20), Sir John Rogerson (£23), Sir Humphrey Jervis, Sir Mark Rainsford, the Lord Mayor of Dublin, the two Sheriffs of Dublin, several Dublin merchants three Aldermen, a local farmer Thomas Browne, and the local innkeeper Wolfenden. One merchant, Pat. Lattin, pledged 20 "deals" worth 18s, and another, Jos. Clarke, pledged 10 "deals" worth 9s.

Maintenance and repairs

There were recurring problems with the building for two decades afterwards. As early as January 1708 the windows were damaged by the wind "through weakness of the barrs" and repairs had to be organized hurriedly. Even the bell needed recasting or replacement on some occasions.

In 1713, money had to be raised for repair of the window frames, plastering, a new bell, flagging the church and rails and bannisters for the Communion Table. The costs were as follows:

Grant (from the City) towards flagging the church: £10
To John Waters for flagging the church: £7-10s
Balance of the City £10 paid for railings and banisters: £2-10s
John Johnson and Chris Jones for the Bell and Rope: £6-5s

The new porch

In the original Church, the entrance was on the south side. In March 1725, it was decided to move it to the west end beside the tower and thereby provide more room inside. Subscriptions from twenty-two donors raised £4-11s-11d for building the new porch, and the expenditure on materials and labour was as follows:

In 1742, the church needed repairs once more, and the porch then was described as being in "ruinous condition". Again, in 1765, the porch and belfry were described as being in a ruinous condition. The tower did not undergo restoration "for want of money", according to a report to Parliament by the Curate in 1777, and it was not until the end of 1896 that this was eventually carried out when the present porch was built, along with the new chancel (see below).

The Church silver

In 1724, a group of prominent parishioners presented the church with a large silver salver, two silver chalices and two patens.

The donors were: The Curate Rev J. Travers, Doctor Delany, Sir John Rogerson Junior, Mrs Rogerson (widow), Isaac Ambrose (Clerk of the Irish House of Commons), Captain J. Davis, J. Knightly, Mr. Rupert Barber Senior, Hugo Batho, Messrs Settle, Flack, Board, Power, Chantry, Mrs. Dorothy Berkeley (widow).

The silver and its costs are listed on 17th May 1725 as follows:

One chalice and patine (sic) with Latin inscription weighing 19 ounces, 15 penny wt. at 6s-8d per ounce: £6-1s-4d

One chalice and patine with English inscription weighing 19 ounces 18 penny wt at 6s-8d per ounce: £6-12s-8d

One large silver salver weighing 16 ounces 3 penny wt at 6s-8d per ounce: £5-7s-8d

The English inscription on one chalice is "Humbly dedicated to the service of the altar (sic) in the Church of Glasnevin by the curate and parishioners". The Latin inscription on the other chalice is "In usum Ecclesia et Parochialis de Glassineven Johannes Davys Armiger ("Captain") humilimi dedicavit Anno Dom 1724".

Two other items were presented later: A silver flagon inscribed "Glasnevin Church Anno Domini 1868" and a silver salver presented by Derek Henry Caldwell Cooper in 1966.

Pews

On the completion of the Church, a number of prominent parishioners presented the first pews, for which they were rewarded with the right to occupancy thereof with their heirs "forever". These were Sir John Rogerson, Terence Reyly, Solomon Fairweather, Charles Ryves and David Thomas. The pews constituted part of their estate, and could be handed over or sold to others, subject to approval by the Vestry. For example, on 20th July 1716, Mr. Jjaack (sic) Rabateau was "installed in the pew belonging to William Pedy, having purchased the same from Margaret Tickell, sister to the same Pedy". In 1723, Doctor Delany was granted liberty to build two pews "on the remaining ground westward uniform to the pews already built".

Over time, the ownership of pews became more casual. Some pew-owners no longer resided in the parish, while some residents were denied the use of pews. Arising from this situation, in 1789 the Vestry set up a committee to inspect claims to seats and pews. In 1815, Pew No. 11 was granted to Rev. Robert Walsh, the historian, who lived in Church Hill House nearby.

The vestry room

As long ago as 1730 it had been intended to build a vestry room on to the church, but it was not started until 1815 when a special cess was organized to pay for it.

The gallery

In April 1831, a committee was set up to erect a gallery in the church, and £20 was collected for the purpose. A petition was sent to the Archbishop to obtain his consent, and the matter was submitted to the Consistorial Court of the Diocese. A citation approving the erection of a gallery was obtained, and it was completed within twelve months. (Consistorial Courts dealt with matters such as wills, matrimonial disputes, clerical misconduct, and tithe disputes. They were abolished in 1869 under the Irish Church Act).

Claim for a glebe

The history of the glebe in Glasnevin, and the circumstances surrounding, are rather unusual. In 1664, Daniel Hutchinson (q.v.)acquired the lease of a large area of Glasnevin. Under the terms of the lease, Hutchinson had to provide six acres as a glebe for the Curate, convenient to the Church, or if the Curate should not reside there, he (Hutchinson) had the use of it for a rent of 40s. (This is roughly the area now occupied by a group of modern houses off Mobhi Boreen called "The Haven"). At the time, there was no resident Curate in Glasnevin, so that the matter of a glebe did not arise. In any event, he would have had no tithe under the terms of his curacy.

In 1719, some lands were set to Lady Altham paying £10 to the Curate and rent of £280 to the Dean and Chapter. In the 18th century this appears not to have been a matter for concern for the clergy then, who seemed to have been largely self-sufficient.

On 18th June 1803, the new Curate Rev. Dr. Hume wrote to the Dean of

Christ Church drawing attention to the terms of the original Hutchinson lease, and asking for the six acres of Glebe which he would exchange for the means to erect a Glebe House, or some equivalent compensation. Nothing came of his approach.

Notwithstanding this failure, a later Curate, Philip Ryan, in 1809 took up the matter with a submission to the Dean and Chapter, complaining of the "peculiar hardships" under which the Curate of Glasnevin labours in consequence of the manner in which the land is withheld" His point was that he was excluded from the Board of First Fruits by reason of his having only a nominal glebe - in effect no glebe at all - albeit with compensation.
The matter was put to a lawyer, William Saurin, who gave a judgment against the Curate dated 24th September 1809 as follows:

I do not have the smallest doubt that nothing in the clause in favour of the Curate can prejudice the lease. It is not the object of this case to dispute the right of the Curate. It would be inadvisable to enter controversy and we should abide by the matters as they have been.

The transfer of part of Glasnevin Parish to St. George's Parish

One of the major events in the parish was the transfer of the area of Glasnevin Parish on the south of the River Tolka to the newly-formed Parish of St. George, an area of 86 acres. This was effected by an Act of Parliament in 1793, but the actual transfer did not take place until 1798 when the cess ceased to be taken for the area ceded.
St Georges Church was built in Hardwicke St. ("George's Pocket") and completed in 1802. Its churchyard is some distance away, off Whitworth Road and behind the former Drumcondra Hospital).

Disestablishment 1869

The Board of First Fruits was established in 1711 to deal with church finance, buildings land and tithes in Ireland. ("First Fruits" originated in the time of Henry VIII when they replaced the annual payments to the Pope, called "annates").

In 1833, the Church Temporalities Act re-organized the temporal affairs of the Church of Ireland, abolished the First Fruits Board and established Ecclesiastical Commissioners in its stead. The Irish Church Act of 1869 disestablished and disendowed the Church of Ireland and sundered the union with the Church of England. A new corporate body, the Representative Church Body (RCB), replaced the commissioners and took over the finances and ownership of church buildings, glebes and schools. This brought to an end the civil role of the Church of Ireland.

The Union of Glasnevin and Santry Parishes

In 1876, the RCB decided that, for financial reasons, the Parishes of Santry and Glasnevin should be united. This was opposed by the Glasnevin Vestry, who tried to have the decision rescinded. They were informed that this would cost them an amount of £1500. On 17th September 1886, they resolved to do everything in their power to "preserve the individuality of the Parish of Glasnevin, and so far as is possible to raise the balance of the capital".

They were unsuccessful in their attempt, but the union did not come into effect until after the death of the Rector, Reverend H.G. Carroll in 1896. The Rectory on Ballymun Road (Melville) was sold, and the Rectors thereafter lived in Santry, until the Union with Finglas. The Parish of Cloghran was included shortly afterwards.

The union with Finglas Parish

In 1991, due to diminishing numbers of parishioners, the Parish of Finglas was united with the United Parishes of Glasnevin, Santry and Cloghran.

The first extension to the church building.

In the 1880s, the increase of population in Glasnevin seems to have more than compensated for the loss of the townlands south of the River Tolka, and the need for enlarging the church building became pressing. In 1887, the Vestry decided that the accommodation of the parish church was inadequate, and that steps be taken to reorganize the seating, and to extend the building eastwards to accommodate a choir of twelve (i.e. a chancel). It took another nine years to bring this to fruition, by which time it became clear that more room would be needed. This would involve a new transept on the south side. In 1896 it was decided to proceed with the following:

- building a new chancel at the eastern end
- arching the space under the tower to accommodate the baptismal font
- building a new porch
- replacing the windows in the nave in with a gothic design and cathedral glass or stained glass panels
- moving the organ to a new chamber on the right-hand side

- moving the tablets from the east wall to the west wall
- providing a gothic table for the chancel
- installing a new gas heating system.

The new transept was deferred for the time being.

The original baptismal font had been in the Claremont Deaf and Dumb Institution for many decades, and in 1888 this was returned to the church after repair and re-cutting by Harrisons, stonemasons, of Brunswick St.

The work was completed in 1898 at a cost of £1235-12s-2d. The money was raised from bazaars, sale of stocks and a contribution of £150 from the widow of the late Rector Henry George Carroll towards the arching of the tower and a memorial window therein to her late husband. This became the new baptistry. The pulpit had then to be moved to its present position beside the north wall.

The south transept

Planning for the new transept went ahead which would substantially increase the seating. The work encompassed enlarging the existing organ chamber, and it was completed in December 1908 at a cost of £898-18s-4d. The stained glass windows on the south wall were transferred to new transept. The new design, by architects Benjamin Pemberton and Son, altered the appearance of the building to a significant extent. One unfortunate result of erecting the new transept was the removal of some of the very old headstones and their dumping at the far end of the churchyard. They included the headstones of some very prominent personages.

A bazaar was held in July 1907 on the grounds of Claremont Deaf and Dumb Institution in aid of the church building fund. A photograph taken there shows a gathering of people and, what may be noteworthy for that time, a banner proclaiming in Gaelic the text "Glasnaoidhean Fete".

Figure 76: St. Mobhi's Church Entrance and Tower

The windows

The windows in the original church rebuilt in 1707 were of a simple multi-paned type, with curved top, When the chancel was built in 1896, all the simple 18th century windows were replaced with a more elaborate gothic type with mullions of Portland stone and "cathedral glass" at a cost of £36 each.
It was around this time that a number of parishioners and some others donated stained-glass windows as memorials to their departed relatives.

The window in the baptistry commemorates the Reverend Henry George Carroll, the last Rector of Glasnevin before its union with Santry. It depicts The Good Shepherd and The Light of the World. The window in the chancel at the opposite end commemorates Mary, the young wife of Lindsay Fitzpatrick, who died in 1895. It depicts The Ascension.

On the north wall are two memorial windows. One, depicting The Ascension, commemorates James Hannan and his family, and the other, by Edward Frampton of London, depicting the Resurrection, commemorates Jervis and Esther Birney.

On the south wall, in the transept, are two memorial windows one depicting the Resurrection commemorates Robert Briers and his wife, and the other depicting the Gospel scene "Suffer the little children" commemorating the Hon. Ellen Lindsay, wife of H.G. Lindsay of Glasnevin House.

The furniture

The old pulpit was replaced in 1909 by one of carved wood made by the pupils of the Claremont Institute for the Deaf and Dumb, as were the organ screen and one of the hymn boards. The organ was built by William Benson of Manchester in 1893, and moved to its present position in 1897. The communion table was presented by two members of the Lindsay family in 1897.

The church bell

The present church bell was made by John Sinclair of Dublin in 1779. It carries an incised inscription   "F. Nettervill W, Fanning Churchwardens 1779 I:S" and sounds to Note C. It has had a long history of repair and re-casting over its lifetime.

Restoration

As with any building, maintenance is a continuing burden. A major restoration was carried out in 1962, which included the replacement of the roof. The baptistry was dedicated to Canon Bond in 1966.

Pastors from early Christian times to the Reformation

St. Mobhi, Abbott and Bishop, 12th October 544 A.D.
St. Cialtrog, Abbott and Bishop, d. 741 A.D.
St. Maolbuille, Abbott and Bishop d. 552 A.D.
Sir David the Chaplain c.1344 A.D.
John Neile, Chaplain c. 1442 A.D.
John Wolfe, Curate d. 1481 A.D.
Patrick Lowe, Curate d. 1514 A.D.

Pastors from the Reformation to 1700

Richard Wyburne (or Wybrants) " a preacher" c. 1615
John Allen, Perpetual Curate, also of Clonturk d.1639
Laurence Wogan, Perpetual Curate, also of Clonturk, d. 1645
Henry Brereton, Licenciate to the Care of Souls in Glasnevin, Clontarf, Raheny and St Dolough's d.1646
Michael Clenahan, do. Drumcondra and Glasnevin, d.1684.
Joseph Espin do. Drumcondra and Glasnevin d.1697.

Rectors of Glasnevin from 1700 and dates of appointment

Ralph Darling 1708.
William Wolsey 1709.
Robert Echlin 1710.
Michael Hartlib 1711.
John Travers 1719.
William Pountney 1729
Richard Parker 1735.
Dr. Patrick Delany 1745.
John Boyle 1754.
Theobald Disney 1779.
Travers Hume 1785.
Crinus Irwin 1805.
Charles W. Wall 1809.
Philip Ryan 1809.
James Smith 1822.

Reginald Greer 1827.
John West 1829
Walter C. Roberts 1830
Charles Standford 1835
Charles H. George 1843
Moses Margollouth 1844
Henry George Carroll 1847, died 1896.

Henry George Carroll, the last Rector of Glasnevin, born in 1820, was scholar of some distinction who won the Berkeley Gold Medal. He was previously Chaplain to Steevens' Hospital.

Rectors of the United Parishes of Glasnevin and Santry

Canon Richard A Byrn 1896
Rev. Gordon Stuart McPhail 1936
Canon W.R.A Bond 1940
Canon Allen Wilson 1964
Rev. R. Desmond Harman 1973
Rev. Victor G. Stacey 1986.

A remarkable fact is that between 1847 and 1936 – a period of eighty-nine years -there were only two Rectors, possibly a record.

Rectors of the United Parishes of Glasnevin, Santry and Finglas

Rev. Mark Gardiner
Rev. David Oxley

Chapter 48:
St. Mobhi's churchyard

Ancient history

The site of St .Mobhi's has been a place of Christian burial since the sixth century, and Annals of Ulster record the death of the saint on 12th October 544. The early Christian slab graves discovered in 1914 on the site of the present Met. Eireann Office indicate that the monks had a separate burial place some distance away.

Up to the Middle Ages, it was a widespread custom to inter the dead from the wealthier families under the church floor rather than outside, and two ladies, Jonet and Agnes, successive widows of Geoffrey Fox of the Great Farm, in their wills in the 15th century specified that they be buried in the nave of the Parish Church of Glasnevin "before the image of St. Mary". It is certain that burials continued to be carried out in the church and churchyard over the centuries, but no records, if any existed (which is doubtful), survive from the period up to 1700.

The churchyard

The churchyard of St. Mobhi's is quite small and quaint, and it is now closed to any future burials. It is bounded by a laneway, and the walls of the Bon Secours Hospital. At the eastern wall behind the church building is a postern gateway now bricked-up.

The disease and famine of the late 1700s and early 1800s sent the death rate in Dublin soaring and burial space became scarce. In St. Mobhi's, at one stage, four or five burials were registered every week, but it appears that some more were interred clandestinely outside the churchyard. In 1951, during the excavation of soil preparatory to making the foundations for the new Bon Secours Hospital a few burials were discovered, which were inspected by Mr. Lucas, of the National Museum. In June 1956, excavations in Mobhi Boreen ("The Cinder Path") for a new flats development revealed human bones of at least five skeletons probably dating from that tragic period (National Museum Registration 1956:16). The bodies were not laid in any particular direction.

To cope with the demand, some time after 1830, the level of the churchyard was raised at the eastern end to half-way up the postern gate, as may be seen today. When the south transept was built in 1908, several headstones, some commemorating notable people, were removed and they now repose against the eastern wall of the churchyard.

The oldest headstones

The oldest headstones in Glasnevin are set in the base of the church tower. They bear the names George Clayton (1695) and Walter FitzSimons (1699), and date from the time before the church was rebuilt.

Memorials to persons of note

The best known deceased, perhaps, is *Doctor Patrick Delany FTCD*, of Delville whose grave is at the north-eastern corner. He died in Bath in 1768, and was buried here beside his first wife Margaret (nee Tenison). A large vertical slab in the wall commemorates his life.

On the north side of the churchyard is a horizontal slab, now broken in two parts, over the grave of *Dr. Jacky Barrett D.D.*, one- time Vice Provost of Trinity College and Professor of Oriental Languages. He was a scholar of some distinction, and an astrologer, but he is remembered in Trinity lore mainly for his wit and eccentricities. Having endured poverty in early life, he became a miser that scrimped and saved, and on his death in 1821 he left the very considerable sum of £70,000, most of it to the Claremont Institution for Deaf and Dumb, with three hundred pounds to Glasnevin Parish. His sister Catherine Guinness (1826) and her family are also buried there.

Further along the north wall is the railing-enclosed family grave of the Caldwell Family, notably that of *Andrew Caldwell* (1683-1731), a solicitor and his son, also *Andrew* (1732-1808). Andrew junior studied law but was more prominent as an architect, literateur, antiquarian, and patron of the arts. He amassed a large library of works on botany, natural history and architecture which was his main interest. He published his "Observations on Public Buildings in Dublin". Another notable member of the family was *Admiral Benjamin Caldwell*. The Caldwell family maintained its connection with the Parish well into the 20th century, and Derek Caldwell presented a silver salver to the church in 1967. The family is also commemorated by two tablets inside the church.

At the far end, adjoining the grave of Patrick Delany, is the family plot of the Lindsay Family, who were the principal landowners in Glasnevin from 1806 until the late1920s. The founder of the Lindsay "dynasty" was the Hon. Charles Dalrymple Lindsay, son of a Scottish nobleman (the Earl of Belcarris), and many of his descendants are buried here. He was Bishop of Kildare and Dean of Christ Church wherein he is entombed. The best-known of his descendants was his son *Lieut. Colonel Henry Gore Lindsay* who died in 1914.

Just inside the gate to the right is the family plot of the *Craigie family,* founders of the Merville Dairy (afterwards Premier Dairies).

Among the many headstones on the south side of the churchyard is one to *George Henry Grattan*, (b.1787) of Cullenswood, who died in 1819. He was a young painter of great promise who was considered "one of the brightest flowers of Irish genius", according to the inscription. His most famous painting *Beggarwoman and child* hangs in the RDS. He may have been the son of Dr. Richard Grattan of Hampstead. Nearby is the grave *of Henry George Carroll,* the last Rector of Glasnevin Parish before its union with Santry.

Many of the large landowners of the 18th and 19th century are buried here. These are *Thomas Howey* (Claremont), *William Elliot, John Croker* (in a family vault), *William Hayes* (Daneswell), *John Christian Chesnay* (West Park), *Major Arthur Howard Gorges* (in a family vault) (West Park).

The unmarked graves of the famous

With the building of the south transept in 1908, the headstones on its site were taken up and piled against the east wall beside the postern gate. We cannot tell now where the graves were, but we know from the records whose they were. They include *Thomas Tickell*, friend of Joseph Addison, (who is also commemorated by a plaque inside the church), the members of the *Barber Family* (Rupert Senior, Mary the poetess and friend of Swift, Rupert Junior the portrait painter, and General Lucius Barber). Their headstone is visible at its edge only.

Sir Henry Jebb was a very famous physician associated with Mercers Hospital, "a physician of the less-guilty class who contributed rather to the births than to the deaths of the community" (d'Alton's History of County Dublin). He was Professor of Midwifery in the Royal College of Surgeons, and later its President. He died in 1811 and is recorded as being buried on the north side of the churchyard, near Jacky Barrett's grave.

Others whose headstones were removed are *James Belcher,* patron of the literary arts and his protégée *John Winstanley, Samuel Fairweather,* publisher and friend of Swift, *Henry Singleton*, Master of the Rolls and Chief Justice (of Belvidere, Drumcondra).

Robert Emmet

The whereabouts of the grave of Robert Emmet has intrigued historians for two centuries, and many books have been written after extensive research, propounding a variety of theories, some fairly convincing, but none conclusive.

The churchyard of St Mobhi's is one of the dozen or so reputed locations. Dr. George Petrie, the noted historian, believed that Emmet was buried somewhere there, near the eastern wall. Dr. Richard Madden, FRCS spent a lifetime in the quest for Emmet's body, and a photograph exists of him in the churchyard, beside what was thought to be Emmet's grave.

A local tradition handed down through successive owners of Delville tells of the patriot's headless body being brought into Delville, taken out by a side window, and carried up the garden path to pass through the postern gate of the churchyard. Although the story may well have some substance, there is no evidence that the headless body was actually that of Robert Emmet. It is quite probable that the British authorities deliberately caused confusion concerning the burial place in order to prevent Emmet's grave from becoming a nationalist shrine.

The story of the alleged grave was perpetrated and embellished over the years by various locals' expounding it to visiting Irish- Americans and others in the local hostelries, who expressed their gratitude in the customary fashion.

City tradesmen

Many headstones from the 1700s commemorate tradesmen and merchants from Dublin City, for example Henery(sic) Ford of King Street (1743), Chris Monck of Dirty Lane, Vintner, Daniel Hogan, Fishamble Street, Terence Reilly of Pill Lane, (1761), Laurence Connell, Baker, of S. Earl Street (1793), Mick Penroney, Manufacturer, of May lane (1786), and Joseph Archdeacon, collar maker, Church St.(1750).

War graves

There were three headstones for soldiers killed in the First World War, formerly supported by the Imperial War Graves Commission with an annual grant of 7s- 6d. Only one of those, Rifleman R. Manly of the Royal Irish Rifles, who lived on Botanic Road, is to be found today, a modest stone near the eastern wall. He was killed on 10th July 1915 at the relatively mature age of 46.

Glasmanioge

Several people buried here are shown as coming from Glasmanioge (or Glasmahonoge), as the area of Lower Phibsborough Road was called before 1900, for example, M. Clarke (1750), William Hanelon (1754), and Mathew Eves (1777).

Claremont Institute pupils

Deceased pupils of the nearby Claremont Institute for Deaf and Dumb were interred here (Chapter 42). There are no headstones marking the graves.

Body snatchers – the "Sack 'em Ups"

The early 18th century was very busy period for body snatchers, or "Sack 'em Ups" as they were called, with a plentiful supply of corpses and a high demand by the medical profession. Perhaps the most notorious of these operators were Burke and Hare who emigrated to Edinburgh to ply their trade. Dublin had its share of these activities, as, for example, the watchtowers of Prospect (Glasnevin) Cemetery bear witness.

The churchyard of St. Mobhi's did not escape their attentions, as Saunder's News Letter reported with the following headline in January 1830:

"DESPERATE ENGAGEMENT WITH BODY SNATCHERS".

According to the report, after the burial in Glasnevin churchyard of Edward Barrett, Esq. during the previous month, a nightly guarding party was mounted by armed local vigilantes to thwart any body snatchers. An attempt one wintry Saturday night by some of these gentry was abandoned when they saw the guard. Nothing daunted, they returned around two o'clock the following snowy Tuesday morning with augmented forces and well armed. On being challenged, the raiders opened fire from behind the wall, which was returned by the guard party who took cover behind the tombstones. The engagement lasted more than a quarter of an hour until one of the defenders rang the church bell, bringing the police and a crowd of local people despite the severe weather. The raiders made their retreat, one of them severely wounded, judging by the great quantity of blood on the snow.

Despite their previous rout, "those humble friends of science and humanity" (sic) made yet another attempt the following Sunday night. Again, they were repulsed by the guard party, who succeeded in wounding some of them, as would be verified later by the blood on the wall. Many of the headstones bore the marks of damage from the shooting afterwards. No further raids on the churchyard were reported.

The Fitzwilliam St. connection.

Number 29 Fitzwilliam St. was restored by ESB and the National Museum to become an exhibition of Dublin middle-class life around the 1800 period. Its first occupant was a Mrs. Olivia Beatty, a widow with seven children. One of her daughters, Maria, died in 1794 and was buried in St. Mobhi's Churchyard. The headstone was recorded in 1922 as being fractured, and cannot be identified today.

Closure

Shortly after 1990, the churchyard was officially closed to any burials, following the last two interments of people with burial rights.

References:
Saunder's News Letter January 1830,
Journal of the Associations of Memorials to the Dead in Ireland 1907- 1909,
The Irish Body Snatchers, by Dr. John Fleetwood (Tomar Publishing)
The Irish Independent, 8th June 1956, "Human bones unearthed"
Dublin burial grounds & graveyards, by Vivien Igoe (Wolfhound Press.)
The History of 29 Fitzwilliam St., by Kevin Burns (Dublin Historical Record Spring 2004).

Chapter 49:
THE ROMAN CATHOLIC CHURCH AND GLASNEVIN 1620-1900.

The Old Catholic families of the Pale

Apart from the native Irish, many of the aristocratic Anglo-Norman families of the Pale held on to the old faith. Separated for two centuries from their ancestral English origins, they had become increasingly isolated from their English cousins in their ways and even in their speech. When their ancestral country abandoned the Catholic faith they felt betrayed and dismayed. They were determined to hold on to that faith.

The names of County Dublin families such as Talbot of Malahide, St. Lawrence of Howth, the Hollywoods of Artane (or "Tartane") are part of history. Closer to Glasnevin, there was the Bathe Family of Drumcondra (one of whom is suspected of being a spy for the English authorities) and the Ball family of Ballygall (or "Ballinegall" as it is shown on an early map). Margaret, Matron Ball is perhaps the best known of those today since her beatification.

The resurgent Catholic Church: The Parishes restored

In 1618, a synod of the Leinster ecclesiastics was held in Kilkenny. The synod decided that re-organization should be done on a diocesan basis, but, that the original parish system should be reviewed, taking into account the changed circumstances and the financial support needed for the clergy. In Dublin, This involved amalgamating the original parishes into viable economic groups. Around this the time, the term "Parish Priest" and the address "Father" were introduced, replacing "Vicar" and "Rector".

The Parish of Coolock: A new beginning

In North County Dublin, the new Parish of Coolock comprised the entire area of the Barony of Coolock, combining eight of the original parishes of Fingal. These were: Coolock, Clontarf, Artane, Drumcondra, Santry, Glasnevin, Raheny and Killester. It was to remain a single parish until 1879.

The first Parish Priest was a Fr. James Drake, appointed in 1619, and described as "a Mass priest resident at Tartane, and commonly saith mass here. There is also his brother Patrick, a Popish schoolmaster". In common with most of the Catholic clergy, Fr. Drake had to work in defiance of the civil power which proscribed the practices of Roman Catholicism. The law was not always rigidly enforced and so he had to take his chances. Mass was celebrated in private houses and covert "Mass Houses" all over County Dublin, there being no Catholic churches at the time. Fr. Drake lived to see the coming of Oliver Cromwell and his army of Roundheads, and he died in 1650.

Between 1650 and 1680, there is a gap in the records and there may well have been no parish priest during the post - Cromwellian period.

Richard Cahill P.P.

Fr. Richard Cahill was ordained in 1674, and appointed Parish Priest of Coolock around the year 1680. He resided with the Hollywood family at Artane, and he is listed in 1697 as a "Regular Priest for the Parish of Santry". He built the first Roman Catholic chapel in Coolock during a period of relaxation of the laws following the restoration of the English monarchy under Charles II and the subsequent accession of James II. A curate, Cormack Cassidy, appears in the Government register for 1709.

After the end of the Williamite wars, there came the notorious Penal Laws in Ireland (interestingly, no such laws were enacted for the minority of Roman Catholics in England). Vindictive penalties were enforced for the public observance of Catholic practices. The chapel in Coolock was closed and Mass was once again celebrated in private houses. Records tell of the prosecution in 1714 of several people for attending Mass in Raheny and Coolock, who were fined £40, a huge sum in those days. Fr. Cahill died in 1720 and his successor was Nicholas Gernon who died in 1733, and of whose pastorate we know nothing.

Andrew Tuite P.P.

In 1733. Archbishop Luke Fagan appointed Andrew Tuite Parish Priest of Coolock (the original deed of appointment is preserved in Fairview Parish). It was around this time that the enforcement of the Penal Laws began to ease and the severity of the first three decades was not to return.

Fr. Tuite resided at Artane, as did his predecessors. About this time, returns were made by an Order of the House of Lords of "all incumbents, Mass Houses, Popish Schools, and priests. Under "Raheny", appears "one priest at Coolock and chapel, and several (unnamed) itinerant (sic) priests".

Andrew Tuite was responsible for developing the Catholic parish to an extent not witnessed since the Reformation. A major concern was that the location of the parish church in Coolock was not convenient for most of the parishioners, especially those in the distant Drumcondra and Glasnevin areas. Fr. Tuite decided to build a second chapel in the western area of the parish, midway between Glasnevin and Santry. In 1745 or perhaps a little later, a small chapel and school were built in Ballymun. These buildings were located on the Naul Road, a short distance north of the present Ballymun town, and strategically near the old Charter School which had been established in the previous year by "The Incorporated Society for Promoting English Protestant Schools in Ireland". The chapel was rebuilt and enlarged in 1797. It appears to have been a thatched building, surmounted by an ornate cross of wrought iron. This cross is the only artefact to have survived and it is now in private ownership.

In 1766, a census was taken of all religious denominations by the Church of Ireland. It states that Glasnevin and Drumcondra had a preponderance of Protestants, and refers to "Andrew Tuite and James Murray his assistant, and two Popish chapels". Andrew Tuite died in 1771.

Terence McLaughlin P.P. and John (Canon) Larkin P.P.

Fr. Terence McLaughlin succeeded Andrew Tuite, and he resided in Coolock. As part of the deal for the relaxing of the Penal Laws, the Archbishop of Dublin and his clergy accepted the Oath of Allegiance in 1782. Canon McLaughlin, as he had become, died in 1785, and was succeeded by John Larkin P.P (later Canon) who lived in Donnycarney and died in 1797.
Succeeding parish priests were Patrick (Canon) Ryan, 1797-1805, Daniel (Canon) Murray (for only one month in 1805), Patrick Long D.D. 1805-1829, and James (Canon) Callanan 1829-1846.

The curate at the time was a Fr. William Green, who lived at Black Bull in Drumcondra, and ministered there and in Glasnevin. He died in 1798. The next two curates were Fr. Strong O.P. and Fr. Ham O.P.

James Canon Callanan P.P.

James Callanan became parish priest in 1829, when the name of the parish was changed to "Clontarf". Having enlarged the church in Coolock, he built the church of St. John the Baptist on the site of "The Sheds" a settlement of poor fisher folk on the sea front in Clontarf. The church was opened in 1838. In 1834 he re-opened the old chapel in Fairview which continued in service until 1846, in which year he died.

Callanan was succeeded by Canon Rooney. There were two curates here at this time, Frs. Kennedy and McCabe, the latter of whom would later rise to the rank of Cardinal.

In 1848, the old thatched chapel in Ballymun was closed and a new church dedicated to St. Pappin was built, the gift of James Coughlan, a wealthy Catholic merchant. Canon Rooney died in that year.

The Catholic clergy and Glasnevin

By the middle of the 19th century, Catholics comprised one half of the population of Glasnevin, an area hitherto predominantly Protestant. In 1853, a Fr. William Purcell was appointed curate to the Parish of Clontarf as it was now styled) and in the following year he was appointed chaplain to the newly-arrived Sacred Heart Sisters in Glasnevin. He lived in the area and became a full-time resident curate there, serving Glasnevin and Ballymun. He was succeeded by Frs. T. Morin (1856-1858), Philip Carbery (1858) and later J. Farrell in 1879.

The new Parish of Fairview

After the death of Canon Rooney in 1878, Edward, Archbishop McCabe, decided to divide the parish in two, using the Malahide Road as a dividing line. The new parish was called Fairview Parish. There were now two new parishes as follows:

Clontarf: Comprising Clontarf, Killester, Coolock and Raheny.
Fairview: Comprising Fairview, Artane, Glasnevin and Santry.
.
The first Parish Priest of Fairview was William Keon P.P. Archbishop McCabe had expressed concern that there was no Catholic church in Glasnevin, nor any within a reasonable distance. He gave instructions to Fr. Keon who straightaway undertook the building of a chapel in Glasnevin.

The Church of the Seven Dolours of Our Lady (The Wooden Chapel)

Fr. Keon acquired a piece of waste ground beside Glasnevin Bridge, a part of the old Common beside the old parish school (the "Inkbottle") Here he erected a "temporary" church in 1881. Money was not plentiful, and Fr. Keon had to build the church from "bits and pieces". He acquired a temporary wooden building that had served as a church on Berkeley Road in Phibsborough since 1871, and, following the building of the new St. Joseph's Church, it was "going a-begging". Originally located in Glasthule, it was now to receive a third lease of life. A local builder,

Thomas Conolly, was employed to erect and complete the building.

The church was a plain rectangular building, with a corrugated- iron roof and seating for 150 people. The reredos, altar and tabernacle were acquired from City Quay church, but they were originally in the chapel of Newgate Prison in Little Green Street. The first Mass was celebrated there on 18th September 1881.

The Church of the Seven Dolours, or the Wooden Chapel, as it became known familiarly (or "The Woodener" in local parlance) lasted ninety years before a new church was built. By that time, the people of Glasnevin had contributed to the building of no fewer than three other churches in the area.

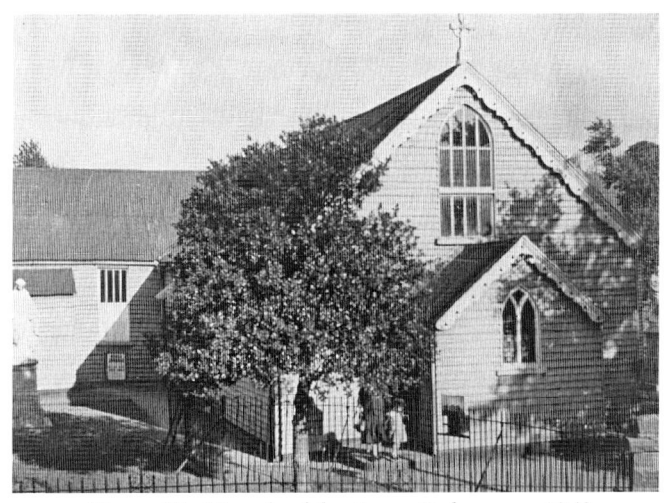

Figure 77: Church of the Seven Dolours c. 1960

Figure 78: Church of the Seven Dolours: Interior c. 1943

Chapter 50:
The Roman Catholic Church in Glasnevin in the twentieth century

The Parish of St. Columba's (Iona)

In 1902, Archbishop William Walsh (a man famously referred to by James Joyce in his poem "Gas from a burner") decided to carve out a new parish to be known as St. Columba's, or more familiarly, Iona Parish. This took in a large part of Drumcondra, and Glasnevin areas south of the River Tolka as far south as Whitworth Road and west as far as Botanic Road.

The new Parish Priest Fr. John Byrne had no church at the beginning of his appointment, and he was permitted to use the Wooden Chapel for the duration. This made him technically a curate of Fairview Parish. He enlarged the Wooden Chapel by adding two transepts in 1904, thereby enlarging the seating capacity to 400, at a cost of £650. He also built the Parish Hall, a timber building beside the church.

St. Columba's (Iona) Church

Fr. Byrne proceeded straightaway with the building of his new parish church. His first act was to purchase two acres of land from the Redemptoristine Sisters in the nearby Convent of St. Alphonsus. In 1902 a fund-raising meeting was held in the Wooden Chapel, presided over by Archbishop Walsh, which managed to raise £4,500.

On 7th August 1903, the foundation stone of the new church was laid. The builder was Thomas Conolly and it was completed (except for the spire) within three years. It was dedicated to St. Columba and consecrated on 15th October 1905 followed by Mass celebrated by Dr. Nicholas Donnelly, Auxiliary Bishop and historian. At the time, some locals considered the church much too large for the population, but within two decades it was just adequate. The spire was never completed.

Iona Church, as it is popularly known, is a good example of the classical 19th century style of Hiberno-Romanesque church building, and the interior is ornamented with Celtic-style patterns. Its architect George Ashlin. of the firm of Ashlin and Coleman, had served an apprenticeship to the famous English church-architect Augustus Pugin.

In 1926, the sacristy was added, and, in 1933, the mortuary chapel which in the 1980s became the Blessed Sacrament Chapel. One of the Parish Priests, Dr. Francis Wall, was afterwards elevated to the rank of Titular Bishop of Thasos and Auxiliary Bishop of Dublin.

Figure 79: St Columba's R.C. Church, Iona Road .2010

The Parish of Glasnevin and Ballymun.

Glasnevin remained part of Fairview Parish under Canon Pettit until 1912. In that year the Parish of Glasnevin and Ballymun was created and St. Pappins Church became a chapel-of-ease for the Parish. On 27th March 1912, Fr. Henry Dudley was appointed the first parish priest, with curates Frs. Doherty and Fitzgibbon. He had been a curate first in St. Michan's in Halston St. and afterwards in St. Agatha's in North William St.

Fr. Dudley (later Canon), spent much energy and all of his considerable private means on the embellishment and improvement of the Wooden Chapel. One of his achievements was the reinforcement of the river bank which had been a cause of ongoing concern due to risk of flooding. He provided the famous Christmas Crib with half-scale figures which, unfortunately, were dumped when the church was demolished in 1970. He died in 1932 and was succeeded by Fr. Joseph Dwyer.

Corpus Christi Church

The development of areas in Glasnevin, Drumcondra and Whitehall caused a large rise in population, needing more room. To this end, a temporary "chapel of ease" was erected on a three-acre site between Home Farm Road and Griffith Avenue which was acquired from Hampstead Farm in 1923. This church, dedicated to Corpus Christi, was a timber structure with roof and cladding of corrugated iron, known as "The Tin Church". Fr. Dudley himself contributed £10,000 to the fund.

Fr. Joseph Dwyer, (later Canon), set about the building of a new church there, and in 1939 the present Church of Corpus Christi was consecrated. It is an impressive and very large domed building of white granite and with an ornate marble interior, which was for many years a somewhat incongruous "chapel of ease" to the little Wooden Chapel. The architect was a Mr. J.J. Robinson.

The Parish of Glasnevin after the War: the break-up

After the Second World War, the development of Dublin's suburbs resumed, and by the mid 1950s the fields to the north of Glasnevin were occupied by hundreds of new houses. Once again, a re-organization of the parishes became necessary. The first change was in 1944, when St. Pappin's Church was separated from Glasnevin to serve the new Parish of Larkhill/Whitehall.

With the development of Ballygall and the area around St. Canice's Road and Ballymun Avenue, another church was found to be necessary.

The Church of Our Lady Mother of Divine Grace, Ballygall

In 1958, Curate Fr. George Henry emulated his predecessor when he acquired a temporary building for use as the new Church in Ballygall. A timber structure with a corrugated iron roof, it was erected in 1959 on the corner of Ballygall Rd. East and St. Canice's Rd. and dedicated to "Our Mother of Divine Grace". A new parish of Ballygall was created in 1964 by the Archbishop, Dr. J.C. McQuaid. The timber structure was replaced by a permanent building in 1988.

Following the detachment of Ballygall Parish, Glasnevin Parish had shrunk to an extent that it was no longer viable. This state of affairs was ameliorated by transferring part of Iona Parish to Glasnevin, to wit roughly an area bounded by Botanic Avenue and the northern end of Botanic Road, and including the area at the western end of the Old Finglas Road which includes Violet Hill. Glasnevin still remains the smallest parish in Dublin City.

The Church of Our Lady of Dolours, Glasnevin

Towards the latter end of the 1960s, approval for the building of a new church came from Archbishop McQuaid. In 1970, the Wooden Chapel was dismantled, ninety years after it was erected, watched by nostalgic parishioners. A temporary church was provided in the grounds of the hospital pending completion of the new church.

The foundation stone was laid by Archbishop McQuaid on 25th March 1971, and the church was dedicated to Our Lady of Dolours (a change of name) on Sunday 25th March 1972. The cost was £170,000. The new church, designed by architect Vincent Gallagher, is of a stark modern design with two interlocking semi-pyramids of black slate supported by a heavy steel frame. It did not meet with universal approval in the area at the time among those who had hoped for something more traditional. The warm-air heating system proved to be ineffective on account of the height of the building, and the vast expanse of slating would prove a continuing maintenance problem. The basement area under the church building was designated a parish centre to replace the old timber building adjoining that had served as the parish hall.

The main features of note are the suspended iconic Sanctuary Cross depicting the crucified Christ with Our Lady and St. John (painted by Patrick Pollen), the Stations of the Cross which are etched on the windows (the work of Ronan Jacob), and a statue of Our Lady of Dolours designed by Sr. Clair from Loretto College and executed by Noel Hoare.

Figure 80: R.C. Church of Our Lady of Dolours 1992

The clergy

Glasnevin Parish has been remarkable for the longevity of its Parish Priests. In course of the twentieth century, the total number was six: Henry, Canon Dudley (1912-1932) Joseph Canon Dwyer (1932-1953), Very Reverend Michael Gleeson (1953-1958), Michael Canon Geraghty (1958-1973), Very Reverend John F. Kennedy (1973-1988) and Very Reverend Hugh Daly (1988 – 2005). Very Rev. Fr. Sean Mundow succeeded Fr. Daly.

Of the many priests that served in Glasnevin, two in particular deserve mention. Rev. John Cahill (1925-1939), a chaplain in the British Army during the First World War, he served in the trenches where he suffered serious injuries. Dr. Winder, a local doctor who had served with him, described Fr. Cahill as "the bravest man I have ever met". Fr. John Kennedy was an extremely erudite scholar and a particularly fine preacher who is remembered for his sermons that were meticulously crafted and delivered in fine style.

Placenames
GLOSSARY OF PLACE NAMES

This glossary is a collection of all the known place-names in Glasnevin, past and present. The archaic names are taken mostly from the Deeds and other documents of Christ Church Cathedral in Dublin, and in many cases they bear no relation to the present-day names and places. Some older place-names listed are purely local slang, most now obsolete

The reader will find further information in the main text of this History.

A

Addison Lodge: Botanic Road opposite the Gardens. Lounge bar and public house. c. 1850. Formerly a family residence.

Addison Park: Old Finglas Road, apartment building scheme 2002.

Addison Place: Terrace of 19th century houses behind the Dispensary on Botanic Avenue

Addison Terrace: Nos. 160-179 Botanic Road (Opposite the Botanic Gardens)

Albert College: (*The Model Farm*) Ballymun Road, now part of DCU

Albert College Park: Ballymun Rd./Hampstead Avenue

Alms House/Poor House: Former building on Glasnevin Hill, on site of River Gardens (1723-1869)

An Grianan: House in the grounds of *Albert College*

Ardmore: Former Jacobean House Glasnevin Hill south side, 1710-1962

Avondale: Botanic Villas (cul-de-sac)

Aylward House: Holy Faith Convent Residence

B

Ballinagall: Ancient designation of Ballygall (Survey 1640)

Ballygall: Townland (part of)

Ballygall Road East (part of): Thoroughfare from Old Finglas Road to Beneavan Road.

Ballygall shopping centre: FitzMaurice Road east end

Ballymun Road (part of): Southern part of the R108, formerly *The Naul Road*

Bank Farm: Townland north of the River Tolka, site of Colaiste Caoimhin.

Beechmount Villas: South side of Glasnevin Hill, Nos. 45-51 c.1912

Beechmount: North side of Glasnevin Hill. Jacobean House c. 1710

Beechmount: North side of Glasnevin Hill Modern scheme of town houses

Beechview Terrace: Former terrace of Georgian houses on south side of Glasnevin Hill, partly replaced by Beechmount Villas

Bengal Terrace: Finglas Road adjoining the Cemetery (east side)

Bishop's Road: Former name for Whitworth Road *(after Bishop Lindsay, Landlord)*

Bloody Acre: Field on south bank of River Tolka adjoining the cemetery

Bon Secours Hospital: Entrance Glasnevin Hill (1951)

Botanic Avenue: (Corey Lane). Road from Glasnevin Bridge to Drumcondra Bridge

Botanic Gardens: Botanic Road, 1795

Botanic House: Public House adjoining Prospect Cottages

Botanic Mews: Modern development off Prospect Avenue

Botanic Park: Modern development off Botanic Avenue

Botanic Road: Main road from Cross Guns to Glasnevin Bridge

Botanic Square: Modern apartment complex. Entrance from Botanic Avenue

Botanic View: Terrace on Botanic Rd. adjoining the Gardens

Botanic Villas: Cul-de sac adjoining Botanic Villas

Brian Boru: Public house on Prospect Rd. (1852)

Brighton Terrace: Nos. 86-92 Botanic Road (east side)

Broughall's Farm: See *Foster's Farm*

Bull's Field: Formerly a field between Cliftonville Road and Fairfield Road

Bull's Head, the: Former name of Tolka House (1700-1883)

Bull Ring: On the *Common,* the site of the present National School, Botanic Avenue (1500s)

C

Canal – see Royal Canal

Carlingford House, - Cottage: Former Georgian house and cottage on site of River Gardens, Glasnevin Hill   (c.1760 –1965)

Carmelite Convent: Formerly on site of present Holy Faith Convent (1829-1849)

Carroll Estate: Area on east side of Botanic Road now vacant development site

Castle: See *Glasnevin Castle* and *Hampstead Castle*

Cemetery: See Prospect   (Glasnevin) Cemetery

Cemetery- early Christian : On site of present Met Office

Cemetery Lane: Prospect Avenue (q.v.)

Charles' Farm: See *Gogh's Farm*

Charleville LTC: Whitworth Road

Church (R.C.): Seven Dolours of Our Lady (1881-1971) / Our Lady of Dolours : Botanic Avenue (1972)

Church (R.C.): St. Columba ("Iona Church") Iona Rd.

Church (R.C.): Our Lady Mother of Divine Grace: Ballygall Rd. E

Church (C. of I.): St. Mobhi : Church Avenue

Church Avenue: Cul-de-sac off Ballymun Road, leading to St. Mobhi's Church.

Church Hill House: Ballymun Road east side

Church Hill Terrace: Ballymun Rd, east side (Nos. 1-11)

Churchill Villas: Terrace of 2 houses Ballymun Road east side (Nos. 40. 42)

Church Lane: Former name for Church Avenue

Church View: Former house on Ballymun Rd. facing Church Avenue

Cinder Path : Former local name for Mobhi Boreen (Boithrin Mobhi) (q.v.)

Claremont:
(1) Large townland in north- west area of Glasnevin
(2) Georgian house, formerly the *Deaf and Dumb Institute,*
(3) Modern estate, off Finglas Rd., opposite Glasnevin Cemetery

Claremont Avenue: Cul-de-sac off Ballymun Road, beside former Enterprise Ireland

Claremont Cottage: Former Georgian house, on the site of the present Ballygall shopping centre.

Claremont View: 18th century house on Claremont Avenue

Clareville Grove: Cul-de-sac off Claremont Lawn. Finglas Road (N2)

Claude Road: Cul-de-sac off Whitworth Road (after Lieut. Claude Gore-Lindsay, d. 1886)

Cliftonville Road: Cul-de-sac off Botanic Road east side

Clonmel: Medieval farm and later estate.

Clonmel: The most northerly townland in Glasnevin

Clonmel Cottage: Former Georgian farmhouse on Clonmel estate

Clonmel Road: Clonmel estate.

Cloonoons House: Former house on present site of St.Michael's School, Ballymun Rd.

Coffee Cabins: Former row of 18th century mud cabins on site of Botanic Road Nos 161-179 and shops adjoining.

Colaiste Caoimhin: Dept. Of Defence, St, Mobhi Road, formerly *Marlborough Hall*

Colaiste Einde : Former training college in *Glasnevin House,* on site of former Enterprise Ireland premises (1920s-1930s)

Common: Small area beside the River Tolka, now the site of the R.C church and the national school

Convent Cottages: Row of labourers' cottages, Holy Faith Convent grounds, Old Finglas Rd.

Convent of the Holy Faith: Glasnevin Hill

Convent of the Sacred Heart Sisters: Formerly on the site of the present Holy Faith Convent (1849-1864)

Corey Lane: Former name for Botanic Avenue *(also called Gorey Lane).*

Crawford Road: Original name of Lindsay Road, for a brief period.

Crawford Avenue: From Iona Road to Hollybank Rd.,(beside the Church)

Cremore Avenue, - Crescent, - Drive, - Park & - -Road: Off the Old Finglas Road, / Ballygall Road.

Cremore Lawn: Part of former Glasnevin Demesne (Holy Faith Convent), Old Finglas Rd.

Cremore Heights: St. Canice's Road, west end.

Crescent Villas: Iona area

Cross Guns (1): Former tavern on site of corner of Finglas Road and Prospect Avenue, later site of Hart's newsagents shop. (Styled "The Cross Guns" in Parish records for 1721)

Cross Guns (2): Former name for village in the area of the present Hart's Corner

Cross Guns (3): Townland lying on east side Prospect Road/Whitworth Road area.

Cross Guns Bridge: See Westmoreland Bridge

Cuilin: Georgian House in the grounds of DCU.

Cullenagh: The name given to the present Wadelai area in the 1640 Survey.

D

Dalcassian Downs: Apartment scheme Hart's Corner / Finglas Rd. (site of former orphanage)

Daneswell: Townland (19th century) comprising two areas, the larger one stretching from Greenmount to Cross Guns area (also referred to as *Cross Guns North* and *"The Lynch Estate"*) the smaller one located due south of *Fair Field (q.v.)*

Daneswell House: Former Georgian house on site of shops between Lindsay Rd. and Whitworth Rd.

Dane's Well: see Deane's Well

Daneswell Road: Link-road from Fairfield Rd. to Botanic Avenue (see Deane's Well)

Daneswell Villas: Terrace on Whitworth Rd.

David Road: Off Whitworth Rd.

Deaf and Dumb Institute (Claremont): Now St. Clare's Hospital, Griffith Avenue

Deane's, the : Parcel of lands, largest part in Botanic Avenue area on south bank of the River Tolka, also called *the Lord's Mede in medieval times, later Drishoge.*

Deane's Well: "Curious well" in Fairfield Road area, on private property *(after the Dean of Christ Church)*

Dean Swift Green, Road: The Wadelai area

Dean Swift Avenue: Original name proposed in 1930 for St. .Mobhi Road

De Courcy Square: Between Finglas Rd. and Prospect Avenue

Delville: Former house and estate on site of Bon Secours Hospital *(1719-1951)*

Delville Lawn Tennis Club: rear of St. Mobhi Drive *(1930s)*

Delville Road: The Wadelai area

Demesne: See Glasnevin Demesne

Dispensary: Botanic Avenue/Addison Place,(formerly on Glasnevin Hill up to c. 1900).

Dollar, the: Former tavern on Finglas Road at Cross Guns end (1800s)

Drapier Green, - Road: The Wadelai area

Draycott's Farm: Ancient name for the Wadelai area, *((also Wadd's Farm, North Farm, Cullenagh)*

Drishogue : Townland south of the River Tolka in the Botanic Avenue area, (*also called The Lord's Mede and The Deane's)*

Dublin Industrial Estate: Extensive industrial estate off Finglas Road, containing roads named after Irish rivers

E

Elmhurst: Part of Hampstead estate (Eustace Family)

Enterprise Ireland: Occupied premises on corner of Ballymun Rd and Old Finglas Rd. From c.1990-2008

EOLAS: Former name for *Enterprise Ireland,* Ballymun Road

F

Fairfield: Townland, former small estate with Jacobean house (c.1712-1928), now the Fairfield Rd. and Daneswell Rd. area

Fairfield Road: Off Botanic Rd /St Mobhi Rd. junction

Fee Farm: Parcel of lands spread over central Glasnevin

Ferndale: End house, David Terrace

Finglas Road: part of, (Slane Road) from Cross-Guns to Finglas Bridge

Finglas Road, Old: See Old Finglas Road

Finglas Road North: Former name for the Old Finglas Road

Florence Court: Original name for *Carlingford House*, Glasnevin Hill (1738)

Foster's Farm (also "Broughall's Farm"): Parcel of lands spread over Glasnevin

Fourteen Fields: Part of West Park Estate (1800s)

Frank Cooke Park: Sports club premises ("Tolka Rovers") Griffith Avenue.

G

Gartan Road: Off Iona Road/Lindsay Road

Glasilawn Road, - Avenue: Off Ballygall Rd.E

Glasmeen Road: Off Glasilawn Avenue

Glasnamana Road: Off Glasilawn Avenue

Glasnevin Castle 14th cent): Ruin, formerly in the grounds of *Delville*, now the Bon Secours Hospital. Also termed *Manor Hall and Grange Hall*

Glasnevin Cemetery: (1832) *Prospect Cemetery* Finglas Rd.

Glasnevin Demesne: Former designation for the lands of the Holy Faith Convent *(also called the "Mitchell Estate")*

Glasnevin Football Club (est. 1896): St. Mobhi Rd.

Glasnevin Hill: Centre of Glasnevin Village *(also Glasnevin Street)*

Glasnevin House: Name formerly applied to the Georgian house in the grounds of the Holy Faith Convent up to c.1830, subsequently given to the house built by the Lindsay family c. 1840, taking in an older house called "The Turrets" in the grounds of the present Enterprise Ireland..

Glasnevin Lawn Tennis Club: Ballymun Rd. (1912)

Glasnevin Lodge: Former early Georgian house adjoining Addison Lodge, Botanic Rd.

Glasnevin National School: Botanic Ave. *("The Ink Bottle").*

Glasnevin Road: Former name for Botanic Rd & part of Phibsborough Rd. up to c.1900.

Glasnevin Streete: Former name for Glasnevin Hill

Glebe, the: Field, now the site of The Haven and Mobhi Boreen *(also The Vicars' of Glasnevin in the 1640 survey)*

Glen, the: 4 acres of *the Delville estate* on banks of the Nevin Stream

Gogh's (or Gough's) Farm: Former parcel of three small farms including Goose Acre (also "Charles' Farm")

Golden Acre: Terrace on Whitworth Rd.

Goose Acre: Townland between Addison Lodge and Botanic avenue

Grange, the: See *Glasnevin Castle*

Great Farm: Former name for the area of Glasnevin lying east of the Ballymun Road

Great Meadow ("Moch Mede"): Former name for the area of the Botanic Gardens nearest the road, and shown as a triangular field, part of the Dean's Farm (D3), in the 1640 Survey

Greenfield: Former name for pair of houses on Ballymun Rd., east side

Greenmount: Former Georgian house, estate and townland between Botanic Avenue and Iona area.

Grianan - An,: formerly the Albert National Agricultural Training Institution, Hampstead North

Griffith Avenue (part of)

Griffith Park: Botanic Avenue

H

Hampstead South: Townland, area east of Hampstead Hill, site of hospital

Hampstead Hill: Townland, area south of Hampstead Avenue

Hampstead North: Townland, area on north side of Hampstead Avenue, site of former Albert College etc. and part of DCU land.

Hampstead Avenue, -Park: Off Ballymun Road

Hampstead Castle: Former tower house in the grounds of Hampstead South estate.

Hanna Villa: Former name for pair of houses on Ballymun Road east side

Hart's Buildings: Curved red-brick row of shops and apartments at Hart's Corner/Prospect Avenue

Hart's Corner: Junction of Finglas Rd, and Botanic Rd. *formerly Cross Guns*

Haven, the: Modern housing development in Mobhi Boreen (q.v.) (see "*Glebe*")

Hayes' Estate: Former name for estate lying east of Botanic Road

Holy Faith Convent: Glasnevin Hill

Home Farm Road: (part of) (after *Home Farm* on the Upper Drumcondra Rd.*)*

Howth View: Former name for terrace of two houses on Prospect Road, west side

I

Industrial Research Centre: Former name for the location of Enterprise Ireland and former *IIRS*

Institute for Industrial Research and Standards IIRS: Former name for *Enterprise Ireland.*

Iona Crescent, -Drive, -Park, -Road, - Villas: Iona district.

Iona National Airways: Former garage premises (Cahills') on corner of Prospect Rd. and Whitworth Rd.(now Porterhouse, a restaurant).

Ink Bottle (school): See Parish School

Ivy Cottage/Lodge: Former house on Ballymun Rd. facing Church Avenue

J

Johnstown Lane: Former name for Ballygall Rd. East.

James's Terrace: See St. James' Terrace

K

Katherine Terrace: Botanic Rd. east side

Keegan's Buildings: Former name for terrace of 3 houses on Prospect Rd. beside present Brian Boru public house, *Cross Guns.*

Kelleher's Corner: Local name for the junction of St. Mobhi Rd. and Ballymun Rd. (1940s)

Kincora Terrace: Former name for terrace on Botanic Road west side

Koh i noor Villas: Former name for pair of houses on Ballymun Rd. east side

L

Lambay Road: Road between Home Farm Rd. and Griffith Ave.

Lindsay Road: Road from Hart's Corner to St. Patrick's Rd. Drumcondra

Lindsay Terrace: Former name for the first houses built on Lindsay Rd.

Lord's Mede, the: Ancient name for Drishogue.

Lynch Estate: see Daneswell.

M

Maher's Cottages: Former row of cottages on the site of Nos.1 to 10 Botanic Avenue

Manor Hall: See Glasnevin Castle

The Manse : (1930: 1, Cremore Park, former residence of the Presbyterian Minister)

Maolbuille Road: Clonmel estate

Marlborough Hall: Formerly a teachers' college, afterwards a military hospital, now Colaiste Caoimhin and the Dept. of Defence, St.Mobhi Rd.

Marlborough House: Formerly a student residence, a remand home, now the site of Met Eireann

Margretta Place: Former terrace of three houses behind the Brian Boru, Cross Guns

Marguerite Road: Cul-de-sac off Botanic Road

Melville: Ballymun Rd /Claremont Ave., formerly the Rectory of Glasnevin

Meteorological Office/Met Eireann: Corner of Glasnevin Hill/ Ballymun Rd.

Mill of Glasnevin: Ancient watermill formerly in the area immediately on west side of Glasnevin Bridge (c. 800 – 1830 A.D.)

Mill Field: Part of the Botanic Gardens, between the mill stream and the River Tolka

Mill stream: In the Botanic Gardens

Mitchell Estate: Former name for the site of present Holy Faith Convent, Old Finglas Rd. (also called *"Glasnevin Demesne")*

Mobhi Boreen: Between St. Mobhi Rd. and Church Avenue (formerly called " *The Cinder Path"*)

Moch Mede: See *Great Meadow*

Model Farm: The Albert College (now DCU)

Model School: Church Avenue, now a preparatory school .

Monastery, early Christian (St. Mobhi's): Site of present Bons Secours Hospital

Monastery, St. Joseph's : See St. Joseph's Monastery

Motte: Mound, extant Norman (?) artifact in River Gardens, Glasnevin Hill

Mount Michael: Former name for terrace of nine houses on west side of Botanic Rd.(between *Prospect Cottage* and *Sunnybank)*

N

Na Fianna GAA club: St Mobhi Rd. *(Bank Farm)*

Naul Road,The : Former name for Ballymun Rd. (up to 1900)

Nevin Stream: Tributary of the River Tolka

Newton House/Newtown Cottage: Former early Victorian house, c.1800- 2004, Ballymun Rd. adjoining Melville (q.v.)

Norah Terrace: Former name for terrace on Botanic Road east side

North Dublin National School Project (NDNSP): Ballymun Rd.

North Dublin Union Huts (auxiliary workhouse): West end of Whitworth Rd., an arrangement of wooden huts. c.1850-1890

North Farm: See *Draycott's Farm*

Northland Drive, - Grove: Off Tolka Estate Rd

O

Old Finglas Road: Road from Glasnevin Hill to Finglas Bridge, formerly *Finglas Road North"* (19th century)

P

Player's houses: Botanic Avenue (1920s) (distinctive "English Cottage" style)

Players' Tobacco Factory: Botanic Rd. (offices and chimney still extant)

Poor House: See Alms House

Poor Lotte: Formerly a plot of land now part of River Gardens, Glasnevin Hill

Pound, the Parish: Formerly at the bottom of Glasnevin Hill, east side.

Primrose Terrace: Former name for a row of small cottages on Prospect Ave. (pre-1900).

Prospect Avenue: Hart's Corner to Prospect Square formerly *Cemetery Lane*

Prospect Cottages: Former name for row of early 19th century dwellings on Botanic Rd..

Prospect Monastery (Boarding School) Also called St. Joseph's Monastery: Prospect Avenue (1845 –1900s)

Prospect Road: From Cross Guns Bridge to Finglas Rd.

Prospect Square: North. end of Prospect Avenue, location of the old gate to the cemetery

Prospect Terrace: Botanic Rd. west side

Prospect Way: By-pass connecting Finglas Rd. with Botanic Rd.

Q

Quarry: Former field beside Botanic Avenue south side (*Rowland Parker's Quarry)* Now Botanic Park.

R

Railway station: Extant building adjoining Charleville LTC Whitworth Rd.(in operation from 1908 – 1925)

River Gardens: Glasnevin Hill apartments, on both west side and east side

River View, River View Cottage: formerly on Botanic Ave., river side

Rise, the: Off Griffith Avenue and Ballymun Rd. (1930s)

Roaches Hole: Former inlet on the north bank of River Tolka , east of bridge on St. Mobhi Rd.

Rookery, the: Former pair of houses on Glasnevin Hill south side adjoining *Beechview Tce.*

Rose View: Former (Georgian?) house Incorporated in Marlborough House (q.v.)

Roseville: Former Georgian house, Old Finglas Rd. opposite HF Convent (c.1730-1982)

Round House: Designation given to the former *Parish school* ("*The Inkbottle*") (1730-1900).

Royal Canal: Fifth lock at Cross Guns Bridge (*Westmoreland Bridge*)

S

St. Andrew's Terrace: Former name for a pair of houses on Ballymun Rd., east side

St. Brigid's National School: Old Finglas Rd.,

St. Canice's Road: Road between Ballygall Rd. East and Ballymun Rd.

St. Clare's Hospital: (formerly the Claremont Deaf and Dumb Institution)

St. David's Terrace: Terrace at rear of the Met. Eireann Office

St. Ita's Road: Cul-de-sac off Botanic Ave. north side

St John's Villas: Former name for pair of houses on Ballymun Rd. east side (Nos. 36-38)

St. James' Terrace: Botanic Rd. west side

St. Joseph's Cottages: Former row of old dwellings on Botanic Rd. west side.

St .Joseph's Crescent: Terrace of single-storey dwellings on Botanic Rd. west side

St. Joseph's Monastery: (Prospect Monastery): Former boarding school on Prospect Ave.

St. Malachy's Road: Cul-de-sac off Botanic Ave. north side

St. Maolbuille's Road: Clonmel Estate

St. Mary's Secondary School: Holy Faith Convent, Glasnevin Hill

St. Michael's House (Special school): Ballymun Rd.

St. Michael's Road: Cul-de sac off Botanic Ave. north side

St. Mobhi's Church (C.of I): Church Ave.

St. Mobhi Boithrin: see Mobhi Boreen

St. Mobhi Road: Main thoroughfare from Botanic Rd. to Ballymun Rd. (1925)

St. Mobhi Drive: Connecting road between St. Mobhi Rd. and Glasnevin Hill

St. Mobhi Grove: Cul-de-sac off St. Mobhi Rd.

St. Pappin's Road, - Green: Wadelai area

St.Philomena's Road: Cul-de-sac off Finglas Rd.

St. Teresa's Road: Road from Botanic Rd. to Prospect square

St. Teresa's Place: Parallel road off Prospect Square.

St. Thomas' Terrace: Glasnevin Hill north side

St. Vincent's School (CBS): Finglas Rd.

St. Vincent de Paul Orphanage: Former building on present site of Dalcassian Downs, Hart's Corner .1863-1980.

Seven Farms: Parcel of lands distributed over the Parish.

Sharpe's Bank: Ancient name for field on bank of River Tolka (1600s, exact location unknown)

Slab grave: See cemetery, *early Christian*

Slut's Alley: Local name for part of Botanic Avenue (*Corey Lane, 1800s*)

Slough's (or Slut's) End: Townland in neighbourhood of Finglas Rd. and Hart's Corner (also called *West Farm*)

Springmount: Former name for terrace of 2 houses adjoining Sunny Bank, Botanic Rd.

Stella Avenue: Off St. Mobhi Rd. near Home Farm Rd.

Stormanstown Road: Wadelai area

Sunny Bank: Botanic Rd. west side, Hotel, former 2-house terrace and maternity home

Sunny Side : Former row of mud cabins on site of Players' Houses, Botanic Ave.

Sunday School/infant school: Former establishment on Glasnevin Hill on present site of "The Gem" (c.1834- 1910)

T

Thom's: Former printing works (Alex. Thom) Botanic Rd., later Browne and Nolan, and later Smurfits

Teeling's Tenement: Former name for holding acquired for the Botanic Gardens in 1795

Tolka Bridge House: Former house in the present Rose Garden, Botanic Gardens

Tolka Cottage: Former name for the old single-storey dwelling on Botanic Ave., near the junction with St. Mobhi Rd.

Tolka Estate Road: Road on "parliamentary boundary" between Glasnevin and Finglas Parishes, from Old Finglas Rd. to Glasmeen Rd.

Tolka House: Public House beside Glasnevin Bridge (formerly *"The Bull's Head"*)

Tolka River: Principal river running through Glasnevin, *(also " Tolekan", "Tulkan", "Tulga" etc)*

Tolka Rovers: Sports club on Griffith Avenue (Frank Cook Park)

Toll gates (Turnpikes): Formerly on the site of present Hart's Corner (Cross Guns), one on Finglas Rd., and one on the present Botanic Rd. (c. 1725-1850)

Towerview Cottages: Finglas Rd., cul-de-sac facing Glasnevin Cemetery

Triangle, the: Former local name for piece of ground off Botanic Ave., now Botanic Square

Turrets, the: Former Jacobean house c.1710, later incorporated in *Glasnevin House* (q.v.)

V

Vera Terrace: Terrace of houses on Botanic Avenue, opposite Players' Houses

Vicars of Glasnevin: Former name for the *Glebe*, now the site of The Haven, Mobhi Boreen

Vicars Choral: Former name for the Mill Field (q.v.)

Villa Park: Iona area, off Iona Crescent (1940s)

Violet Hill: Townland outside and adjoining the parliamentary boundary, but now included in the Glasnevin R.C. Parish area. Also former *Violet Hill House* on Finglas Road.

Vincent Terrace: Former terrace of early 18th century houses on Glasnevin Hill west side

W

Wad (1): Townland forming the furthermost north-east area of Glasnevin

Wad (2): Stream formerly marking northern and eastern boundary of Glasnevin, now culverted

Wad Bridge: Former bridge, on Ballymun Rd. over the Wad River

Wadd's Farm: Also called *Draycott's Farm(q.v.)* included the present Wadelai area

Wadelai: With Clonmel, the most northerly area of Glasnevin, after *Wadelai (House)*. Also Wadelai Green, - Road.

Wadelai (house): Former residence situated between Walnut grove and Ballygall townlands. C. 1890 – 1950. Name possibly derived from the words "Wad", and "Ellis", the name of the resident family.

Walnut Grove: Townland, with former house of that name, lying north of St. Canice's Rd., formerly part of *Draycott's Farm*.

Washerwoman's Hill: Very old local name for Glasnevin Hill (after the inmates of the Alms House q.v.). Name probably dates from before 1770.

Watch House: Former constabulary house in west end of *Glasnevin Demesne* (c. 1800-1950)

Westmoreland Bridge: Original (and official) name for "Cross Guns Bridge", Royal Canal fifth lock.

West Farm: See Slut's End

West Park: Georgian house on Ballygall Rd. East (still extant)

West Park: Modern estate off Ballygall Rd. East

West Park Farm: Formerly on Ballygall Rd. East / Griffith Ave. area (Coyle family)

West Park House: See *Claremont Cottage*

West Park Road: Former name for Ballygall East Road (1920s-1930s)

Whitworth Road: (Part of) after Charles, Earl of Whitworth (*formerly The Bishop's Road)*

Wigan Road: Off Whitworth Rd.

Willows, the: Cul-de-sac off Finglas Road

Wooden Chapel: R.C. Church of the Seven Dolours, Botanic Avenue (1881-1971)

Wyckham's Farm also Wicomb's Farm, etc.: See Clonmel

Sources for the Illustrations

In this history, the following illustrations are reproduced by kind permission of the following institutions and individuals:
Figures 7, 18, 67:   National Library of Ireland (Brendan Scally Collection).
Figures 16, 46: The National Library of Ireland.
Figures 9, 13, 14, 15: The National Gallery of Ireland
Figure 6: Representative Church Body
Figure 77: Architectural Archive.
Figure 28: Papers of late Oliver D. Gogarty
Figure 29: The late Pat Coyle, Glasnevin
Figure 68: "The Silver Lining", by John Houghton
Figure 74: Michael Corcoran.
Figures 30, 48: The Ordnance Survey Ireland Permit No. MP 001411
Figure 73: Evening Herald 1/11/1937
The following are reproduced from old post cards:
Figures 38, 39, 50, 53, 61.

The remainder are from the author's private collection.

LIST OF HISTORIC MAPS OF RELEVANCE TO GLASNEVIN

The Plott of the Lands of Glassnevin in the Countie of Dublin belonging to the Deane of the holy Trinity Dublin, performed by Richard Francis in 1640. (RCB Library). ©Representative Church Body
The Plott of the Towne and Lands of Glasnevin in the County of Dublin, belonging to the Dean of the holy Trinity Dublin, performed by Richard Francis, in the year 1640 and now traced out in February 1719 by me, John Greene. (St. Mobhi's Church).
Actual Survey of the County of Dublin, by John Rocque 1757.
William Duncan's Map of County Dublin 1821.
Ordnance Survey Map Dublin (1834-1842) 6" and 25" and subsequent issues
Ordnance Survey Map Dublin 1936.

Deed maps of leases in Glasnevin held in the National Library, Dublin: (from 1767)
21 F 51/86: Forster's farm 1768
21 F 51/87: Turret House
21 F 51/88: Hampstead
21 F 51/91: Botanic Garden 1800
21 F 51/94: Claremont Demesne 1819
21 F 51/95: Commissioners for Education (Met Eireann site) 1831
21 F 51/96: A field in Glasnevin between Claremont Avenue and the Nevin Stream 1829
21 F 51/98 and /99: The mill and mill dam
21 F 51/100: Fairfield etc. with "Curious Well"
21 F 51/107: Mill Field, to Royal Canal Co.
21 F 51/108: Map of part of the lands of Glasnevin .held by John Bayly 1806
21/51/148: Map showing all Glasnevin properties and tenants.
21 F 51 (106) Map of Part of the Lands of Glasnevin let to William John Gore Esq. 1807 (John Longfield).
21 F 53(51) Delville Demesne, the Seat of David Babingham, 1799. National Library
Glasnevin Demesne, for George Putland Esq., 1799 by Thomas Logan.